Media Studies

Media Studies

Texts, Institutions and Audiences

Lisa Taylor and Andrew Willis

BLACKWELL
Publishers

First published 1999

2 4 6 8 10 9 7 5 3 1

Blackwell Publishers Ltd
108 Cowley Road
Oxford OX4 1JF
UK

Blackwell Publishers Inc.
350 Main Street
Malden, Massachusetts 02148
USA

British Library Cataloguing in Publication Data

A CIP catalogue record for this book is available from the British Library.

Library of Congress Cataloging-in-Publication Data

Taylor, Lisa, 1966–
    Media studies : texts, institutions, and audiences / by Lisa
  Taylor and Andrew Willis.
        p.   cm.
    Includes bibliographical references and index.
    ISBN 0-631-20026-6 (hc. : alk. paper). — ISBN 0-631-20027-4 (pbk. : alk. paper)
    1. Television broadcasting. 2. Motion pictures. 3. Mass media.
  I. Willis, Andrew, 1962 Nov. 17– II. Title.
  PN1992.5.T28   1999   98-30067
  302.23—dc21   CIP

Typeset in 11 on 12½ pt Palatino
by Newgen Imaging Systems (P) Ltd, Chennai, India
Printed in Great Britain by TJ International Ltd, Padstow, Cornwall

This book is printed on acid-free paper

Contents

Introduction

Media studies is a rapidly growing area within higher education, with a range of media-based courses on offer to undergraduates. This book is designed to service some of the needs of students undertaking such courses. It aims to provide a comprehensive introduction to the key areas of study within the field. Ideas are presented in an accessible way and wherever possible key concepts and critical approaches are applied through the use of examples or case study material. However, while the book is aimed in the first instance at students who are new to media studies, it might also be used by those further on in their studies, who seek to reinforce or build on their knowledge of particular approaches or areas.

The book is divided into three parts – on texts, institutions and audiences – covering the major approaches to the media within media studies. This division is created to enable students to dip into each part and, with this in mind, each one stands alone as well as being integral to the overall book. Broadly, these parts represent the most common approaches within the subject. It is not a division that is designed to make false distinctions within the subject area; rather, students are encouraged to draw on the approaches dealt with in all three parts. We would argue that a fully comprehensive understanding of the media requires a knowledge of all three.

Part I, 'Texts', offers a range of textual tools, such as semiotics, *mise-en-scène* analysis, narrative and genre, which students might use as approaches to understanding the vast range of media texts encountered daily. Part II, 'Institutions', focuses on the organizations which produce media texts. It introduces students to the dominant critical frameworks used for understanding media industries. It also examines some of the key institutional debates in media studies: for example, the impact of the partial deregulation of media organizations and the meaning and status of independent media production. Part III, 'Audiences', investigates a range of diverse perspectives on media audiences, from the effects tradition to the ethnographic cultural studies approach. It also investigates debates about the media and consumption: for instance, how the purchase and appropriation of media programmes and media technologies, from satellite dishes to 'quality' drama, can be used as a means to indicate social status. By examining these three interlinked areas the book provides the reader with a comprehensive overview of the main strands within media studies at an introductory level.

This book also acknowledges that study at undergraduate level is very different from that undertaken at earlier stages. It is therefore designed to help students to make the change to the new and different kinds of learning methods encountered in higher education. The first year in higher education is often a moment of transition, during which students become accustomed to these different study methods. This book, and in particular the final research chapter, aims to help students move on from the activities which might have characterized their work on, for example, an A-level or Access course, to the kinds of assignment which are typical on the first year of a degree programme. Study at university is generally less directed. Students will find themselves encouraged to develop independent study skills and take responsibility for their own learning. Perhaps the most fundamental change is that they are expected to research topics on their own. In the research chapter we provide some strategic suggestions for how to work successfully with the new challenges and expectations demanded by higher education.

A new media studies student will not necessarily have encountered the subject prior to arriving at university. This book aims to introduce the central ideas and concerns that may be encountered on a media studies course, and to illustrate the sorts of research assignment that will be set. Furthermore, we aim to show that investigating the media means gathering particular kinds of research material. This may include finding appropriate media texts such as films, specific episodes of television programmes or editions of magazines, as well as more traditional resources like government reports that relate to media policy. For this reason, each chapter concludes with suggestions for further work and reading which should encourage students to apply critical approaches in contexts that will help to develop their own independent learning.

Part I
Texts

1

How the Media Communicate

This chapter introduces the idea that each medium communicates differently, using a distinctive set of production codes and conventions. This is important to acknowledge, particularly when our subject of study – the media – is comprised of so many different forms, such as photography, radio, television, film, advertising, newspapers and magazines. Each medium requires analysis that takes the different and unique aspects of each form into account. Roy Armes in his book *On Video* (1988) issues a warning about the pitfalls of simply using the tools of film analysis to explore a related but crucially different medium, video: 'My initial difficulties in coming to terms with the new medium stemmed, largely, I now believe, from attempting to define it in ways more appropriate to film ... aspects of this theoretical work make its direct application to video hazardous' (p. 2). There may be the temptation, for example, to think of television as a miniature film screen, yet film and television are two very different mediums. As specific forms they are distinguishable in a range of ways: their screen ratios are quite different; while films are often shown as discrete texts, television, as Raymond Williams argues, can be thought of as a 'flow' of images which seem to merge almost indistinguishably together in continuum (1974, pp. 91–2); and both television programmes and films are produced with their contrasting contexts of consumption in mind. Film and television, even while they converge in terms of some of the visual strategies they use – invisible editing, for example – also have different conventions.

From the outset, therefore, it is vital that any textual analysis of a media product takes into account the specifics of the medium in which that text appears. In doing so, it is important to consider the formal aspects of media texts alongside any consideration of their content. The way in which a message is communicated within the media therefore becomes as important as the message itself. In other words, the form in which a message appears contributes a great deal to the way in which we are able to decode and understand any media text.

Media forms and conventions

Debates and discussions about the media often cite a divide between form and content. Form may be defined as the way in which a particular medium packages its message using its particular technologies and codes and conventions. The message itself, the ideas within, are the content. Each works using accepted methods of communication, often termed conventions, which are particular to the medium in question.

The textual strategies used by media forms establish currency by becoming conventional over time. New media texts require the social sanctions guaranteed by convention to ensure audiences will be able to read them. Mediums such as comics and radio exist almost within a predefined tradition of textual norms or conventions which generate audience expectations. Andrew Crisell in his book *Understanding Radio* (1986) discusses the role silence plays on radio. Silence is a signifier, Crisell argues, since its 'absence of sound can also be heard' (p. 55). On a station like Radio Four the use of silence signifies serious and dignified breaks before an important moment; silence falls before the five strokes of the time announcement, for example. As Crisell argues, 'silence can resemble noise (that is sounds, words and music) in acting as a framing mechanism, for it can signify the integrity of a programme or item by making space around it' (p. 56). In this sense, our acceptance of this particular function of silence is conventional, precisely because it has become an orthodoxy through repeated use.

Sometimes, however, texts play with convention, slightly altering the expected formula, while remaining for the most part within sanctioned boundaries. Manipulating what they have come to expect can be a source of pleasure for audiences because the text plays on, and indeed complements, the reader's knowledge of its conventions. The 1980s situation comedy, *The Young Ones*, is an example of a text which set out to break away from, and ultimately challenge, the formal conventions of its genre. Most notably, it refused to abide by the conventions of realism that dominate mainstream television production. Situation comedies conventionally construct the audience as the fourth wall, the unacknowledged observers of a slice of 'real' life. The direct address of the characters in *The Young Ones* destroyed the illusion of realism. Yet more anti-realist were the cartoon-like scenes where the student characters committed seemingly irreparable acts of violence against each other, only to survive completely unscathed. Flouting the fundamental rules of the form added a new dimension of comedy and gratification for audiences of this text; their laughter came from *The Young Ones'* departure from expected conventions.

The most straightforward method of exploring the ways in which these formal differences manifest themselves is to take a closer look at the ways in which a particular idea or content is realized in different mediums.

Different mediums, different conventions: *The X-Files*

The X-Files is a popular 'cult' science-fiction thriller. Because of its perceived cult status the programme has been used as the fictional base on which a plethora of other X-Files commodities, such as comics, T-shirts, mugs and posters, have been produced. *The X-Files*, like a number of other media texts since the mid-1980s, has been successfully diversified into interrelated technologies and areas of entertainment so as to elongate the exposure of the text in all its different aspects. In so doing, the producers have been able to reap the maximum profit by presenting the text across multiple media (see illustration 1.1). Product diversification has meant that *The X-Files* exists in separate media forms: primarily the television serial, but also a comic entitled *The X-Files* and tie-in paperbacks such as *Whirlwind* (1995). All share the same fictional concept, but they present them using different codes and conventions. *The X-Files* is consequently

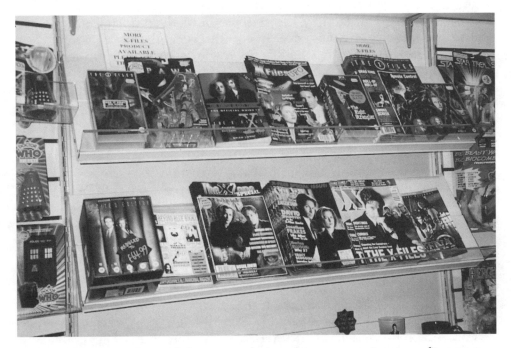

Illustration 1.1   'Concepts' are now designed to reap maximum profits across multiple media.
Source: The authors.

an interesting case study for analysing how these formal conventions operate.

The familiar *X-Files* viewer will have a number of expectations concerning its manifestations in different mediums. A number of the elements the viewer becomes accustomed to can be categorized as the narrative conventions of the science-fiction thriller. However, several of these conventions appear in ways specific to *The X-Files*, hence its off-beat 'cult' status. In the programme, FBI detective partners Scully and Mulder investigate crimes with a difference; a question-mark always hangs over the perpetrators of the crime at hand – though rationality dictates that a logical explanation can be uncovered, cues in the text invite the viewer to entertain the idea that an alien, paranormal force may be responsible. In the case of the television programme, the opening credit sequence, which is repeated before each episode, feeds the conviction that the alien source is the one to be taken seriously. The credit sequence opens with a series of computer-enhanced images which all suggest the existence of extra-terrestrial life: the opening shot shows the scanning and enlargement of a piece of footage of a moving UFO; another scans the eye of a creature unknown to humankind.

As FBI agents, Scully and Mulder break with the conventional gender mould of the ordinary crime series investigators. The character of Dana Scully is a challenging representation of a female detective. As a highly educated woman, marked by her status as a medical doctor, she always seeks rational scientific evidence. In contrast, it is the male partner, Fox Mulder, who has intuitive beliefs in the existence of extra-terrestrial activity. In this type of programme it is usually female characters who are seen to use so-called 'feminine' powers of intuition. As a result, dramatic tension emanates from the conflicting explanations each character produces for the crimes they are assigned to investigate and solve.

The FBI as an institution is represented as a secretive, suspicious organization. Because the government is repeatedly shown to be obstructive to the detectives gaining access to the information it holds about extra-terrestrial activity, the reader anticipates the intervention of the FBI whenever Scully and Mulder begin to uncover aberrant causes for the crimes they investigate. Constantly implied in the text is the state's desire to guard and ultimately control this information in order to pave the way for experimentation and research into the ways in which the power of the paranormal might be used as a means of extending both the state and the nation's power.

These narrative conventions are realized differently in each medium by the use of distinct formal conventions. With the use of an episode from the second season of the television series, a story from *The X-Files* comic and an advertisement for Vodaphone which uses the concept of the X-Files, the specific modes of communication adopted within each medium can be explored in some detail.

The television X-Files

The television episode *Die Hand Die Verletzt* opens in a school in Milford Haven, New Hampshire, governed by a board whose members are involved with the occult. One night, a group of youths meets in a nearby forest to recite a Satanist chant. Seemingly as a result, one of the boys is choked to death. The FBI is called in and Scully and Mulder inspect the crime site and question the school's staff. From an analysis of this episode it is possible to see that there is a range of visual strategies being utilized to infuse meaning into the text. Within television, the selection of close-up or mid-shot is crucial to the director. Close-ups often emphasize particular events with special narrative or thematic significance. In addition, this way of editing or juxtaposing one frame next to another enables the director to make heavy implications about who the viewer should suspect.

At one point Mulder and Scully walk down the school corridor troubled after their interview with the board members. In mid-shot, the camera tracks in front of Mulder as he walks ahead to drink from a water fountain. Mulder exclaims as he lifts his head after drinking; the water, counter to the norms of the northern hemisphere, travels anti-clockwise. 'That's impossible', remarks Scully. A close-up focuses on the small stainless steel sink; the image works to emphasize the strangeness of the water movement, impacting on the viewer as the camera dwells on the water for a few seconds. The grey sink is hard and shiny; the water's movement is cold material fact. The edit works both to reinforce Mulder's claim and to discount the rationality of Scully's reply. The following mid-shot shows Mulder turning from the sink to look at Scully: 'Something is making these things possible.'

A cut to the substitute teacher Phyllis Paddock, in long shot behind her desk, strenuously suggests an answer to the assertion made by Mulder in the previous shot. Moreover, her status as a substitute teacher raises questions about her reliability as a character. Her background is totally unknown, lending her character a transience which is open to foreboding speculation. The shot lingers to show her ending the class then cuts to show the girls present at the murder the previous night walking towards the classroom exit. The overlaying of synthesized music as the girls walk towards the teacher creates anticipation and furthers the viewer's suspicions that the teacher is not to be trusted. A mid-shot from a side angle shows the teacher speaking with the girls, asking them to confide in her if they need support; the choice of a mid-shot creates an intimacy which will be open to re-reading after the following series of shots; as the girls leave expressing thanks, the camera cuts to the teacher's hands and arms. She briskly gathers the assignments, banging them on the desk to neaten them into an ordered pile. The frame composition is sinister: to focus on the teacher's body without her face creates a feeling of dislocation. This, coupled with the briskness of her movement is potentially threatening.

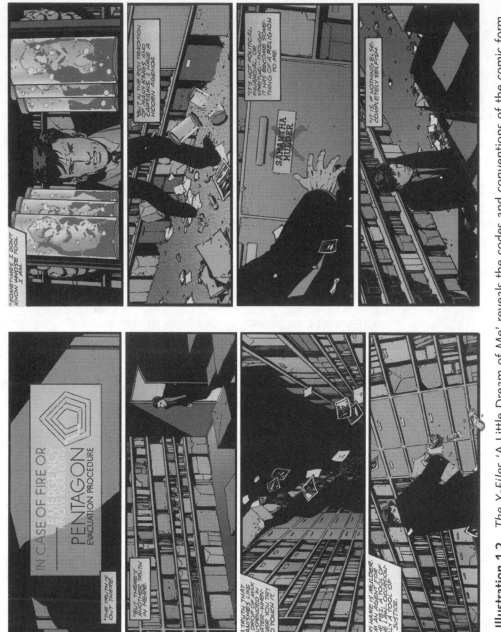

Illustration 1.2 *The X-Files* 'A Little Dream of Me' reveals the codes and conventions of the comic form.
Source: 20th Century Fox and Topps Comics. Reprinted with permission.

The final shot confirms her connection with the occult or an alien force. As she places the assignments in the desk, the camera moves to a close-up on her face. The teacher smiles while staring off-camera towards a presence, leading the viewer to question the 'straightforwardness' of the previous shots.

Phyllis Paddock's offer to counsel the students is no longer reassuring; it is, instead, set up as a terrifying catalyst for furthering the satanic events of the narrative. The method of framing and editing utilized within this episode reflects the ways they are used more generally within television production. The fact that these techniques are being used conventionally allows the audience to comprehend their implications for the future development of this episode of *The X-Files*.

The comicbook X-Files

In 'A Little Dream of Me', the third 'all-new case' for Scully and Mulder in *The X-Files* comic, there is an opening sequence of graphic frames which introduce the narrative. These are comparable to the sequence which introduces the story of each episode before the familiar credit sequence of the television series. In 'A Little Dream of Me' these graphic frames show Mulder breaking into the Pentagon's chamber of files with a view to opening an X-file with personal significance (see illustration 1.2). It deals with the disappearance of his sister Samantha. In much the same way that viewers of film and television must learn to decode moving images, the comic reader becomes competent at building a relationship of meaning between the montage of separate graphic frames which constitute the narrative sequence. Narrative captions 'place' each frame and speech or think bubbles allow the characters to communicate directly with the reader. These are examples of the technical codes and conventions at work in comics. The framing of each image, the colour used in the graphics, the typography used to create the impression of sounds, such as 'POW', 'BZT WHRRR', or speech bubbles, can be designed to produce a variety of connotations by the producers. In this particular opening, each still offers a view which operates rather like the viewfinder of a camera. The first picture shows Mulder's point of view as he stands in front of the door to the Pentagon file chamber. The second picture features an omniscient position, showing Mulder entering the room. The eight stills which make up the initial double spread all show Mulder from different angles penetrating the files until he finds the one marked with a red X entitled 'Samantha Mulder'.

Specific to comics in general, and to this one in particular, is the digression away from a strictly realistic mode of presentation. As a form, comics encourage an imaginative, active reader, who must fill the narrative 'gaps'. At the same time the still graphic images are open to moments of exaggeration which are not usually available or used in television.

In just eight graphic frames Mulder's emotional, even manic, mind-state is conveyed, as files, photographs and even pickled aliens tumble out from the shelves amidst fragmented viewpoints of Mulder's taut body and anguished facial expressions. The larger-than-life images conveyed within the comic would be unsuitable for television because they fall outside the conventions of realism required for mainstream productions. Yet within comic pages they are perfectly acceptable, as they exist within the limitations imposed by the codes and conventions of the form. Once again, we can see the ways in which very similar content is presented to the audience differently, depending upon the medium in which it appears.

Advertising and The X-Files

The enormous popularity of *The X-Files* not only led to very rapid repeats of early episodes on both satellite and terrestrial television channels in the UK, but to a vast expansion in the tie-in market of which the comic book is a very visible and prominent example. The circulation of what might be labelled the X-Files concept in the public imagination has meant that advertisers have confidently capitalized on the meanings generated by that concept. Vodaphone, a large telecommunications company, have utilized the X-Files concept of two agents searching for unexplained phenomena in their attempt to create short promotional films, or what are commonly known as adverts. These are texts that will sell products to consumers, heighten their awareness of the product's brand name and create an easily identifiable image for that product. In the Vodaphone advertisements the unexplained phenomena under investigation have included popular mysteries such as the Loch Ness monster and Big Foot. As chapter 7 in this section explains, these sorts of advertisement call upon the audience's prior knowledge of popular culture, in terms of both *The X-Files* and its conventions, and the mysteries the agents investigate, in a playful and celebratory way. Vodaphone is therefore able to cash in on the popularity of *The X-Files*, whilst establishing itself as an up-to-date telephone communication network.

The Vodaphone advertisements also utilize the services of actor Kyle MacLachlan in their equivalent of the Mulder role. MacLachlan appeared in another popular cult television series *Twin Peaks* and brings with him an off-beat persona that allows the audience instantly to key into his character. The advert's production team has been able to construct the narrative economically because it has been able to rely, to some extent, on audience knowledge. It is important to note that both *The X-Files* series and the Vodaphone advertisement are television texts. This highlights the fact that even within a medium, slightly different codes and conventions can be utilized at different moments depending upon the purpose of the text.

It is essential that advertisers can rely on an audience's knowledge of how textually to 'read' an advertisement. The context in which it appears therefore becomes of crucial importance to its textual operation and its effectiveness as an advertising text. For example, audiences will bring expectations to television advertisements: they will be short, they will contain a slogan, they will focus on the product and they will offer some form of brief entertainment. The makers of advertisements must therefore be aware of this when designing such texts, and so a particular set of rules will be followed quite closely. The language of advertising as it is used in the Vodaphone X-Files example is very reliant on a knowledgeable audience which will in some way be aware of the texts being referenced. As advertisement makers know that their products will be repeated a number of times, they are able to infuse elements that will probably only be picked up by viewers after a number of transmissions. In the case of the Vodaphone advertisements, these include references to a number of other prominent science-fiction television programmes such as *Doctor Who* and *V*. The ability to know beforehand that repeated viewing of their text will take place is something that the producers of the television series cannot rely upon; they must work under the presumption that their product may only be seen once and therefore must have a certain level of almost instant coherence. What is interesting in the case of *The X-Files* is that it is probably a name that has meaning and associations for those who have never seen the original series, such is the omnipresent nature of its connotations in the late 1990s.

From the examples cited it is possible to see that advertisements and television series share some clear textual similarities. However, the specifics of each medium, its aims and objectives and the production codes and conventions utilized to realize them, must form a central part in the decoding process of media analysis. These must also be borne in mind alongside the use of the theories explored in later chapters in this section.

Suggestions for further work

Select a contemporary television programme that 'plays' with the codes and conventions of the medium in the manner described in relation to *The Young Ones*. Identify as many examples as you can of how it plays with codes and conventions, and consider the purpose of using such techniques.

Identify as many examples as you can of popular television programmes or films whose 'concept' has been utilized by advertisers. What aspects of the concept do you think made them particularly appealing to those wishing to advertise their products?

Further reading

Crisell, Andrew 1986: *Understanding Radio*, London: Routledge.
Cubbit, Sean 1991: *Timeshift: on video culture*. London: Routledge.
Ellis, John 1992: *Visible Fictions: Cinema: Television: Video*, 2nd edition. London:
    Routledge.

2

Reading Media Images

One of the cornerstones of media studies is the critical analysis of media texts. Often referred to as 'reading' media texts, critical analysis is the close textual examination of the meanings that media output generates. The aim of this chapter is to introduce two key approaches to understanding the textual construction of visual media products: *mise-en-scène* analysis and semiotics. It seeks to show what each approach is capable of revealing about the meaning of textual images and what each can offer to enlighten our understanding about 'what is going on' in the textual organization of a film, a television programme, an advert – indeed the whole plethora of visual media available to us in our everyday lives. These two approaches testify to the interdisciplinarity of media studies. *Mise-en-scène* analysis has its roots in film studies, yet its underlying principles can be used for analysing a range of other visual media. Semiotics, which comes out of linguistics and philosophy, can be utilized in the analysis of sound as well as visual imagery. The two approaches divide and structure the chapter: each section will outline the theory, locate it in historical context and apply it to textual examples.

Mise-en-scène analysis

Mise-en-scène *analysis in context*

In their book *Film Art* (1986) David Bordwell and Kristin Thompson trace the origins of the term *mise-en-scène* as applied to film back to its use in nineteenth-century theatre. In the theatrical sense, *mise-en-scène* was the term used to describe stage direction, or, as Bordwell and Thompson literally translate, ' "the fact of putting into the scene" ' (p. 119). Film critics, they argue, transferred the use of the term to the film medium as a way of understanding the director's input into the construction of the film frame. *Mise-en-scène* is the term used to describe the staging elements which film and theatre share: lighting, costume, setting and the movement of the figures. *Mise-en-scène* is the term one might use to trace back the director's pre-production planning intentions with regard to how each frame will look. In another sense it is a reading methodology which can be used in a consideration of how meaning is constructed within films through the use, for example, of a particular lighting system.

In the 1930s scholars in Europe attacked what they called mass culture. In Britain the most notorious critic promulgating the idea that popular culture was a low and damaging form of culture was the literary critic F. R. Leavis. In Europe the Marxist scholars Herbert Marcuse and Theodor Adorno of the Frankfurt School despised popular forms, arguing that Marxist revolution could never come to fruition because mass culture would effectually numb the critical faculties of the ordinary mind. Mass or popular culture, which included forms such as television and the cinema, were thought to be debased, barbaric forms which dulled the senses of the proletariat. Such forms could never aspire to be called art; they were commercial, mass-produced within industrial constraints and contexts, and could never contain the personal vision and virtues of 'true' art. For them, art, that is works which revealed a personal insight into the human condition, could only be produced by artists who possessed individual genius (see 'The Frankfurt School and its critique of the culture industries' in chapter 8). By the 1960s, however, film critics with a vested interest in redefining the boundaries of what constituted art began to seek new ways of theorizing what forms could reasonably earn the label of 'art'. They set out to mount a critique of the ways in which earlier scholars had lumped all popular art forms together. For one thing, they argued, cinema as a form was able to exhibit to large audiences, and this gave it the ability to disseminate ideas in ways that were closed to more elitist forms such as easel painting. It was in the wake of this challenge that popular cinema, most notably that produced in Hollywood, was reassessed by film scholars.

This group of scholars became known as auteur critics. Their project was to find ways in which film could be found to possess features which could elevate it to an art form. They began to look across the work of certain film-makers in order to ascertain why particular directors could be categorized as great and therefore be placed in a film canon, while others could not. Those who did rise above the majority of practitioners working in Hollywood were deemed auteurs, directors who could transcend the industrial constraints that working within the system imposed. In this way auteur analysis accepted and was predicated on the same high culture / low culture distinction drawn upon by the Frankfurt School critics and F. R. Leavis. As a result, the auteur critics radically retheorized the task of film criticism, as John Caughie argues in his introduction to *Theories of Authorship* (1981): 'The business of the critic was to discover the director within the given framework, to find the traces of submerged personality, to find ways in which the *auteur* had transformed the material so that the explicit subject matter was no longer what the film was really about' (p. 12). Absolutely central to the auteur critics' disclosure of the hidden elements of artistry in film was *mise-en-scène* analysis. For such critics the personal handling of *mise-en-scène* became what has been referred to as the 'stylistic signature' of the director. As Caughie maintained:

> style at least has the possibility of being under the control of the director, and it is here that the personality may be the most legible. Mise-en-scene has a transformative effect. It is with mise-en-scene that the *auteur* transforms the material which has been given to him; so it is in the mise-en-scene – in the disposition of the scene ... that the *auteur* writes his individuality into the film. (pp. 12–13)

A number of the critics in the 1950s and 1960s who embraced auteurism contributed to the film journals *Cahiers du Cinèma* in France and *Movie* in Britain. Examples of this kind of critical practice in the pages of *Movie* were V. F. Perkins's work on Nicholas Ray and Barry Boys's on Vincente Minnelli. In Perkins's piece, 'The Cinema of Nicholas Ray', the commitment to *mise-en-scène*, a term often used interchangeably with style in *Movie*, as the underlying principle of thematic coherence in cinema is clearly central to his analysis of Ray's films. Taking a collection of Ray's films, Perkins charts the recurring thematic concerns embedded in the film texts which point up his 'profoundly personal vision' (Perkins, 1976, p. 257). He argues that Ray is able to express himself through the film medium with remarkable lucidity and directness. For Perkins, this manifests itself in the way in which Ray is able to deliver a great deal of information about his characters and their relationships in the early part of his films. Ray is also able to manifest his 'desire for direct communication' through his use of symbolism, which is often blatantly commenting on the wider themes at play in the films (p. 256).

While there are problems with this kind of analysis, one example being the resultant exclusive and excluding canon of 'great directors', *mise-en-scène* at least offered a specific form of critical analysis which was able to deal directly with the visual aspect of the medium. As Caughie argues, *mise-en-scène*, 'engaging with the specific mechanisms of visual discourse', was at least able to release it 'from literary models, and from the liberal commitments which were prepared to validate films on the basis of their themes alone' (1981, p. 13).

Mise-en-scène: *a definition*

According to Bordwell and Thompson, *mise-en-scène* is a system of staging elements which are shared by theatre. They divide it into four domains:

setting, costume and make-up, lighting and figure expression, and move-ment. Each one hosts a potentially infinite range of possibilities which, when blended with the other elements, combine to give each film its own unique visual style. Reflecting the theatrical origins of the term, their definition is characterized by an emphasis on *mise-en-scène* as a staging technique: 'in controlling the *mise-en-scène*', they argue, 'the director *stages the event* for the camera' (1986, p. 119). Using historical examples drawn from Hollywood, as well as ones selected from a variety of national cinemas, Bordwell and Thompson demonstrate the endless possibilities *mise-en-scène* offers the director when attempting to create meaning within the film medium.

Breaking down the various elements of *mise-en-scène* is a useful pre-liminary exercise for understanding both the specific visual devices at work in the construction of a film and how they then generate meaning for viewers. *Waterworld* (1995), a film reputed to be one of the most costly productions undertaken by Hollywood to date, acts as an interesting example of the use of setting and lighting to create particular effects. Set in a future where much of the earth has become covered by the sea, the remaining world is built out of the remnants of our contemporary land and cityscapes. The 'atoll', which is inhabited by some of the surviving settlers, is a floating encampment built of scrap metal.

The 'smokers', a gang of enslaved pirates who periodically terrorize the atoll colony, live in an enormous, rusted oil-tanker which the viewer learns was once the famous tanker *Exxon Valdez*. The film's set is an imaginative construction which cleverly selects elements of the 'old' dry-land time, which the viewer recognizes as elements of our world. By showing the settlers as survivors who have adapted to their aqueous present with the scarce and at times ill-fitted resources of the dryland past, the set creates a convincing future. The atoll is an enormous construc-tion: part city, part strategic vessel. Fashioned from a vast number of ingredients, from the castle-like gates at its entrance to its water-powered windmill, the set constructs the sense of a people who have been forced to re-evolve. Some aspects of the 'old' time are usefully cast into new roles, others forgotten or unrequired. Since *Waterworld* is a film based almost entirely outdoors, the viewer is encouraged to read the film's lighting as a natural phenomenon, with the sun and sky seeming to light much of the film's action. Yet even while the effect strived for is natural-ism, it is no less a constructed effect than a film which uses coloured filters or strobe lighting. Moreover, a number of the outdoor action scenes would clearly still require standard Hollywood lighting arrangements for close-up or mid-shot framing.

Dawn of the Dead (1979), George A. Romero's zombie horror film, uses costume and make-up effects to distinguish the flesh-devouring undead from the commandos trapped with them in a shopping mall where the zombie pack are forever doomed to hunt for human prey. The zombies wear everyday clothes signifying their status in the society they once occupied while alive. Not only does the relatively simple use of an eventone skin make-up, which varies from pale aqua to greenish grey, serve to render bloodless the flesh of the zombies, it also emphasizes their flesh-ripping mouths. The fact that all the zombies share the greenish hallmark of zombie-like skin tone also highlights, not without a touch of comic wit, the fact that people from all walks of life have been zombified – from old people, to hippies and even Hare-Krishna worshippers. The result is horrifyingly repulsive, for while their flesh is given a mouldy, decaying hue, their mouths in contrast are bright pink, active and undoubtedly hungry. Yet while the make-up is in part responsible for the creation of these monsters, it is impossible to discuss the meaning created by these creatures without reference to the expressive movement of the actors. When unaware of nearby flesh, they amble forward in hordes, some of them rocking from side to side as they walk, their faces hung and expressionless. Their simple movement signifies their status as bereft of life. But when live human bodies are nearby they still move slowly, but much more surely and with arms outstretched, unerringly making an advance towards their human prey. Even when they encounter an obstacle, like a shop window which at one point stops their advance towards the commandos, they continue to take steps and reach out against glass towards the live bodies they instinctually desire. In this example figure movement is an essential ingredient in generating the idea that these monsters are terrifyingly unstoppable.

While Bordwell and Thompson separate the four 'general' elements of *mise-en-scène*, they stress that its elements rarely act alone to create effects. In most cases the basic elements act together to form a system of meaning, with each film text arguably the result of the individual staging procedures conceived by its director. Film also sets out to construct a sense of space in which the 'world' of each film is set. Unequivocally, the screen onto which a film image is projected is flat, yet the medium is able to represent screen space as though it were three-dimensional. Bordwell and Thompson suggest that this is achieved on two levels. First, there are compositional elements: movement, colour, balance and size which are at the director's disposal and which draw the eye and guide the viewer's perception of screen space (1986, p. 136). While compositional elements are working to cue our looking around the space created by film, a second layer of strategies used to create the illusion of three-dimensionality operates simultaneously (p. 137). By manoeuvring the staged elements of the *mise-en-scène* already explored – lighting, setting and so on – the director is able to imply that a scene has volume and depth. The viewer, already familiar with the conventions in other arts which construct three-dimensional space – theatre, painting and photography, for example – is persuaded to look through the flat screen plane into the action depicted in imagined 'real' space. The impression of the solidity of objects in film gives each frame volume, suggested by their shape, shading and movement.

Bordwell and Thompson define *mise-en-scène* through a combination of separate elements, working in systematic combination to create meaning in the cinema, whereas other critics argue that *mise-en-scène* ought to be linked to the wider issues involved in film production. Richard Maltby and Ian Craven in their book *Hollywood Cinema* (1995) argue that an understanding of how *mise-en-scène* is organized by Hollywood film-makers must be tied to the financial constraints practitioners working within the mainstream industry encounter: 'We should think of mise-en-scène less as a list of devices, or techniques such as set design, lighting, or camera placement, than as a form of textual economy, comparable to … financial and generic economies' (p. 200). Bordwell and Thompson's account of *mise-en-scène* as a system open to infinite possibilities is countered by Maltby and Craven's argument, which theorizes such possibilities as partially constrained within the realms of what audiences can recognize. The generic conventions of film types set boundaries around what possibilities, are open to the director. While the staging of elements provides endless possibilities for the director, work within a particular genre will inevitably impose limits onto the range of staging devices available.

So far this chapter has explored the ways in which *mise-en-scène* analysis might be used to explore the connotative effects of the staged representational elements of film images. Indeed, there is no reason why *mise-en-scène* analysis cannot be used for approaching the textual construction of a range of other visual media forms, for example television drama, soap opera, television current affairs and the quiz show, as well as photographic media forms such as advertising. However, if *mise-en-scène* is utilized as an approach for forms other than film, Maltby and Craven's argument that the form in question must be related to the financial and generic specificities which structure its production are important factors to take into account. Whilst much can be gained from applying *mise-en-scène* analysis to examples such as the BBC's production of *Pride and Prejudice* or Granada television's crime thriller *Cracker*, there are specific factors to be borne in mind. For example, the generic conventions of either period adaptation or of the crime serial which shape and delimit the choices the director can make about the visual style selected for the programme.

While it is agreed among film scholars that *mise-en-scène* is a reading strategy which examines the staged aspects of the film image, there is a degree of uncertainty about whether the term includes the technological properties of the film medium which form an integral part of the film image. Such elements – image framing, editing, the duration of shots or camera movement – are missing from most accounts which define the term. It is only in the work by some auteur critics appearing in *Movie*, in which the term *mise-en-scène* is used interchangeably with visual style, where the technical specificities of film are mentioned as aspects of *mise-en-scène*. For example, in the discussion of Ray's work mentioned earlier, V. F. Perkins includes the use of editing as an essential component of his unique visual style. Yet Bordwell and Thompson in *Film Art* exclude the technological elements of film from their model of *mise-en-scène*. Taking the point further, Pam Cook in *The Cinema Book* (1987) concludes her definition of *mise-en-scène* by arguing that attention to film form requires it to be an approach used in conjunction with others if a complete understanding of a film is to be achieved. Some of these complementary approaches are discussed in the following chapters. However, it is clear that the framing, editing and effects created by the technological properties of visual mediums are crucial aspects of any analysis.

Semiotic analysis

Semiotic analysis in context

The body of critical work on semiotics credits the American philosopher Charles S. Peirce and the Swiss linguist Ferdinand de Saussure as the thinkers who laid its foundations. It was not until the 1950s, however, when Roland Barthes began to apply the theoretical principles of semiotics to various aspects of French popular culture, from the new Citroen car to steak and chips, in his book *Mythologies* (1972), that the approach gained currency among academic audiences. Semiotics, or the science of signs, is primarily the study of how signs communicate. It is also the study of the rules which regulate the operation of each system of signs. Unlike *mise-en-scène* analysis, which has historically been used to analyse the film medium almost exclusively, semiotics, as Ellen Seiter argues, 'is the study of everything that can be used for communication: words, images, traffic signs, flowers, music, medical symptoms, and much more' (1992, p. 31). Seiter's examples demonstrate the assertion made by Liesbet van Zoonen that 'almost anything can be considered a sign' (1994, p. 74). More specifically for media studies, it is an approach suitable for analysing how meaning is produced by media texts from a diverse range of media. Seiter argues that, as an approach, semiotics made a radical break with more traditional forms of criticism. Instead of asking what meanings an aesthetic art form conveys, as many elitist forms of art criticism tend to do, semiotics asks how the mechanics of signs in all texts, including art objects, communicate, thereby bringing a more scientifically methodological analysis to bear on texts. Furthering her point, Seiter identifies the benefits of semiotic analysis: it 'allowed us to describe the workings of cultural communication with greater accuracy and enlarged our recognition of the conventions that characterize our culture' (1992, p. 32).

The key concepts of semiotics

Semiotics is based on Saussure's 'discoveries' about the sign in language, the main tenets of which are to be found in a series of published lectures entitled *Course in General Linguistics* (1974). Saussure argued that the sign is made up of two elements: the signifier and the signified. These two elements are inseparable. The signifier in word form is made up of a combination of letters, for example 'house'; the signified is the concept of the dwelling place summoned in the mind of the reader. The relationship between the signifier and the signified in the case of words as signifiers is entirely arbitrary. The word 'house' and the mental concept it refers to have no natural relationship to one another. Indeed, it would be wholly possible for the members of a speech community to use 'spleep' as a stand-in signifier to replace 'house', as long as the users of that system became acquainted with its usage. It therefore follows that signs and their relation to external referents (the actual objects to which signs refer) are arbitrary. We can look to other languages to sanction further the arbitrary link between the signifier and the signified; if there were any-thing inherently house-ish about the external referent, all languages would use the term, yet in French the word *maison* is used.

According to Saussure, signs make meaning relationally. The signified, or the meaning of 'house', has nothing to do with its status as a building; instead it is the way in which our linguistic sign system divides the meaning of other kinds of dwelling place. We understand the meaning of 'house' because of its difference from other words in the linguistic sign system: it is neither mansion, nor cottage, nor shack, nor maisonette. Jonathan Culler in his book *Saussure* (1990) explains the same idea, using colours as an example. He suggests that if one were explaining the meaning of 'brown' to a non-English speaker, the wrong thing to do would be to take that person into a room full of brown objects. Instead, other colours need to be introduced into the field of meaning because brown can only be meaningful in relation to other colours: 'in order to know the meaning of brown, one must understand red, tan, grey, black etc.' (p. 25). As John Hartley argues, 'What determines the value of any sign, then, is not its degree of fit with some pre-existing entity or concept (whether of thought or of nature), since signs *themselves* define what is and what is not a concept. The value of signs is determined wholly by their relation-ships with others in a system' (1982, p. 18).

Central to the semiotic approach is the idea that language, signs and their meaning are historically, culturally and socially produced. Consider, for example, the historical and social change the word 'queer' has been subject to. Twenty years ago the word was used pejoratively to describe lesbians and gay men. Yet in the early 1990s the term was reappropriated by gay groups who worked to change its meaning. Since heterosexual society has oppressed gay groups the term 'queer' was seized upon as the label which symbolized the very discrimination the groups have chosen to rally against. 'Queer and proud' became a slogan for groups which aimed to resist the oppression against non-heterosexual sexualities which exists in mainstream culture. The fact that words can be subject to such radical change illustrates the point that signs and their meanings are historically, socially and culturally contingent.

Furthermore, Saussurean linguistics holds that signs rarely make meaning as solitary units; instead they generate meaning in relation to other signs. Saussure argued that languages and their codes are constructed from two axial dimensions: the paradigmatic and the syntagmatic. John Fiske defines the paradigmatic as choice and the syntagmatic as combination (O'Sullivan et al., 1994, p. 216). He goes on to offer a man's wardrobe as an example of a set of paradigms: 'one each for shirts, ties, socks – which are combined into a syntagma (his dress for the day)' (p. 216). A paradigm is therefore a set of units which hold some kind of generic likeness – like the set of shirts that the man looking into his wardrobe can choose from: the Hawaiian shirt, the grandad-style shirt, the checked shirt. Yet each unit, or shirt, is distinguishable from the rest since it derives its meaning from the others that it is not, the white long-sleeved Oxford-style shirt is not the checked shirt and it is not the grandad shirt, nor is it a range of other possibilities. It can also be seen from the example given by Fiske that a man's dress or syntagma is made up from a number of paradigms, or choices – not just the shirt, but trousers, jackets, cuff-links, shoes and so on.

In semiotic analysis, it is possible to conduct what is called a commutation test. Such a test involves taking one paradigmatic choice out of a syntagma and replacing it with another. The result demonstrates that the meaning of the syntagma changes. If we refer back to a man's dress once more and think of complete conventional evening wear and replace the paradigmatic choice, a dickie-bow tie, with another paradigmatic choice, a boot-lace tie, then the meaning of the syntagma is entirely altered. What the commutation test further underlines is that signs and their combinations are often highly conventionalized, hence the social unacceptability of the boot-lace tie with evening wear. Commutation tests are also useful devices for media analysis because of what they can tell us about the conventions which structure the meaning of media texts.

While Saussure concentrated on symbolic signs (language), Peirce was interested in working on the relationship between pictorial signs and their meaning. In some sign systems, for example drawings, photographs and television images, the relationship between the signifier and the signified is less arbitrary. Peirce called signs in which the signifier resembles its signified in some way iconic. Yet iconic signs are no less conventionalized than words in language. Just as the meaning of words becomes prevalent through recurrent, learned and collective use, the resemblance that pictures have to their referents comes from learned recognition. Seiler illustrates this point by using the example of the different drawings of a dog that might be produced, each relying on the recognition of sign conventions:

> The drawing could be skeletal or anatomical, in which case it might take
> a trained veterinarian or zoologist to recognize any structural similarity
> between the drawing and the signified 'dog'. The iconic sign could be a
> child's drawing, in which case another expert decoder, for instance the
> child's parent or teacher, might be required to detect the structural resem-
> blance. (Seiter, 1992, p. 35)

A key point about the features of representational codes, from words in
language to the iconic signs of photo-journalism, is that they become
naturalized. Van Zoonen argues: 'semiotic analysis can be seen as a formal-
ization of the interpretative activities ordinary human beings undertake
incessantly' (1994, p. 77). As highly skilled users of signs, whether linguistic or iconic, their use becomes so normative that there is a danger of
believing that signs are the most natural, most 'correct' way to represent
our environment. Yet what must be remembered is that the link between
signifiers and their signified is made purely by convention. Even while
there exists a belief that a camera gives us access to highly objective
accounts of the world, its images are as subject to codes of signification as
drawings are. Semiotics enables us to realize that all media texts are
mediated, using the codes and conventions of the sign systems in which
they communicate. They can therefore never simply be transparent
mediums through which we have access to a 'truth'.

Barthes made a differentiation between first- and second-order signification, or, as he labelled them, denotation and connotation. Denotation is
the image or signifier – what is contained in the image. The denotative
meaning of 'red rose' would be a flower of a particular colour. Connotation
takes the first-order signification – signifier and signified – and attaches an
additional second-order signified to it. The connotative meaning of 'red
rose' is romance. Importantly, it is our culture which surrounds the red
rose with the connotative meaning of romance. Second-order signification
emanates from the imbued cultural meanings within a sign system, and
a knowledge about the values and beliefs of a particular culture are
necessary if connotative readings of signs are to be successfully arrived
at. It is because connotation is so saturated with cultural meaning that
Barthes argued that it is always ideological, expressing what he called the
'myth' of a society. In so doing, the connotative meaning of signs is often
attempting to make culturally constructed societal power relations of, for
example, class and gender, seem natural, universal and inevitable. By
logical extension, Barthes's argument about connotation, myth and ideology can also be applied to the images that the media directly trade in: it
is through connotative meanings that the media, at certain moments,
communicate ideologically.

Semiotic analysis: the front cover of Cosmopolitan

Van Zoonen argues that while semiotics does not offer a definitive methodological approach to analysing texts, what it does provide is 'a means for a systematic assessment of the processes of signification in the text' (1994, p. 78). Furthermore, she suggests that a semiotic analysis can be organized into a series of working 'steps'. Using van Zoonen's 'steps', we now want to provide a semiotic analysis of a front cover of a copy of the general interest women's magazine *Cosmopolitan* (see illustration 2.1).

The first step for van Zoonen is to 'identify relevant signs and their dominant aspects', a step that requires that the kind of signs used are categorized, and, with particular regard to media texts, some are likely to be iconic signs (1994, p. 78). The front cover of *Cosmopolitan* is made up of a number of signs. The photographic representation of a woman is an iconic sign. Words as signs are used for the title, cover lines and the date and price, which overlay the iconic sign of a woman. These signs are featured on glossy paper, another signifier offering meaning about the product.

Having established the various signs we wish to examine, van Zoonen recommends that 'one continues with examining the paradigmatic combination of these signs, for instance by asking what their absent opposites are, and how they relate to each other syntagmatically' (1994, p. 79). In making a choice from a set of possible units or paradigms, as in the example of the shirts in a man's wardrobe cited earlier, meaning is being made by selecting a unit that derives its meaning from what it is not. Syntagmatic meaning, or the relationship each sign has with others in the same text, is crucial, but absent paradigmatic opposites also make meaning in a text. Syntagmatically, in the case of the front cover of *Cosmopolitan*, the constraints of the genre of the general interest magazine impose a coded order of signification on the producers, so that certain elements must feature in conventionally organized ways. As *Cosmopolitan*'s readers would expect, the model centres the image, the cover lines appear at the sides and the title heads the page. Within these boundaries, the elements, the cover lines and choice of model, for example, signify slightly differently because they change each month, but always within the relational limitations of the genre. Identifying paradigmatic opposites amounts to carrying out a commutation test on various elements in the syntagma. The meaning of what has been selected can be arrived at by questioning what other paradigmatic units have been rejected. In this edition, as is the case with most other issues of *Cosmopolitan*, a white Western woman centres the cover, as opposed to a Chinese or Afro-Caribbean woman. It might therefore be argued that the magazine is Eurocentric in outlook. The clothes worn by the model, a vest with two overshirts, one crimson silk the other a white translucent fabric, are casual yet physically revealing. And while the combination of dress codes is in itself a syntagma, the

Illustration 2.1   Magazines such as *Cosmopolitan* can fruitfully be analysed using semiotics.
Source: National Magazine Company Limited. Reprinted with permission.

combination chosen is not executive meeting wear, nor is it what one might expect to find a female engineer wearing. So a particular kind of female dress, one possibly signifying modern, casual sexuality, is being presented. A consideration of the paradigmatic opposites therefore throws the meanings of the text sharply into relief. Van Zoonen argues that having carried out those first two 'steps' of semiotic analysis, 'One thus arrives at an understanding of the different processes of signification in the text: denotation, connotation, myth and ideology' (1994, p. 79). The *Cosmopolitan* front cover on a denotational level or first-order signification carries the following: cover lines, all of which are about sex, 'SEX lives of the rich and famous', 'The world's most wanted men talk about ... SEX'; a title *Cosmopolitan*; typography of differing styles; a colour scheme of red, white, blue and yellow; a photographic representation of a blond, white, young woman, who looks out to the viewer with lips parted and who poses side on, with arm raised above her head to lift her left breast into view. This denotational list is in no way exhaustive – there is much more to say about what the cover denotes; semiotics as a tool tends to leave no sign unexamined, hence its usefulness as an approach.

On the cover of this edition of *Cosmopolitan* the second-order signification or connotations generated by this particular syntagma are predominantly concerned with specific meanings about femininity and sexuality. The cover lines all advertise features about sex, which hold contradictory messages about how women and sexuality are represented in mainstream culture. Some of the features clearly show that feminism in a popular form has reached mainstream audiences – '*Sexually Assertive Women*. How do men feel when you come on strong?' This kind of cover line connotes sexually strong-minded women, thereby dispelling the dominant idea that women are sexually passive. On the other hand, the fact that all the features in the magazine are about sex, some of which are operating on an instructional level – 'Transform your performance on the job' – tends to connote the idea that women are not much more than sexual beings, since there are no features about, for instance, women and work or women and politics. The title, *Cosmopolitan*, creates the sense that the kind of femininity represented in the magazine is outgoing, gregarious and sophisticated. The colour schemes and typography also signify. The bold, fearless reds and blues give weight to meanings of sexual freedom and permissiveness being generated by other signifiers in the text. The simple, clear, crisp typography creates a modern, urbane feel. It is the photographic image which is arguably the most significant sign on the front cover, not least because it is the one that readers focus much of their attention on when deciding which magazine to buy from the range of competing titles on the news-stand.

The white, slender, European-looking young woman selected to centre the front cover is heavily made-up despite her regular features: small nose, white straight teeth, full lips and flawless skin, features which are all part of the cultural conventions of feminine beauty in the West. The woman's posture, clothing and facial expression signify sexual confidence and availability. The hand held above the model's head forces her breasts forward, the open shirt carries the eye downwards across the model's body. The confident gaze at the viewer invites the approach of the female consumer, who in turn might wish to make herself more consumable for men in the same way the model does. In this way the connotations of the photograph of the model tie in with the connotations of the cover lines: while sexual confidence emanates from the image of the model, conversely the image renders insignificant the woman's identity or anything else she might achieve beyond attracting men.

The signifiers in this text which are linked by the theme of sexuality might, arguably, be categorized as trading on the myths about women that pervade our Western culture: that before anything else women must strive to be sexually attractive for the sake of male, patriarchal pleasure. And, by privileging particular types of femininity above others, white, thin, conventionally beautiful, sexually confident women are confirmed as the most desirable, thereby reinforcing myths about what constitutes desirable femininity.

The polysemic nature of signs, or the ability signs have to carry multiple meanings, amounts to the fact that a singular or definitive reading of a text is impossible. Signs also change according to the context in which they are placed. Imagine the differences in meaning if the photograph on the front cover of *Cosmopolitan* were to appear on the front of a magazine aimed at a lesbian readership for example. Moreover, the social position of the reader, arising out of factors such as class, gender, sexuality, race, education and occupation, impact on the kinds of reading produced. The reading of the front cover of *Cosmopolitan* therefore offers one possible way of interpreting its signs, but there is a range of other available readings.

Semiotic analysis is, as van Zoonen argues, a 'powerful tool to understand how sign systems in mass media can evoke emotions, associations, fears, hopes, fantasies and acquiescence' (1994, p. 79). Semiotics has this effect because, as an analytical approach, it insists on cracking open layers of meaning which reside in texts. Indeed, the study of connotation refuses merely to describe media content. However, semiotics does assume a well-acquainted knowledge of the text's host culture if rigorous analysis is to take place. What semiotics cannot provide, as van Zoonen asserts, is any kind of statistical information about how often particular meanings re-occur in the media. It might be useful to build up a sense of how often and in what ways female sexuality is represented on the front cover of *Cosmopolitan*, for example. Content analysis, an approach considered in more depth in chapter 4, aims to provide such information. Some media researchers, for example the Glasgow University Media Group in its work on television news in the 1970s and 1980s, used a combination of both semiotics and content analysis to argue that news presented a distorted view of industrial relations, which served the ideological interests of the ruling class. In order to reach those conclusions they measured their semiotic and content analyses of the news over a given period, and compared it to empirical data of actual strike events. For their project they needed to move beyond just textual readings of the news.

The problems with textual analysis

Textual analysis, or the practice of questioning the meaning in magazines, films or even junk mail to name but a few examples, might be described as the starting point of media studies. Approaches such as *mise-en-scène* analysis and semiotics offer an invaluable understanding of the construction of textual meaning. Textual analysis used in isolation, however, tends to confine meaning solely to the text. Historically, *mise-en-scène* analysis made no direct mention of possible audiences, but instead assumed the audience to be an abstract given, unresearched and entirely unspecified. While semiotics theorizes signs and their meaning as cultural and open to change, and the reader as a negotiator of textual meaning, it remains a text-based approach which requires theoretical extension if it is to include some analyses of the interdiscursive ways audiences make meaning. There now exists a whole body of work in media and cultural studies which has sought to challenge the previous assumptions made about audiences within theories of textual analysis. This work, which used empirical data and ethnographic study, as well as textual analysis, is typified by the analysis undertaken at the Birmingham Centre for Contemporary Cultural Studies (BCCCS). Some of the most significant research on audiences undertaken at the centre was carried out by David Morley. In *The 'Nationwide' Audience* (1980a) his project was initially to test out empirically some of the theoretical assertions made by Stuart Hall in his seminal paper, 'Encoding and decoding in the television discourse' (1973). What is central to the approach used by the members of the Birmingham Media Group and to the research carried out by Morley is the focus on examining the social position of the reader, and how those social factors impacted on the meaning specific audiences made of media texts. As Morley argues in 'Texts, readers, subjects', 'other discourses are always in play besides those of the particular text in focus – discourses ... brought into play through "the subject's" placing in other practices – cultural, educational, institutional' (Morley, 1980b, p. 163) The main principles of Hall's argument in 'Encoding and decoding in the television discourse' and the importance of a variety of work carried out at BCCCS will be investigated further in Part III. A truly thorough analysis aims to incorporate other factors into the investigative arena besides just the meanings either overt or latent in media texts; factors such as institutional constraint on textual meaning as well as the ways in which audiences actively negotiate and read media output as a result of a whole range of social variables.

Suggestions for further work

Select and analyse a short sequence from a popular television programme using the elements of *mise-en-scène*. How useful do you feel this kind of analysis is in relation to other mediums apart from film?

Look at a number of editions of the same women's magazine (for example, over six months). What versions of femininity and female sexuality are present, and how often are they present over the period of your study?

Take an example of a men's general interest magazine and use semiotics to analyse its front cover. Consider particularly how it presents masculinity and male interests.

Further reading

Bordwell, David and Thompson, Kristen 1986: *Film Art: An Introduction*, 2nd edition. New York: Alfred A. Knopf.
Culler, Jonathan 1990: *Saussure*. London: Fontana.
Strinati, Dominic 1995: *An Introduction to Theories of Popular Culture*. London: Routledge.
van Zoonen, Liesbet 1994: *Feminist Media Studies*. London: Sage.

3
Ideology

Theories of ideology have been some of the most influential in the analysis of the media. Many of the approaches detailed in this book draw upon theories of ideology in some way. This chapter will introduce some of the central ideas most commonly used in what can be termed ideological analysis. Beginning with a brief definition of ideology, the section goes on to explore the ideas of two major figures often cited as being pivotal to the development of theories of ideology: Louis Althusser and Antonio Gramsci. Two case studies will show how theories of ideology can be utilized in the analysis of media texts. The first will be an exploration of news coverage, and the second a consideration of the Hollywood film *Demolition Man* (1994).

What is ideology?

Ideology is a complex term and literature in the field demonstrates that it can have a number of sometimes contradictory meanings. Mike Cormack in his book *Ideology* (1992) begins by quoting four competing accounts of the term (p. 9). Terry Eagleton in *Ideology: An Introduction* (1991) lists as many as sixteen definitions currently in circulation (pp. 1–2). This makes it a difficult and wide-ranging area of study. However, it is fair to say that the most influential accounts of the workings of ideology, and those most useful for analysing the media, come from what may broadly be labelled a Marxist perspective. At its most basic level ideological analysis attempts to understand how dominant social groups are able to reproduce their social and economic power. It does so by focusing on both the material and intellectual manifestations of this reproductive process. A great deal of ideological analysis aims to show how the dominant ideas in a society at any given moment are formulated and perpetuated by the ruling class in order to maintain its control. These ideas were originally derived from the work of Karl Marx, who argues, 'The ideas of the ruling class are in every epoch the ruling ideas, i.e. the class which is the ruling *material* force of society, is at the same time its ruling *intellectual* force' (Marx and Engels, 1974, p. 64). Ideological approaches to the media are concerned, therefore, with revealing the ways in which the media assist in the maintenance of ideas and beliefs that work to reproduce the existing social order and the dominance of the ruling class. This has led to two types of media analysis. First, one that looks at the content of the media and how it works ideologically to reinforce dominant ideas and beliefs. And second, one that concentrates its focus of analysis on the economic structure of the media industries and investigates their position within the broader capitalist system. The latter approach argues that media organizations have a strong desire to maintain their place within the capitalist economic order and, as a result, work to reproduce it.

The base-superstructure model

Both of the above approaches relate in some way to what is known as the base-superstructure model. This model is an attempt to reveal how society is structured. The base refers to economic production. The super-structure refers to the political and cultural ideological institutions that make up society – for example, the family, religion, the state and education. In traditional Marxist thinking the economic base is held to be the most significant, important and deterministic. If one considers these approaches in relation to the media, the organization of the media industries and the texts they produce are both considered to be determined by the economic base. In the case of Western Europe the economic base is capitalism. The production and distribution patterns of the media industries are organized within capitalism and therefore can be seen to work to maintain the capitalist economic order. However, this model has been widely criticized because it is considered to be too economically deterministic. In other words, too much emphasis has been placed on the ability of the economic base, upon which society has been built, to influence the production of culture and ideas. Some criticism has therefore attempted to move away from the crude economic determinism of the base-superstructure model in order to find more useful ways of developing an understanding of the contribution of institutions such as the media in the reproduction of dominant ideas and beliefs. Louis Althusser's account of ideology still operated within the base-superstructure model. However, he rejected strict economic determinism and instead argued that the superstructure had a degree of relative autonomy from the base.

Althusser

Louis Althusser (1918–90) was a French philosopher and Marxist. In his writings he wanted to expand Marxist theory in order to understand how societies reproduced their social formations. In doing so he was addressing what he saw as the limitations in traditional Marxist thinking. Althusser challenged the view that everything in society could be reduced purely to the economic, arguing for an approach that took twentieth-century changes in the state and social institutions into account. As a result, his account challenged the traditional determinist Marxist link between the economic base and the superstructure. He argued that in advanced societies, such as those in Western Europe, the superstructure could be theorized as having a relative measure of independence from the base. Althusser therefore placed more emphasis on the superstructure, theorizing it as not simply dependent upon economic relationships. He believed that it was only through a more detailed consideration of these aspects of society that a complete understanding of the ways in which existing social formations reproduced themselves could be reached.

In his influential essay, 'Ideology and the ideological state apparatuses' (1971) Althusser argued that the social relations necessary to uphold capitalist production were maintained by what he called ideological state apparatuses. These consisted of the family, the judiciary, schools, the church, the political system, culture and the media. These were supported by repressive state apparatuses: the military and the police. For Althusser, it was the ideological state apparatuses, previously untheorized by other Marxist thinkers, which played a key part in governing individuals in the interests of the ruling class.

According to Althusser, it was through an understanding of the workings of ideology in everyday life, or lived experience, that earlier Marxist views could be challenged. These had, as Graeme Turner notes, seen ideology as 'a kind of veil over the eyes of the working-class, the filter that screened out or disguised their "real" relations to the world around them' (1990, p. 25). Althusser's break with this position centred on an acknowledgement that ideology in fact played a part in people's everyday perceptions of the world. For him, rather than being a 'false consciousness', ideology in fact structured people's lived experience.

What an ideological analysis of the media, influenced by Althusser's thinking, attempts to reveal is how certain ideas and beliefs are legitimized and 'made real' through their media representations. This occurs as much in factual media texts as it does in fictional ones. For example, many media texts revolve around individuals, either as the focus of news reports or as the central characters in fictional stories. According to Althusser, the centrality of individualism assists in the reproduction of existing social formations. It prevents people seeing or thinking of themselves as members of a collective group, such as a social class, which if acknowledged may cause them to resist their 'given' role and seek to challenge the capitalist values that oppress them. Individualism, and our experience of the world as being made up of discrete, free-thinking individuals, is, according to Althusser, an ideological rather than a natural phenomenon. Following this argument, the emphasis the media put on individual actions can be construed as ideological. Textual analysis can reveal the ways in which news reports, television programmes and feature films are structured around this 'common-sense' centrality of individuality. The construction of a society of individuals tends to mask the power relations at work at a given historical moment. To individualize a subject is to ignore the relations of class, race and gender which govern the amount of social power to which an individual can gain access. To individualize is also to make the individual finally accountable for his or her actions, which discounts the differences of class, race and gender which affect the opportunities an individual can actually exploit.

Interpellation

Althusser argued that one of the chief ways in which ideological state apparatuses position individuals is by the process of interpellation or hailing. The media and other cultural texts 'hail' or 'call up' readers, and in the process position them in relation to what they are consuming. As a result of interpellation the individual sees him or herself as a sovereign, autonomous individual. In so doing the individual recognizes him or herself as the subject of ideology, but at the same time, in Althusser's terms, the individual also misrecognizes him or herself. As Chris Weedon explains, 'the individual, on assuming the position of the subject in ideology, assumes that she is the *author* of the ideology which constructs her subjectivity' (1987, p. 31). Yet at the same time, as Mark Jancovich argues, 'These positions are not normal and inherent to individuals, but individuals "misrecognise" or mistake these positions as being natural and inherent in themselves' (1995, p. 128). As a result of misrecognition, individuals become the active agents of ideology, giving power and sustenance to the very ideologies that work to exploit them. Ideology negotiates the relationship between individuals and their actual conditions of existence. Yet, as Althusser argues, the connection between the individual and the subject position taken up in ideology is an imaginary one. Advertisements, for example, continually offer the individual consumer a clear, ideological definition of who or what they should or may be. They invite him or her to see themselves, or a potential self, in the advertising images as autonomous individuals who can make consumer choices. They are 'called up' to the advertisement and invited to see it as representing their interests and desires. Yet in Althusserian terms their identification with the ideological subject position offered by advertising is a misrecognition. The consuming individual is only really given a choice within the interests of those who rule. It is this naturalization of particular interests, beliefs and desires, which are closely connected to the values of consumer capitalism, that leads people to argue that advertisements really work to sell the dominant ideology, as much as they sell consumer goods.

However, the idea that consumers are simply duped by the power of ideology has since been widely contested by a number of writers who have attempted to offer a less passive view of the consumers of popular culture (see, for example, Nava and Nava, 1992).

Hegemony

Althusserian versions of ideology are not the only ones to have had a significant impact on the way people have thought about and analysed the media. Writers such as Stuart Hall (1982) have argued for an approach that is more influenced by the work of Italian Marxist Antonio Gramsci. Although writing a number of years before Althusser, Gramsci's work, and in particular his concept of hegemony, had its greatest impact later on English language critics. One of the reasons for this is that Gramsci's notion of hegemony can be seen to offer an alternative to some of the perceived limitations of Althusser's ideas. In so doing, it proved appealing to a number of Marxist critics uneasy with the ways in which Althusser's ideas were being used to suggest that subordinate social groups were the passive receivers of dominant, capitalist ideology. The concept of hegemony offered another explanation of how the dominance of certain class values came about. Gramsci suggested that this dominance occurred not simply through the imposition of the will of the dominant class through ideology, but by its presentation of itself as the group best able to fulfil the interests and aspirations of other classes, and, by implication, a whole society. In this way, the dominant class can be said to rule through consent rather than coercion. It must be stressed that, according to Gramsci, consent is not simply given without question; rather, it must be continually renegotiated and re-established, since however much the interests of the ruling class are presented as accommodating those of the subordinate classes, their interests are in opposition. In response to the continual challenges to the dominant class's presentation of itself as best able to deliver the interests of other groups, it needs constantly to assimilate these challenges to some degree within the dominant ideology in order to pacify and appease them. For example, it has been argued that the impetus of the women's movement in the 1960s and 1970s has been assimilated into the mainstream via what has been labelled 'popular feminism', as it became clear that, as society changed, it was no longer in the interests of the ruling class completely to marginalize women's experiences. However, it was also not in its interests to accommodate and legitimize radical ideas alongside popular feminism. As a result, 'watered down' and 'sanitized' versions of feminism are to be found in the pages of popular women's magazines such as *Marie Claire* and *Cosmopolitan*, and in the women's pages of newspapers such as the *Daily Mirror*. However, it is worth bearing in mind that the concept of hegemony is not much of an advance on interpellation. The subject who consents to be ruled is surely no more or less passive (as long as he or she consents) than one who misrecognizes itself as the author of ideology.

Using an approach informed by the concept of hegemony it is possible to argue that virtually all mainstream media texts are part of a changing historical process which maintains the interests of the ruling class through the reproduction of values and beliefs. These values and beliefs are not fixed but are open to change in order to support the interests of this group, thereby presenting them as concerned about, and caring for, subordinate groups. Therefore, it is no longer viable for media texts to be considered as simply imposing ideas upon those who consume them; instead, it is necessary to investigate the ways in which the reproductive powers of ideology succeed through a process of negotiation. As Stuart Hall argues: 'Hegemony … is not universal and "given" to the continuing rule of a particular class. It has to be won, reproduced, sustained. Hegemony is, as Gramsci said, a "moving equilibrium containing relations of forces favourable and unfavourable to this or that tendency"' (Hall et al., 1978). One of the main sites of this hegemonic struggle is the media. It is in this area that it is possible to see dominant ideas and values presented in a form which allows them to seem as though they are working in the interests of those they in fact help to subordinate. This view is at the centre of much analysis which has investigated the workings of popular media texts. The following sections on the media presentation of news and the popular Hollywood film *Demolition Man* (1994) will explore a hegemonic approach further.

Factual media output: the news

The presentation of news has been of particular interest to those under-taking media analysis because of the ways in which it can be seen to work ideologically. John Hartley, in *Understanding News* (1982), argues that one of the most significant ways in which television news can work to re-inforce dominant ideas and beliefs is through the way it makes sense of events for the viewer. News broadcasts, in his view, attempt to position viewers in relation to their content. This is achieved by presenting an ideological position for the viewer to assume, and from which they consequently consume information. The viewer, in this model, is invited to see this ideological position as natural and in their own interests. One of the ways in which this is achieved is by placing the viewer 'in' the events being reported, thus making the reports seem straightforwardly transparent. Again as Hartley notes, in relation to the ITN coverage of the 1980 storming of the Iranian embassy in London by the SAS: 'the voice-over commentary by Michael Sullivan on the ITN bulletin was presented entirely in the present tense: talking us through the screams, shooting, attack, dogs barking, sirens, fire, firemen and hostages' (p. 145). Because of this use of the present tense, the voice-over, he argues, was presented in such a way as to seem unconstructed, natural and transparently truthful. In this way the ideological content of news reports is masked by the conventions of the television news format. It is simply expected that news will be presented in this way, therefore there is no invitation or reason to question its truthfulness, or its construction as 'news'. Furthermore, audiences are invited to think that the form cannot dictate the content, and that news programmes simply just present us with the 'truth'.

The Glasgow University Media Group undertook a series of investigations that set out to prove that news coverage in the media was not simply 'truthful'. Broadly speaking, their research was concerned with the ways in which news coverage could be shown to be, on many occasions, biased. A self-proclaimed Marxist group, they argued that bias in television news was class-based, and much of their early research focused on the ways in which industrial disputes were reported. They concentrated their efforts on the close textual analysis of news and argued that it could be seen that coverage of industrial disputes was indeed biased against strikers in favour of management. This work clearly relates to the ideological content of news reports, and the Glasgow University Media Group's analysis exposes the ways in which news is often not merely a truthful reproduction of facts. Their work indicates how a process of selection, construction and presentation helps to reinforce dominant negative ideas and beliefs about industrial action and strikers. As Nick Stevenson argues, their conclusions reveal the ways in which the uncovered bias worked to uphold the dominant ideology: 'television news can be described as biased according to the extent to which it reaffirms or leaves unquestioned the central economic relations of capitalism. The media works within a dominant ideological consensus, where strikes are never justified, and are always the fault of the workers' (1995, p. 27). However, Stevenson also identifies problems in the work undertaken by the Glasgow University Media Group. His main criticism is that they make several assumptions about audiences' interpretations of television. His criticism, which is representative of a number of writers, can be levelled at a good deal of ideological analysis of the media, which assumes that all viewers will be successfully positioned by the text, and that they uniformly accept the position in relation to events offered. However, it is useful to note, as John Hartley does, that due to a preponderance of male presenters and correspondents it is possible to argue that the news appeals less, and therefore perpetuates ideologies less successfully, to women. This view might today seem dated because there is a greater number of female news readers. However, van Zoonen argues that female news readers are often used for their traditional feminine characteristics; bad news, she suggests, can be softened by the nurturing, comforting qualities of women. The use of more women news readers is therefore hardly radical; rather, it affirms the traditional attributes of femininity (1991).

Hartley quotes David Morley, who argues that, 'Ideologies do have to function as "descriptions" or "explanations" of the "reader's life", and it is in so far as they succeed or fail to do this that the "ideological viewpoint of the text" is accepted or rejected' (1982, p. 122). The model of all readers responding uniformly to the ideological position offered by a news text is limited. News and ideology can be explored more fully by acknowledging the variety of 'readers' lives' and by incorporating them into the analytical equation.

Ideology and fictional media output: Demolition Man

Demolition Man (1994) is a Hollywood science-fiction film which follows the exploits of a late twentieth-century cop, John Spartan (Sylvester Stallone), and master criminal, Simon Phoenix (Wesley Snipes). The main action of the film takes place after the pair are 'defrosted' in the twenty-first century, after being cryogenetically frozen for anti-social activities. One of the most significant ways in which the film creates its future society is by presenting its value system as different from that of today. The futuristic setting and the logic of the film's narrative allow a presentation of today's dominant values and beliefs, as personified by John Spartan, as ahistorical, logical and correct. Within *Demolition Man* this is achieved through humour. A 1990s audience is invited to laugh at the 'futuristic' value system on view; it does not correspond to their own and is presented in such a way as to be both strange and recognizably naive. The early part of the film is used to establish the future's dominant beliefs and for the most part uses the character of John Spartan, who is continually confused and amused by its laws and morality. The audience is invited to empathize with his reactions, the future's lack of toilet paper for example, since his reactions probably mirror their own. This is typified by the 'sex scene' between Spartan and Huxley (Sandra Bullock), a young police officer from the future, where she informs him that the transfer of bodily fluids has been outlawed. His amazement that sex could be outlawed in the future can be read as another strategy designed to invite the audience to see Spartan's responses as similar to their own. This in turn has the effect of placing the audience in a sympathetic relationship with the character and, importantly, the ideas, values and beliefs he represents. After all, what could be more natural and timeless than heterosexual sex?

Another way in which the film operates to support the values of the present is by slowly revealing that the initially peaceful and idealistic city of San Angeles in fact contains a social underclass which lives in the sewers beneath the city streets. This rebel force is led by Edgar Friendly (Dennis Leary), who claims that all they desire is food and the right to live as they want. The dominant ideas of 1990s 'free' America are clearly presented as those that this social underclass aspire to. When Spartan visits the rebel underworld society he finds that they eat hamburgers and drink beer: things that are banned as unhealthy in the 'utopia' of San Angeles. Of course, for the audience who live within a Western capitalist society the freedom to consume what one might wish is taken for granted. Following this less-than-serious reinforcement of the dominant ideas and values that underpin America, we are told by Edgar Friendly that all this underclass wants is to be 'liberated, free and equal'. These ideas clearly echo the values that, according to a variety of ideological media sources, built US society and underpin its democracy. The character of Friendly is significant because he represents the desire to return to the perceived values shared by 'normal' everyday members of the audience. Friendly and his comrades are fighting for a form of justice that reflects that thought to be enjoyed by the audience, thereby reinforcing the idea that the USA today is a free and just society. It is through the underground characters that it is possible to observe how it is that many of those watching the film may be invited to see themselves – after all, they may want a burger and a beer after the film and are 'free' to do so. This, however, is taken further: the audience is also invited to see the values represented by the film as operating in their interests, maintaining their freedom to act as they wish. It is possible to argue that it is through the values that the central characters Spartan and Friendly represent that the film's hegemonic operation can be revealed. What they value is what the audience values, and what they value are the ideals that America has gone to war to protect. It is worthwhile bearing in mind, however, that what the values represented by Spartan and Friendly in fact do is rewrite the present in an idealistic way. It is by acknowledging this that it is possible to see how the film constructs a position in relation to contemporary capitalist values. What the audience is not invited to bring to a reading of the film and its support for contemporary capitalist values is a knowledge and experience of the poverty and injustice that exist within the contemporary USA. In fact, it is a consideration of the marginalized experiences and knowledge in *Demolition Man* that makes it possible to read the film as having a clear ideological function.

The operation of these ideological aspects of *Demolition Man* is masked by the speed and excitement offered by the narrative. The action here, as with other pieces of Hollywood entertainment it may be argued, carries the audience along without giving it the time or the inclination to question or challenge the values being presented. Finally, the ways in which

Demolition Man can be argued to operate ideologically are most clearly demonstrated at the very end of the film when Spartan and Huxley kiss, something previously banned by the oppressive regime. This heterosexual kiss marks the final defeat of the old order and releases people to act 'naturally'. This may also be read as the final reinstatement of today's dominant ideology in the film's future. It is significant that this takes place in the realm of the personal, since it links with the view, constructed through ideology and explored earlier in this chapter, that within Western capitalism everyone is a free-thinking individual who can make decisions about his or her personal actions and private life.

Suggestions for further work

Select an example of both print and television advertisements. How do they interpellate consumers, and how far do they speak to them as 'individuals'?

Watch an edition of television news. How far do the stories attempt to create an ideological position for the viewers to assume?

Watch a contemporary Hollywood film. How far do you agree that popular forms such as this work to naturalize certain ideas and beliefs? It may be useful to list the moments when it is most clearly doing this.

Further reading

Cormack, Mike 1992: *Ideology*. London: Batsford.
Eagleton, Terry 1991: *Ideology: An Introduction*. London: Verso.
Thompson, John B. 1990: *Ideology and Modern Culture*. Cambridge: Polity.

4
Representation

This chapter begins by defining what is broadly meant by the term representation in media studies. It goes on to outline a specific kind of representation – stereotypes – and through an examination of the debate that surrounds these images asks if they are necessarily always, as they are so often assumed to be, inherently negative. The chapter also outlines and assesses the two dominant approaches that have been used to analyse and evaluate media representations of social groups: content analysis and what might loosely be termed an ideological approach. This is followed by an examination of contemporary media images of youth, drawing on the paradigm developed by Dick Hebdige in his article 'Hiding in the light: youth surveillance and display' (in Hebdige, 1988). Hebdige argues that young people are more often than not represented in two dominant ways: 'youth-as-trouble' and 'youth-as-fun' (p. 19). The examples explored assess the pertinence of his model while drawing on Gramsci's notion of hegemony.

Representation: a definition

Sign-users, as communicators, wish to convey meaning about their social environment. Representation is the term used to describe the practice of placing different signs together in order to render complex abstract concepts intelligible and meaningful. This sense-making practice is a fundamental cognitive process.

It follows that all signifying practices are capable of, indeed are concerned with, representing, and it is possible, strictly speaking, to represent all social concepts, however intricate. Representations can be: of states of mind or emotions – love, happiness, anger; social groups – white women, the disabled; or social formations – the family, the working class. Most often, the act of representing requires the gathering together of sometimes

quite disparate elements into a tangible form. This process is often referred
to as one of selection and construction, and since choices must be made
about what signs are to be selected and welded together to create meaning
about the object or idea in question, the resultant text tells the reader
something about those representing as well as those being represented. In
this sense representations are ideological.

At any one moment there are a number of representations of the same
thing in circulation; there is no singular, 'natural' way of representing
single parenthood, for example. If one were to examine a range of contemporary signifying practices it would soon become apparent that there are
in fact competing versions of single parenthood residing in the media as
well as in legal and social policies and practices: all are vying to authenti-
cate their own account above others. The feature film *Kramer vs. Kramer*
(1979) represents the intentions of fathers separated from their children
very differently from the ways in which, it has been argued by its critics,
the new social policies enacted by the Child Support Agency serve to
present 'absent' fathers. The very fact that representations, when set
alongside one another, do amount to different, sometimes even contradictory versions of an event or group, serves to highlight their construction.
No cultural representation can offer access to the 'truth' about what is
being represented, but what such representations do provide is an indication about how power relations are organized in a society, at certain
historical moments. Glenn Jordan and Chris Weedon argue that: 'All signifying practices – that is all practices that have meaning – involve relations of
power' (1995, p. 11). Some feminists, for example, have attacked what they
believe to be damaging representations of female sexuality in pornography,
advertising and mainstream cinema. For them, representations which
present women as readily 'available' for the sexual advances of men testify
to the power mechanisms of patriarchy which pervade our culture. Similar
arguments have been mounted about other social groups which hold less
social power in society than others. For example, black people, old people
and the disabled have all been represented in pejorative ways. Yet the signs
which construct representations are subject to historical, cultural and social
change. Representations are therefore a site of struggle about meaning. In
recent years, alternative representations have been produced which have
arisen partly in response to the political agitation of, say, feminists and black
activists who have sought to challenge dominant representations. The fact
that representations are changeable is potentially positive for those whose
identities are actually at stake within them.

Stereotypes

A widespread form of representation, which appears most commonly but
not exclusively, in popular media texts is the stereotype. A stereotype is

the selection and construction of undeveloped, generalized signs which categorize social groups or individual members of a group. The crude selected signs used to construct stereotypes usually represent the values, attitudes, behaviour and background of the group concerned. Implicit within the stereotype is the fact that the signs chosen make common assumptions about the group in question. Indeed, Tim O'Sullivan suggests that what distinguishes stereotypes from other kinds of representation is that they, 'carry *undifferentiated* judgements about their referents' (O'Sullivan et al., 1994, p. 300). Instead of expressing a diversity and difference between members of a group or community, stereotypes, by the nature of their simplicity, focus on broad similarities and identifying characteristics. The social groups often stereotyped are, for example: nationalities (such as the Germans), the disabled (the visually impaired), sexualities (transsexuals) and race (Jews). The process of stereotyping renders each member of these groups 'all the same'; so all Germans become disciplined and arrogant, all visually impaired people have super-senses of touch and hearing, all transsexuals are gay and all Jews are wealthy and have large noses.

As these examples show, in one sense stereotypes serve to indicate the social distinctions at work in a society, in that they act as indicators about power structures and existing social conflicts. The stereotyped examples above show relations of domination and subordination; the groups have been defined as such not by themselves, but by those who hold greater degrees or dominant forms of social power. Moreover, the repetition of stereotypes, which makes the type of knowledge about groups so prevalent (the Irish are stupid, blondes are dumb), serves to perpetuate and reinforce those ideas about people, until they have entered the ideological realm of 'common sense'. For commentators and critics of stereotypes, one of the more worrying aspects about them is that for those who gain no further knowledge about the group being represented, limited and potentially damaging assumptions remain intact and unquestioned.

Stereotypes are frequently used in a variety of media texts. For example, they might arguably be defined as a generic convention within the television situation comedy. Since genre relies on familiar elements, the assumptions conjured up by stereotypes are a short-hand device used by programme producers to draw up characterizations. Bound up with the notion of power is the way in which comedy is often utilized as a means of laughing at the typical traits of 'other' social groups. As Andy Medhurst argues, 'If you want to understand the preconceptions and power structures of a society or social group, there are few better ways than by studying what it laughs at' (1989, p. 15).

Rising Damp, a situation comedy first screened in Britain in the 1970s and since repeated on both Channel Four and UK Gold, centred around the day-to-day life of Rigsby, a white, middle-aged, working-class landlord, and his younger tenants: the black African student Phillip, medical student Alan and Miss Jones. Humour is generated through the tensions within the relationships Rigsby has with each of his tenants. For example, one source of humour stems from the assumptions Rigsby makes about Phillip because he is black, and the challenges Phillip mounts against Rigsby because of his lived experience of racist assumptions. Rigsby articulates stereotypical views about Phillip's beliefs, values and history as a black man of African descent. His comic dialogue, both directly with, and sometimes in relation to Phillip, encompasses a body of assumptions. For Rigsby, Phillip is a member of an unspecified 'tribe', a jungle-dweller innately at one with the culture, superstition and religious beliefs of 'darkest Africa', all of which for him are savage, uncivilized and anxiety-inducing. All these assumptions and their workings into comic dialogue express the power allotted to white people to define black people; the laughter of white audiences, one might argue, expresses complicity in the forms of power which oppress black people. At the same time, *Rising Damp* articulates something more complex about power, comedy and representation. A great deal of laughter emanates from the challenge that Phillip's mental and physical demeanour presents to Rigsby's assumptions. Phillip, with his expensive clothes and received pronunciation, is entirely knowledgeable about the social mores of middle-class English life – far more so than the firmly working-class Rigsby himself. And any actual connection to Africa, since it is only ever evoked by Phillip as a means to mock Rigsby, is presented as ambivalent and so rendered a mythical construction. What the example of *Rising Damp* illustrates is that stereotypes and the use of stereotypical assumptions are more complex than is often thought. A number of critics have argued that the stereotype cannot merely be dismissed as a negative form of representation, while some have even gone so far as to dismiss stereotypes as being redundant for media analysis.

Richard Dyer's article, 'Stereotyping' (in Dyer, 1977) makes an important distinction between stereotypes and what he calls social types. Using Orrin E. Klapp's book *Heroes, Villains and Fools* (1962), Dyer argues that social types are simplified representations of those who are considered to belong to society. Dyer says this about the social type: 'A type is any simple, vividly memorable, easily-grasped and widely recognised characterisation in which a few traits are foregrounded and change or "development" is kept to a minimum' (p. 28). Stereotypes, in contrast, are marked as those who do not belong, those who are thought of as outsiders. The deciding factor in the question of who belongs and who does not is power: those who are powerful are the insiders; those who lack social power are outsiders, as Dyer argues:

Types are instances which indicate those who live by the rules of society (social types) and those whom the rules are designed to exclude (stereotypes); for this reason, stereotypes are also more rigid than social types.

The latter are more open-ended, more provisional, more flexible, to create the sense of freedom, choice, self-definition for those within the boundaries of normalcy. These boundaries themselves must be clearly defined, and so stereotypes, out of the mechanisms of boundary maintenance, are characteristically fixed, clear-cut, unalterable. You appear to choose your social type in some measure, whereas you are condemned to a stereotype. (p. 29)

According to the terms of Dyer's argument, all the characters, including Phillip, in *Rising Damp* are social types, all belong to the fictional world that makes up the set of Rigsby's house. It is the assumptions Rigsby makes about Phillip that are stereotypical, traits that Phillip's character dispels as each episode unfolds. In this way, Dyer's model helps to refine the distinction between what constitutes a type, and what counts as stereotypical in the analysis of a text like *Rising Damp*.

Tessa Perkins's article 'Re-thinking stereotypes' (1979) sets out to quash a number of what she argues to be mistaken claims about stereotypes. For Perkins, subordinate groups are not the only ones to be stereotyped; those who hold the reins of power in society are also subjected to representations of themselves which have been decided upon by others: 'I would argue that there are stereotypes of all structurally central groups – class, race, gender, age. There is the male (he-man) stereotype, a WASP stereotype, a heterosexual stereotype, an upper class (leader) stereotype' (p. 144). Perkins's piece is not only concerned with representations, it is also underpinned by the need to ask how stereotypes function ideologically. While her point that stereotypes are also used by the subordinate seems on the surface to free up stereotypes as a tool for the oppressed, Perkins is at pains to stress that they serve two ideological functions. First, stereotypes of the dominant give meaning to those of the subordinate, therefore carving out societal oppositions. And second, such stereotypes also maintain the socialization of both powerful and oppressed groups. However, it might also be argued that stereotyping those more powerful than oneself serves a hegemonic function. If a worker stereotypes his employer as an 'upper-class twit', he (falsely) imagines himself to be, however momentarily, powerful in some way over his boss. Such moments reinforce hegemonic structures because they make one's place as a subordinate appear appealing, while conversely serving the interests of the powerful who are being stereotyped. Nonetheless, Perkins is right to assert that stereotyping is not only the preserve of the dominant.

Perkins also argues that stereotypes are not always false. To suggest they are, she reasons, is to deny the part they play as socializing agents which construct the identities of social groups (p. 140). She cites instances where empirical evidence has been used by some theorists to push aside claims of the total inaccuracy of stereotypes, replacing them with, 'a "kernel of truth" hypothesis' (p. 140). What such empirical data can provide, she argues, is information 'about the social situation of the group being described', which is not bound to 'imply prejudice or distortion' (p. 139). Yet Perkins steers clear of a reflectionist position on stereotypes; for her, they do not simply mirror group behaviour and their relationship to the power structures in society. Nor do they provide evidence about the essential nature of those being stereotyped. What they do is provide what she calls 'interpretations' of social positions and those interpretations are made more 'real' through the process of representation. To admonish stereotypes as false, therefore, is to ignore the ideological function they perform.

In his book *Comics: Ideology, Power and the Critics* (1989) Martin Barker takes issue with the view that stereotypes themselves are inherently bad and should be removed from texts, a position popular with a number of media researchers. For Barker, the practice of criticizing negative stereotypes and demanding that they be replaced with positive images actually serves to render invisible the 'map' of societal conflict and inequality that stereotypes point up. In this way, the influence of Perkins's argument about the possible truth embedded in stereotypes can be seen in Barker's argument. Using women as an example, Barker argues, 'a good deal of media representation is condemned for showing women in the home, providing services to men – though of course it is in fact true that very many do' (p. 207). Simply to erase the offensive stereotype is also to obscure questions such as: why is this group being represented in this way? who has the power to represent them so? and how can social structures which uphold such forms of power be contested? To cut the racist dialogue that Rigsby speaks, which potentially gives voice to the prejudices harboured by some white audience members, is to refuse to deal with the issue of racism altogether.

Barker also asserts that to protest against categorizing, which some media commentators have argued is the problem with stereotyping, is to condemn a cognitive process which people need in order to make sense of their social world. He stresses that, 'although "stereotyping" involves the simplification of our ideas about other people, nothing says this is unusual or abnormal. Quite the contrary. Many social psychologists say that this is simply part of our normal tendency to categorise, which we can't do without' (p. 201).

The term 'stereotype' is one that is frequently, and sometimes glibly, used in discussions about representation, without any sense of the weight of the issues the debate around it opens up. Yet discussions about stereotypes need initially to set out what is meant by the term, since that question alone is still a site of struggle, before going on to consider the construction of stereotypical images within the media.

Content analysis

Another of the main approaches that has been used for assessing the representation of social groups in media studies is content analysis. As a methodological approach with historical roots in sociology, it is concerned with collating and gauging the manifest content of large amounts of media output over a given time period. Its attention to manifest content makes it different to the semiotic approach which is devoted to analysing the latent meanings in media texts. Content analysis is therefore primarily descriptive and is characterized by its supposed systematic, scientific objectivity. Van Zoonen (1994) describes its ultimate aim, which is to 'compare the features of media output with concomitant features in reality' (p. 69). In this sense it is concerned with asking quantitative questions about how far media representations mirror social actuality.

A number of different projects which have used the approach have been undertaken since it was first developed by B. Berelson in the 1950s: feminists have examined the stereotypes and roles of women in various media forms such as advertising (Courtney and Whipple, 1983) and film (Haskell, 1987; Rosen, 1973); and socialist researchers have scrutinized television news for its class bias in representing industrial disputes (Glasgow University Media Group, 1976, 1982). Many of these analyses have finally concluded that media representations either exaggerate or minimize the 'facts' of social 'reality' in ways which serve the interests of the socially dominant. Rosen and Haskell, for instance, in their surveys of how women are represented in Hollywood cinema up until the 1970s, argue that the majority of roles are inaccurate misrepresentations of the reality of women's historical position in American society. In the 1920s, Rosen argues, Hollywood focused on women who worked in blue-collar occupations which generated the impression that women in this period were non-achievers, yet Rosen cites examples of 'actual' women who did have high-flying careers. Similarly, the Glasgow University Media Group found that there was an incongruence between recorded work stoppages and strikes reported by the news; this had the effect of constructing trade-unionists as 'trouble-makers' who were 'always on strike', thereby highlighting the inconvenience of striking at the expense of analysis that might have served the plight of the workers. Thus, it may be argued, the construction of versions of 'reality' through representations may be revealed.

Methodology and methodological assumptions

All research projects which use content analysis either as the sole, or as part of the methodology share a central aim: they seek to collate a body of solid data. However, before the researcher can begin to compile data, a number of decisions about how the research is to be organized have to be made. Consider hypothetically how a research team might organize a content analysis which aims to test out the claim that women's general interest magazines are predominantly Eurocentric in content. To start with, the team would need to decide on the scope of the project: which magazines should be included? would the study just concentrate on magazines produced in Britain, or could imports which are to be found on British magazine stands be included? should all aspects of the magazine be analysed – the front cover, features and advertising – or might advertising be excluded? The decisions made at this initial stage will impinge on the final claims that can be made at the project's final conclusion. Next, a coding scheme must be drawn up which will enable the researchers to classify their findings into countable units. How that scheme is arrived at is contingent upon what aspects concerning the Eurocentrism of magazines the team wants to find out about. It might be that the team is interested in asking how far class and age are factors which play a part in whether or not black or Asian women are included in magazine features.

The kinds of decision that have been dealt with so far seem straightforward enough. But when it comes to making decisions about how findings are to be classified then the research can run into problems. How, for example, in the hypothetical case above is race to be classified? Is black to be a category reserved for Afro-Caribbean women or should Asian women be included? And, even more problematically, if codings about the physical characteristics of the women included are to be analysed, since a large section of the content of general interest magazines are 'beauty features', then any attempt to arrive at objectivity through subjective classifications seems dubious. Dominic Strinati argues that while content analysis aims to be scientifically objective, its categorization process is often 'loaded' because it might 'embody certain theoretical or political presuppositions which support its more general orientation' (1995, p. 195). This could certainly prove a problem with our example of magazine analysis. If the project's methodology were underpinned by researchers who embraced radical feminist politics, for instance, then presumably the entire project would be imbued with their theoretical conjectures. Yet, as Strinati argues, since one of the primary aims of content analysis is to maintain objectivity, the political assumptions informing the project's decision-making are either undisclosed or implicit and are therefore not open to discussion. If they were, then they 'would often undermine the claims made to objectivity' (p. 195). In fact, a number of the case studies already referred to suffer from the pitfalls Strinati points out. Haskell's study on women and cinema (1987) was undertaken from a liberal feminist perspective, therefore one of her central concerns was whether or not the roles and stereotypes women have occupied in cinema bear an equal relation to the roles men have played. Yet her political position is never made explicit, nor does she attempt to account for the political assumptions her methods embrace. As a result, the possible effectiveness of the politics or the chosen methodology used in the text is unquestioned.

There are a number of other problems with the results that content analysis provides. While the method might show the media researcher how often, say, images of Asian women appear on magazine front covers, the researcher, as van Zoonen argues, 'can't "dig below" the manifest content of analysis' (1994, p. 69). This means that the embedded latent meanings in the images themselves must be left alone, since to analyse these images is to enter the realm of the subjective, which again would undermine the objectivity of the analysis. The insistence that manifest content is privileged over textual meanings can have grim consequences, since the images themselves and how they represent social groups are simply overlooked. Content analysis therefore leaves a whole dimension of media output unquestioned. Yet there are even larger setbacks for this kind of approach. To establish the Eurocentrism of magazine content, having compiled the data's results is to say nothing about how or why some representations are marginalized. Content analysis provides no way of asking what the relationship is between the content of the texts analysed and the social structures which produce them.

Nonetheless, despite the significant drawbacks of content analysis, some critics are keen to assert that some of what it can reveal is valuable. Van Zoonen, for example, argues that in developing countries, where there is a paucity of research into topics such as gender and the media, it can serve as a useful starting point for providing a broad sense of the equalities or discrepancies between how men and women are represented. She also makes the important point that content analysis can be an invaluable tool for feminists working in the industry: 'for policy and programme development – arenas that notoriously prefer "hard data" – content analysis is an invaluable means of convincing decision makers of the necessity for a diverse portrayal of women and men' (1994, p. 73).

A hegemonic approach

Arguably, one of the main weaknesses with content analysis is its lack of engagement with the relationship between representations and the social structures which produce them; it provides no means of understanding why representations of social groups manifest themselves in particular ways. A hegemonic approach is, by contrast, directly concerned with providing a causal analysis for the ways in which representations play a key role in either maintaining or sometimes contesting the existing social divisions in society.

As the previous chapter outlines, hegemony, a central concept in media and cultural studies, provides a way of understanding how, at particular historical moments, dominant social groups are successfully able to govern and rule economically, socially and culturally. Pivotal to the idea of hegemony is the notion that the subordinates in a given society are not brutally coerced into believing and living out dominant ideas or ideologies; instead, they actively concede to them. Dominant ideologies promulgate the idea that social divisions – that men are stronger than women, that white people are more intelligent than black people, that the middle class prosper because it has worked harder than the working class – are natural and unavoidable. One of the main ways in which dominant ideologies pervade our culture is through their existence and perpetuation in the key social institutions which make up the fabric of our society: the family, the judicial system, the education system, the monarchy and, significantly, the media. Moreover, dominant ideas are inscribed in the practices and forms of knowledge each of them produces, from the socialization of gendered forms of behaviour in the family, to the derogatory ways in which gay men and lesbians are often presented in the tabloid press. Hegemonic consent to dominant ideas is won because they become so naturalized that they appear to be 'common sense': gendered forms of behaviour are said to be expressions of 'human nature', for example. Won over by the rhetoric of ideologies, which is constructed through a powerful ability to describe the inevitability of the status quo, the less socially powerful become complicit with their own subordination. As John Hartley argues, the ideological power that works against the interests of the less powerful is masked: 'The upshot is that *power* can be exercised not as force but as "authority"; and "cultural" aspects of life are de-politicized' (O'Sullivan et al., 1994, p. 134).

The hegemonic approach argues that media representations play a central role in winning, securing and maintaining the ideological consent of audiences. Barthes's notion that the cultural connotations of signs perpetuate 'myths' about a society is central to the hegemonic approach. He argued that the meanings and associations generated by signs aim to construct, uphold and reproduce social divisions as natural and unavoidable (1972, p. 11). Subsequent critics who have adopted this approach argue that mainstream media texts, in particular, tend to be constructed out of interests which, on the whole, serve dominant ideas. Gramsci's notion of hegemony was influential at the Birmingham Centre for Contemporary Cultural Studies (BCCCS) in the 1970s, and, as a consequence, a good deal of work undertaken there in both media and cultural studies was characterized by this approach, though it was often used eclectically alongside other theoretical ideas. Angela McRobbie's early work on teenage girls and magazines illustrates the use of semiotic analysis which draws extensively on both Althusser and Gramsci's ideas about ideology. In 'Jackie magazine: romantic individualism and the teenage girl' (in McRobbie, 1991), she argues that the magazine Jackie played a key part in defining ideologically acquiescent modes of femininity in the leisure arena of young women and girls. The codes and values of Jackie, she argued, worked to position its audience into accepting and embracing the dominant roles of wife and mother, and, in so doing, attempted to capture their hegemonic acceptance (p. 91). From this work, one can see the ways in which a hegemonic approach attempts to account for why representations of social groups are as they appear, by linking the representations back to the social structure which frames and produces them.

Images of youth

Some of the most influential work on youth culture was undertaken at the BCCCS in the 1970s and 1980s. Jim McGuigan in his book *Cultural Populism* argues that the innovative work produced there was characterized by 'its distinctive combination of sociological work on deviancy theory, with neo-Gramscian hegemony theory and Barthesian semiology' (1992, p. 89). Work by key writers on youth, such as Angela McRobbie and Dick Hebdige, was chiefly concerned with locating the ways in which young people symbolically resisted the dominant culture. This kind of work marked a radical shift from studies which had previously pathologized the activities of youth movements. For the BCCCS writers, mods, teds, rockers and punks were subcultures which provided important political challenges to the social formation. The studies undertaken at Birmingham University were concerned with the meaning of youth which involved investigating the cultural objects and media artefacts which expressed those meanings. McRobbie, for example, sought to ask why there was a predominance of romance in the photo-love stories of a magazine such as *Jackie* in the 1970s, and what its consequences were for young women; Hebdige, meanwhile, sought to unpack the forms of resistant meanings embedded in the subcultural dress codes and styles of consumption of punks and teds.

In 1988 Hebdige wrote a seminal article about youth, representation and photography entitled 'Hiding in the light: youth surveillance and display'. In it, he argued that, historically, photographs of young people fell into two distinct, yet mutually dependent, arenas of representation: 'youth-as-trouble' and 'youth-as-fun'. The first, he argues, is to be found mostly in documentary forms. These date back to Victorian photographs taken in order to provide surveillance of 'street urchins'. He also cites later examples, sociological ethnographic photographs which begin in the 1920s, which chart youth as a time of painful psychological intensity or youth as victim of social deprivation. For him, 'youth-as-fun' is a later category which emerges in the consumer boom of the 1950s where it is to be found mostly within advertising. It is only then, when advertisers identify teenagers as viable consumers, that images of youth as hedonistic, exuberant and discerning begin to appear.

Hebdige's article firmly places representations of youth within their socio-political circumstances, thereby highlighting the historical legacy images of youth carry. His piece also illustrates the multiplicity of images available of a social group at any one historical juncture: there are no 'true' images of youth which might act as accurate yardsticks against which to measure other representations, but, instead, competing versions out to mark their meanings as somehow more authentic. Hebdige also stresses that photographs of youth have been historically produced out of ideological interests. The photographic practices instigated by the Victorians to 'register' young people in its educational and penal institutions were, as Hebdige argues, 'by no means neutral, representing rather, a particular point of view, particular interests, embodying a desire and a will to know the alien in our midst, the Other, the victim and the culprit' (1988, p. 21). Indeed, the images of fun-loving youth which characterize advertising images of the 1950s are no less ideological, constructed by new markets in an attempt to gain the financial resources young people had gained access to. Hebdige's model of how youth is represented in photographic codes still holds resonance in the media today. In the following sections, we examine the representation of youth using Hebdige's categories.

Youth-as-trouble

Images of 'youth-as-trouble' are still to be found in aspects of the 'factual' media. The mid-1990s witnessed a growth of interest in the debate about how young offenders should be dealt with punitively. Concomitantly, the news media have maintained avid journalistic interest not only in parliamentary discussions surrounding the issue, but also in the extensive coverage they have provided of cases of teenage criminality. The tabloid press often sensationalized the incidents of teenage crime they have featured. Headlines and features in newspapers like the *Sun* and the *Daily Mirror* have been characterized by the idea that many offenders are evil thugs who have been allowed, by 'soft handling', to make a travesty of the judicial system which has been rendered impotent and ineffectual as a result. The criticism of this 'soft approach' took the form of attacking reform programmes which have aimed to offer some type of social rehabilitation to young offenders, in the form of housing or financial allowance. The *Daily Mirror* (26/3/94) featured this report: 'Tearaway, 15, Gets Free Flat and £800', a headline which immediately condemns, by its use of the term 'tearaway', an approach which recognizes, and attempts to remedy, the social causes of crime. Other news articles have used a tone of revengeful relish when some young offenders have been punished in ways which have 'matched the crime' – for example, the headline '10 Years for Car Thug Aged 16', which appeared in the *Daily Mirror* (29/10/94). In such articles, crime committed by white working-class youth is represented as a free-standing social ill, which bears no relation to the possible social context of poverty, unemployment and poor housing conditions with which many working-class people must contend. Instead, young offenders are portrayed as an unfathomable, dangerous and uncontrollable group. By representing working-class youth in this

way, the article can be seen to be operating hegemonically. By individu-
alizing the offender and by rendering invisible the social circumstance
which produced the offender and the offence, the article implies that
society is equal and undivided. It is therefore able to infer that the 'wild'
teenager is at fault, not wider society. The article masks the socio-political
reasons why young people resort to crime and in doing so operates
ideologically. It wins ideological consent from other working-class people,
the implied audience of the *Daily Mirror*, by affirming and reproducing
the ideological beliefs which run counter to their own interests. In this
particular article the reader is told that the offender, having only just been
released after serving a sentence for committing a robbery and drugs
offence, became involved in a car theft and ensuing police chase: 'In a
bid to shake off the squad car he did a hand-brake turn, shot over a
pavement and into an underpass ... There, he *deliberately* ran down great-
grand-father Edwin Shields, 64' (our emphasis). Portrayed as powerless
over the pathologized youth, his parents 'were so frantic at his behaviour
they screwed down windows and locked away his shoes so he could not
leave home on crime sprees'. Interestingly, this report included a head
and shoulders image of the offender, coded in similar ways to that of
prison photography. It is also reminiscent of the photographs of 'street
urchins' that Hebdige argues were used as forms of surveillance in
Victorian Ragged Schools. These articles have the effect of building images
which are often taken as examples of how young working-class people
behave generally. They contribute to an ideological regime of images
which serve to naturalize the media construction of 'youth-as-trouble'.

Images of youth as a problem are not only confined to the 'factual'
media, such as documentaries or news media. British soap operas, often
acting as a forum for raising important issues about 'actual' social problems, have also featured a number of troublesome teenagers. When Tracey
Barlow, a teenage character from *Coronation Street*, was found by her
mother Deirdre to be having under-age sex with her boyfriend, the
breakfast magazine programme *Good Morning* ran a 'phone-in on the issue
with resident agony-aunt Denise. Teenagers who had experienced problems with their parents as a result of their under-age sexual practices were
encouraged to call the 'expert' panel. Incited to confess their practices,
the teenagers, who incidentally were all female, were invited into a
framework already hostile to their experiences, desires and emotional
needs. Representing the 'parent culture' the panel evoked a number of
ideological standpoints on the matter drawn from the family, the police
and the judiciary. As the keepers of normalcy and common sense, it
ideologically serves the interests of these bodies to be against teenage sex.
By bringing these forms of power to bear on the 'problem' situations
presented to them, the panel was able to position offending teenagers in
ways which aimed to control both their actions and thoughts: their ways
of organizing their relationships, their sexual behaviour as well as their

conceptions of themselves as subjects acting in the 'right' ways. Here, deviant youth is represented as ultimately answerable to institutionally sanctioned, predetermined meanings of their sexual identities, meanings which fit the needs of the nuclear family.

However, not all representations of young people are necessarily constructed in ways which serve dominant interests. Some texts actually work to counter hegemonic forces, by revealing the contradictions within ideological ideas. *Suburbia* (1983) an American film directed by Penelope Spheeris, represents the reasons for teenage disaffection as stemming from the contradictory morality of the parent culture. The film opens with two 'ordinary' white brothers, on an ordinary day, living in the suburbs of America. Both are involved in activities which are portrayed as mundane and degenerate: the teenage son sits passively consuming daytime television, and the younger child in another room is seen aggressively interacting with footage from a war film using a toy gun. When the mother returns from work, she violently accuses her teenage son of drinking from a hidden bottle of spirits, and gratuitously lashes out at him for failing to empty the kitchen waste. The son is subsequently seen leaving his suburban home, and, for the viewer, his actions are a welcome means of escape from an intolerable home life. The teenager makes for the city and is shown outside a busy street café, observing groups of urban teenagers who are very different from himself. The punks who pass him in groups are for the teenager and the viewer, who is mindful of the negativity of the power of the parent culture, collective examples of young people who have chosen to resist subordination to the values of the dominant culture. *Suburbia*, as an alternative to hegemonic definitions of youth-as-trouble, attempts to show why young people seek the space to construct a way of living in which they are able to determine at least some of the meaning of their identity.

Youth-as-fun

Images of youth-as-fun are to be found, as Hebdige argues, most easily in advertising. It is in adverts for clothes, music, alcohol and a whole plethora of consumer goods, that young people are portrayed as fashionable, hedonistic and exuberant. They are also, contrary to the examples of youth-as-trouble which tend to be images of working-class youth, often portrayed as a classless, homogeneous social group. Knowing that young people are adept at reading complex visual signs, advertising aimed at young people is also arguably the most textually sophisticated. Banks and other financial services have had the daunting task of appealing to young people to invest in them, a form of spending which is perhaps the least thrilling act of consumption, while also representing them as fun-loving, trendy and 'part of the gang'. One strategy has been to offer young people a package of discounts which enable them to take part in 'fun' leisure activities. One advert for a 'Livecash account' with the Midland Bank, which appeared in magazines like *Smash Hits* (see illustration 4.1), addressed the young consumer in this way: 'Make Yourself More Attractive To The Opposite Sex'. Against a white background, brightly coloured circular photographs show the range of vouchers, surrounded by signifiers of the goods on offer, that can be used once an account has been opened. 'What is going to impress your date more; turning up on your push-bike or arriving in style driving your Mum and Dad's car?' the sell line proclaims. Success in leisure circles is contingent upon young people's spending power, and, careful to make its appeal to the homogeneous category 'youth', the advert attempts to transcend the differences of class, race or gender. In masking those differences the advert is able to play on the most important myth within capitalism: that all individuals can achieve prosperity and success with hard work, and the right attitude to financial investment.

Youth-as-trouble-as-fun

Not all images of youth make their appeal by representing youth as innocent fun. The serialized jeans and work-wear advertising campaign launched by Diesel, a clothes company aimed at young people, appeared mostly, though not exclusively, in style magazines such as *i-D* and *The Face*. The advertisement is number fifteen 'in a series of "How to..."' guides to successful living for people interested in good health and mental power'. Characteristic of a good deal of fashion advertising aimed in the 1990s, this advert represents youth-as-trouble-as-fun (see illustration 4.2).

It is perhaps most disturbing that in 'successful living', a result of 'protecting health', young white masculinity is portrayed killing 'them' before they kill you. Trading on a sense of Americanness, so often appropriated in connection with fashion, especially casual wear, the image of a conventionally attractive young man at a firing range has alluring yet simultaneously disturbing connotations: this might be a trendy young man living in an urban cosmopolitan city (New York, possibly London) but he aims to beat the system before it beats him. This dubious, yet conventional representation of patriarchal, heterosexual masculinity has resonances of male Hollywood film stars and action heroes: Clint Eastwood, Jean-Claude Van Damme and Robert de Niro, actors whose roles have meant defending society against its undesirable elements. Since it is white masculinity which already constitutes the most powerful social group in the West, one might read the idea of 'them' to be those who instil the most anxiety for that group: black people for example, or those who live in poverty.

The use of the female model, who appears 'hip' and fashionable, partly as a result of the juxtapositioning of her body in front of the man as backdrop, and partly because she wears daring, stylish clothing is also

Illustration 4.1 This ad for Midland Bank's 'Livecash account' (1993) represents youth as fun-loving, trendy and 'part of the gang'.
Source: Midland Bank plc. Reprinted with permission.

Illustration 4.2 Here we are presented with youth-as-trouble-as-fun. 'How to teach your children to love and care' – image from Diesel's Spring/Summer 1993 advertising campaign.

Source: Printing authorized by Diesel Sp.A.

highly conventional. In terms of the representation of female sexuality this woman is objectified, dressed for sex, yet conversely vulnerable and dangerously unaware of her potential sexual attractiveness. The images here, while they might appear to be excitingly new and imaginatively presented, are actually predicated on very conventional and conservative ideas about white masculinity and femininity.

Suggestions for further work

Collect some media representations of dominant social groups, for example white middle-class people or the monarchy. Could the images you have found be categorized as stereotypes or social types?

Gather a range of media images of young people, noting their source. How far do these images fit Hebdige's thesis about how youth is represented? Can you draw any conclusions from their sources?

Further reading

Betterton, R. (ed.) 1987: *Looking On: Images of Femininity in the Visual Arts and Media*. London: Pandora.

Hall, Stuart (ed.) 1997: *Representation: Cultural Representations and Signifying Practices*. London: Open University / Sage.

Hebdige, Dick 1988: *Hiding in the Light: On Images and Things*. London: Routledge.

Jordan, Glenn and Weedon, Chris 1995: *Cultural Politics: Class, Gender, Race and the Postmodern World*. Oxford: Blackwell.

McRobbie, Angela 1991: *Feminism and Youth Culture: From Jackie to Just Seventeen*. London: Macmillan.

5
Genre

As a concept, genre is important to both media critics and practitioners. At its most basic level it can assist in an understanding of how media products relate to one another, and how they may, either for analytical or marketing purposes, be grouped together. This chapter will offer a definition of genre before going on to discuss the role of genre criticism within film studies. The application of genre to other media, however, is not always straightforward. Some mediums, it may be argued, offer greater rewards to the genre critic. We use the television western as a test case within which to access the appropriateness of using definitions taken from cinema in the context of television. Finally, the chapter will discuss the ways genre might be considered an agent of dominant ideology.

Genre: a definition

In *Key Concepts in Communication and Cultural Studies* John Hartley refers to genre as the recognized sets into which the output of a medium may be classified (O'Sullivan et al., 1994, p. 127). Individual media products such as films or television programmes can be identified as belonging to a particular genre. For example, a film may fall into the genre of horror, musical or western, a television programme may be labelled a situation comedy, a soap opera or a quiz show, and a musical recording may be categorized as reggae, funk or heavy metal.

In each instance the acknowledgement of the genre is dependent upon an accepted set of generic conventions which enable the audience to key into the text with certain expectations. The pleasure and enjoyment audiences derive from the media often depend upon texts broadly fitting into certain generic groupings. Their judgements as to how successful a text is are formed by generic expectations based upon their experiences as media consumers.

Genres are not fixed and timeless; they are open to historical change. A television soap opera broadcast in 1960 may have important commonalities with a soap showing today, but it will also have significant differences. If we take the first episode of the popular television programme *Coronation Street*, for example, the setting, characters and action are familiar enough for us to label it a soap opera. However, in the early 1960s its working-class characters and milieu had more in common with contemporary 'kitchen-sink' drama, a style marked by its domestic settings and concern with social issues such as class. For audiences today *Coronation Street* has become a benchmark against which other programmes are judged and defined as soap opera. The differences between the American radio shows of the 1930s that gave the form its name because of their sponsorship by soap companies such as Proctor and Gamble and the working-class dramas labelled soaps on British television today are enormous. However, those differences and changes enable us to see a fluidity in the definition of genres.

Whilst genres are historical constructs, at any given moment they never have completely fixed boundaries. It is possible to categorize a media text into a genre if enough recognizable elements are present. However, placing a text within a particular generic category often involves the incorporation of components that also appear within other genres. As John Fiske notes: 'Any one programme will bear the main characteristics of its genre, but is likely to include some from others: ascribing it to one genre or another involves deciding which set of characteristics are most important' (1987, pp. 111–12). For example, whilst *NYPD Blue* has enough generic conventions for it to be labelled a police series, its focus on the personal lives of its characters could be argued to have much in common with soap opera.

To make full use of the notion of genre when analysing the media, generic texts must be placed in a relationship with the industry that produced them and the audiences which consume them. As Stephen Neale argues, 'genres are not to be seen as forms of textual codifications, but as systems of orientations, expectations and conventions that circulate between industry, text and subject' (1980, p. 11).

Genre and production

As well as being an important tool for media analysis genre also relates to media production. The film, television, magazine and newspaper industries may all, to a greater or lesser extent, be said to operate generically (see illustration 5.1). Certain media companies have become strongly associated with products that fall into particular genres. Examples range from Hammer Films, which in the late 1950s became associated with the

Illustration 5.1 Magazines organized along generic lines on the news stand.
Source: The authors.

production of horror films, to DC Thompson, publishers of children's comics, to, more recently, the television company Hat Trick which is most commonly connected with the production of comedy. The way in which genre is able to create a great level of expectation amongst potential audiences means that it is clearly important to producers. The writers and photographers who work on teenage magazines such as *Sugar* and *J17* are expected by their employers to produce work which, broadly speaking, fits the expectations of those who make up the market for teenage girls' magazines. Genre's potential to organize production can also be seen through the example of book publishers Mills and Boon. Dedicated to the production of popular romantic fiction, Mills and Boon have very strict guidelines for potential and existing authors. These guidelines outline the expectations of both the publisher and the reader in terms of the romantic novel, and it is not expected that authors will stray far beyond them. For some producers, then, the organizing categories of genre are imperative for commercial success. It is perhaps in the sphere of television where this can be seen most clearly. The production structure of large organizations such as the BBC is made up of departments that have loose generic titles, each devoted to the production of, for example, news and current affairs, light entertainment, drama and sport.

Genre and film

In *The Hollywood Film Industry* (1995) Richard Maltby and Ian Craven clearly identify the centrality of genre to Hollywood film production. They argue that it is based upon a combination of predictable elements and variation, ordered around familiar cycles and formulae. The familiarity offered by genres plays an important part in the promotion and marketing of new films. It enables campaigns to draw upon audiences' prior knowledge, and in doing so is a useful tool in the construction of, for example, posters and advertisements. The promotional material for new films often contains direct references to other films, thereby asking the potential audience to place the new product in relation to others they are likely to have experienced. Campaigns that foreground the fact that a new release may be similar to a recent popular title achieve this by quoting critics who have placed the film into a particular category. For example, *While You Were Sleeping* (1995) was sold as the 'sweetest romance of the year' and 'a story about love at second sight', whilst *Shopping* (1995) was said to go 'right for the action jugular'. Potential audiences are invited to place these films into the categories of romance and action film respectively. Then, if the romance does not contain action and the action film does not foreground relationships, the audience will not feel cheated.

However, Hollywood also depends upon new films offering audiences something different from previous releases. Generic categories are able to do this because they are unfixed and are flexible enough to accommodate changes. This allows audiences to feel that their expectations of a film within a certain genre will be met, yet there will also be enough that is different for them not to feel that they are simply watching a familiar film again, however similar it may be. Again, promotional campaigns often attempt to offer a combination of similarity and difference, as in the case of *The City of Lost Children* (1995), the follow up film to *Delicatessen* (1991) from directors Jeunet and Caro, whose poster offered a point of recognition, 'from the creators of *Delicatessen*', combined with an element of difference. Here, the claim was that this film 'surpasses its predecessor for pure visual excitement and surreal abandon'. Maltby and Craven argue that a variance of formulae can work to widen and expand audience expectations of genres, whilst still meeting this desire for similarity and difference:

> Generic conventions offer more durable frames of reference, but they also accommodate change: the variations in plot, characterization, or setting in each imitation inflect the audiences' generic expectations by introducing new elements or transgressing old ones. Each new genre movie thus adds to the body of the genre, extending the repertoire of conventions understood by producers, exhibitors, and ticket buyers at a given historical point.
> (1995, p. 113)

Importantly, they make it clear that thinking about genre should incorporate an analysis of its role in industrial production and audience consumption. When considering genre criticism within film studies, these factors have not always been subjects of consideration.

Genre study and film criticism

Genre criticism came to the forefront of film analysis in Britain during the latter part of the 1960s. It was an approach that allowed critics to move beyond the overly individualistic emphasis of earlier approaches to Hollywood cinema. The most influential of these was known as auteurism. As detailed in chapter 2, auteurist critics wanted to equate what they saw as the artistic vision of a select group of Hollywood directors with that of great 'masters' in other forms, such as painting and literature. However, some critics found this emphasis on exceptional individuals problematic and sought other ways of thinking about Hollywood which embraced its popularity rather than praising those perceived as transcending its inherent baseness. Genre study enabled critics to acknowledge fully the significant part played by the industrial context of even the most 'artistic' of Hollywood films. It also placed the work of Hollywood directors into the wider, more collaborative world of the Hollywood studios. Genre, now seen as an important part of the structure and tradition of Hollywood film-making, was acknowledged as playing a pivotal role in the way popular films generated meaning. Reflecting this change, Lawrence Alloway argued that 'the personal contribution of many directors can only be seen fully after typical iconographical elements have been identified' (1971, p. 41).

Alloway's emphasis on iconography as crucial to defining and understanding genre films can also be found in the work of another influential genre critic, Edward Buscombe. For him, it was through iconography that generic definition could best be achieved. This, he argued, was because the medium of film was predominantly visual, and it therefore made perfect sense to 'look for our defining criteria at what we actually see on the screen' (1970, p. 36). Iconography refers to visual motifs that allow audiences to identify certain films as belonging to particular genres. Iconography, then, as Maltby and Craven put it, helps provide a shorthand system that allows the experienced generic viewer instantly to glean a great deal of understanding and information about character, action and setting from costume, sets and familiar objects (1995, p. 117). Iconography, therefore, plays an important role in enabling audiences to make sense of a generic film, and film-makers can make assumptions about and use their audience's experiences of viewing similar films. It is, however, worth noting that whilst iconography can obviously be of crucial importance to critical understandings of genres such as the western or gangster film, the focus of much work in the late 1960s and early 1970s, it is perhaps less useful when considering genres such as the melodrama.

Genre and television

So far we have concentrated on the ways in which genre has been used in relation to cinema. Indeed, most of the substantial academic work on genre has taken film as its focus and there have been far fewer detailed analyses of television genres. A notable exception is the work that has been undertaken around television soap opera. Yet television is very clearly ordered along generic lines. Television is, as John Fiske has argued, 'a highly "generic" medium with comparatively few one-off programmes falling outside established generic categories' (1987, p. 109). These established television genres include situation comedies, soap operas, game shows and daytime magazines. Once again, generic boundaries are established through the identification of similarities between texts, here possibly more clearly connected to industrially defined formulae. There have been few pieces written extolling the artistic creativity of game show devisers, which have attempted to place their work alongside great writers and painters. This perhaps reflects the fact that television has never had the same status as 'high' art, or that critics have never attempted to place its products alongside those of great artists, though arguably an exception might be the television dramas of writers such as Dennis Potter.

Genre approaches to television therefore have not had to employ the political strategies of earlier film critics who sought to use genre as a way out of the individualism of auteurism. Indeed, Denis McQuail argues that genre may not be that useful as an analytical tool in relation to television, because 'one genre shades into another for producers and unselective viewers alike' (1994, p. 265). McQuail's point draws upon the idea that television is not a series of distinct texts, and, as such, breaking it down into genres may prove something of an analytical cul-de-sac. However, many viewers state a preference for certain types of genre and may claim to watch all soaps, or enjoy game shows, and certain producers may be associated with certain television genres such as situation comedies. It could be argued, then, that genre can be of use when thinking about both the production and consumption of television.

The television western

A brief comparison between the western on television and film usefully identifies ways in which the manifestation of the genre in different mediums needs, to a certain extent, to be considered separately. On the level of iconography the two are very similar. For example, guns, locale and costume enable us to read both films and television programmes as westerns. However, with regard to the narrative of each, some significant differences can be identified.

Television westerns were very popular in the 1950s, a period which, as Edward Gallafent observes, was dominated by the series format (1994, p. 3). Very few of the westerns produced for television in this period were conceived as individual texts. Those that were were usually designed as pilots for prospective series that never reached production. The television western did not contain the epic landscapes of the period's cinema films. They also did not have the same drive towards narrative closure that typified the output of Hollywood at the time. Each episode of popular television western series such as *Wanted, Dead or Alive*, *Wagon Train* or *Rawhide* would end in the resolution of the immediate story that was the focus for an episode, but the wider narrative of the cattle trail or wagon train's journey would invite the viewer to tune into another story the following week. The basic structure of the journey would last a whole season and begin again at the start of the next, thus allowing smaller, weekly and independent segments within the larger ongoing narrative. In the case of *Rawhide*, for example, the conclusion of the cattle drive would not provide the great climax of the narrative because there was an assumption that it would begin once again with the programme's return the following season. Gallafent goes so far as to argue that the television western of the 1950s, whilst on the surface looking like a cinema western through its iconography, can most fruitfully be thought of as a generic fusion: 'The episodes were essentially anecdotes, set in the western context, but borrowing elements of their structure from other generic models, such as the family melodrama or even on occasion the horror story' (1994, p. 3).

If this is the case when considering the television western, the idea that iconography is of central importance to an understanding of genre is questionable. And if it is possible to challenge its centrality to the study of television genres, it is therefore important to reconsider its usefulness in relation to film. Many westerns may be better understood by suggesting that they also fuse genres. For example, an analysis of *Warlock* (1959), as David Lusted suggests, benefits from a consideration of it as a melodrama as well as a western (1996, pp. 63–74).

Genre and ideology

One of the most significant ways that genre study moved beyond the simple categorization of films into genres was by considering the role that it may have in the maintenance of 'common sense' ideas, beliefs and values about society. Rick Altman argues that genre classifications work to focus the way audiences read texts and force what he terms a 'pre-reading of the text'. This is due to the well-established visual and narrative codes and conventions of any genre, which ensure that 'it is easy to understand the text in a particular pre-determined way, genres always make it less likely that a film will be construed in a different non-generic way' (1987, p. 5). Altman also states that, 'rather than seeing genres as structures helping individual texts to produce meaning, we must see genres as restrictive, as complex methods of reducing the field of play of individual texts'. He goes on to argue that genres are not neutral; instead, he sees them as 'ideological constructs masquerading as neutral categories' (p. 5). If genres do force a pre-reading of texts, as Altman suggests, this means that the reader is unable or perhaps not invited to read a film or television programme in a wide range of challenging ways. Generic conventions therefore place the audience on a predetermined path, even if they themselves feel they have freely chosen a route through the text. The familiarity of genres may suggest a free choice, yet freedom is something it can never deliver. As Fiske argues, 'Genre spells out to the audience the range of pleasures it might expect and thus regulates and activates memory of similar texts and expectations' (1987, p. 114).

A media text that is new and generic is therefore very likely to conform to already established patterns. In doing so, it delivers already accepted, identified and controlled pleasures to the viewer. At the heart of this position is the argument that generic works cannot ultimately be radical or politically challenging because they conform to already established rules. It is through this regulation of content that genre can be argued to operate ideologically. This idea of regulation can be extended to include the expectations of audiences. It limits the range of readings available from a text and as a result presents certain structures as typical or even natural. Those texts that do not fit into these familiar structures become strange or even deviant, and audiences are continually invited, through advertising, to seek out and enjoy the familiar. This creation of positivity around familiarity can also work within texts. For example, as we have already discussed in chapter 3, in the science-fiction adventure *Demolition Man* the futuristic world has different social values from today. Because they are unfamiliar to contemporary Western audiences, they seem unrealistic, unworkable and open to corruption. In contrast, those of John Spartan, the film's 1990s cop catapulted into the future, correspond to the familiar values of today's capitalist society. Spartan's values and beliefs are presented as more positive and pragmatic, and therefore more workable than those of the utopian futuristic society. In showing them in this way, it could be argued that *Demolition Man* presents these capitalist values and beliefs as always correct, timeless and therefore ahistorical. This view of any value system is highly ideological and open to challenge. However, the familiarity of the generic codes and conventions does not invite the audience to challenge its value system. As John Hartley argues, 'Audiences' different potential pleasures are channelled and disciplined by genres, which operate by producing recognition of the already known set of responses and rules of engagement ... Such is the "contract" of genre. It entails a loss of freedom of desire and demand in order to achieve efficiency and properly labelled packaging' (quoted in Fiske, 1987, p. 114).

Suggestions for further work

Consider the idea of genre in relation to new media forms such as computer games. Identify the possible genres within this form and list their generic conventions.

Look at the TV listings for a day of your choice. Identify all the programmes you consider to belong to a traditional genre and all those that fall outside such categorization. Why do you think television may be so reliant on genre?

Further reading

Fiske, John 1987: *Television Culture*. London: Methuen.
Neale, Stephen 1980: *Genre*. London: British Film Institute.
Winship, Janice 1987: *Inside Women's Magazines*. London: Pandora.

6

Narrative

Everything is narrated – the match, the birth, the funeral, the meal, what so and so said about such and such, yesterday, today and possibilities for tomorrow.
Alverado et al., 1987, p. 120

Narratives are literally ubiquitous. The drive to organize the material of events past, present and future into narrative structures informs virtually all discursive cultural practices: conversation, religion, history, dance, poetry and theatre, to name but a few. Most media products are structured by narratives: the lyrics of popular music, Hollywood films, the television 'talk show', the contents pages of women's magazines and articles in newspapers – all are packaged into coherent story sequences. This chapter introduces various definitions of narrative. It examines narrative conventions across the different mediums of television and film and explores why narrative is important to these industries. Using film studies as a historical case study, the chapter also outlines the impact of structuralism on narrative theory.

Narratives are intertextual. They sometimes overlap other narratives – the same news story across the day's press, for example; or they deliberately reference other texts to 'play' on audience knowledge. Often equipped with a wealth of familiarity about other narrative structures, audience members have differing expectations of the stories they encounter, often producing readings according to their social and personal experiences of narratives.

Narratives tend to appear seamless, natural; they seem to present a story 'as it happened'. A number of media critics have likened the textual organization of narrative to the representational devices used to construct realism. Just as realism's ability to be real-seeming is illusory, so too are the devices narrative uses to organize events into smooth succession. Narrative structures seek to render invisible their processes of selection and alignment of events into a consecutive chain, yet, as Andrew Tolson argues, narratives are 'signs in chronological order' (1996, p. 39). As constructions, narratives are comprised of textual strategies which are meaningful because they are conventional rather than natural. The idea that all narratives are constructed entities or 'sense-making mechanisms' which seek to replace the chaotic randomness of the raw material of fiction or factual events with ordered significance, underpins the narrative theories discussed in this chapter (Fiske, 1987, p. 129).

Beyond sharing the semiotic view that narratives are signs which represent events in a particular way, narrative analysis, as Robert Stam et al. argue in *New Vocabularies in Film Semiotics*: 'seeks to peel away the seemingly "motivated" and "natural" relationship between the signifier and the story-world in order to reveal the deeper system of cultural associations and relationships that are expressed through narrative form' (1992, p. 69). By way of analysing the 'cultural associations' of narrative structures, media critics have used their findings to tackle wider cultural and political issues. Yet, as Sarah Kozloff argues, most narrative theory is, 'unapologetically "formalist" (that is, it concentrates on describing or analysing the text's intrinsic formal parameters)'; as a result, she argues, the onus has been placed on media critics to apply the findings of narrative theory if conclusions about a text's 'content or ideology' are to be drawn (1992, p. 68). This was indeed the case with the application of the structuralist findings of Lévi-Strauss and Propp by a number of film critics in the 1970s, who were interested in the ideological significance of narrative structures in Hollywood cinema. Structuralist applications are dealt with in later sections of this chapter. However, it is fair to say that critics who have used narrative theory for examining media texts have been concerned with analysing how cultures have chosen to represent themselves through their narratives, and with what consequences.

Narrative models: some definitions

Alverado et al. offer a useful starting point for thinking about narrative structures. They begin by defining narrative as 'a kind of corral into which various characters, places and events can be herded' (1987, p. 122). Their definition of narrative as a collection of selected categories of character, place and event, begins to illustrate the selective impetus behind narrative organization. A more detailed model, which claims to encompass broadly what most definitions of narrative fall within, is offered by Robert Stam et al. 'Narrative', they argue, 'can be understood as the recounting of two or more events (or a situation and an event) that are logically connected, occur over time, and are linked by a consistent subject to a whole' (1992, p. 69). They claim that, while most definitions of narrative converge around these three core elements, some writers' approaches are characterized by privileging one of the dimensions as more significant than others. They cite a number of writers to back their case, using Greimas (1966), Prince (1987) and Rimmon-Kenan (1983) as examples of those who broadly comply with their definition but who diverge around specific points. Greimas places greater importance on the drive towards a central goal enacted by the chain of cause and effect; his definition places stronger emphasis on the resolution or closure of the narrative. Prince, on the other hand, places greater emphasis on the linkage of events to one another and on the fact that narratives rely on being told. In their analysis of film, Bordwell and Thompson (1986) also concur broadly with Stam et al.'s encompassing definition. They describe narrative as *'a chain of events in cause–effect relationship occurring in time and space'* (p. 83). They wish to stress two of the elements as crucial to film narrative: 'All the elements of our definition – causality, time, and space – are important to narratives in most media, but causality and time are central' (p. 83). The reason for its divergence around specific points is the specificity of narrative construction in the scrutinized media form. Causality and time are crucial elements of film narrative.

Conventions of narrative across media forms

The idea that definitions of narrative are contingent upon the form in question, be it cinema, television or radio, is crucial to an examination of the conventions of narrative across different media forms. John Ellis, in his book *Visible Fictions: Cinema: Television: Video* (1992), actually warns against the dangers of generalized models of narration. Colin McCabe's contention that the narrational strategies that informed the construction of the classic realist novel were handed down to classic Hollywood cinema and later extended to television is deeply problematic for Ellis (Ellis, 1992, p. 64). He argues that both 'the material and organisational differences between the three media have had a central effect in determining the modes of narration that can conveniently be accommodated in each' (p. 64). While Ellis cannot deny that film and television do contain identifiable resemblances to the novel, he insists that the cinema has 'developed its own procedures and emphases', and, in like manner, that television, 'develops its own distinctive modes of narration' (p. 64).

Ellis devotes two chapters of *Visible Fictions* to examining the formal narrational differences between cinema and television. A key difference between the forms is the way in which they are consumed: a film is a single discrete text and, as such, is viewed with concentration; television appears in unconnected 'segments' and, as a result of its domestic setting, is consumed more casually. These different circumstances of consumption, Ellis argues, directly impact upon the narrational devices each medium can conceivably adopt. For him, cinema recounts events that have already occurred before the audience views the text; television communicates a sense of 'nowness' by presenting events as though alongside their occurrence. Narratorial address in the cinema appears 'as though events narrate themselves', without the use of the 'I' mode or direct address. Television often adopts the first person address in, for example the form of a presenter. And while there is rapid and sustained causation in cinema as the form works towards what Ellis calls the 'final coherent totalizing vision' of closure, the series format, so favoured by television, works in segments which suspend development and resist closure precisely because they are cast indefinitely or across a number of weeks. The series format, delivered in segments, encompasses both fiction and non-fiction programmes: 'there is no real difference', Ellis argues, 'in narrational forms between news and soap opera' (1992, p. 159).

Other critics have mounted similar arguments about the narrative form of fictional and factual media products, giving weight to Ellis's formulation about narrative and form. In *Understanding News* (1982) John Hartley argues that news 'bears a very close resemblance to key types of television fiction, especially the police series' (p. 115). The source material is the only departure point between *Coronation Street* and *The Six O'Clock News*; both must still narrate within the formal constraints of television as Ellis describes.

Why is narrative important to the media industry?

While narrative is a crucial sense-making device for the textual construction of a whole host of media products, narrative devices are also central to the marketing strategies the media industries deploy for advertising their products to audiences. The film posters positioned in cinema foyers, the magazine adverts hammocked between reviews in specialist film magazines such as *Empire* and *Premiere* and the trailers which are screened before feature films at the cinema – all use narrative strategies to offer a partial, yet tantalizing account of the text on sale so as to provoke enough curiosity in the potential viewer to generate commercial success (see illustration 6.1). In similar vein, yet in a way specific to the formal properties of the medium, television programmes are advertised using 'trailer' advertisements in commercial breaks; they, too, are constructed in ways which provide appetizing hints at programme content or development in order to secure audience ratings.

In *Visible Fictions*, Ellis extends his argument about the specific narrative devices used in media forms such as film and television to the advertising each form uses to capture audience attention. The film industry, which is in the business of promoting the 'single text', must create a separate audience for each film. Film-marketing is designed in the knowledge that the audience has never seen the text before. As a consequence, the film's commercial success hinges on the successful marketing of what Ellis calls

Illustration 6.1   Cinema posters offer potential consumers a taste of what
may follow.
Source: The authors.

the 'narrative "image"' (1992, p. 30). This central motif or idea is the
linchpin of the whole advertising campaign, from the film poster to the
cinema trailer. It must be devised, Ellis argues, in such a way as to act as
the 'cinema industry's reply to the question, "What is the film like?"' (p. 30)
The narrative image is therefore the only known commodity that the
cinema ticket's purchase is predicated upon; when thought of in this way,
it highlights its centrality to the film's commercial success. For that reason,
the narrative image must be organized effectively: it must reassure the
audience that it recognizably adheres to some known elements of a generic
formula, while at the same time creating a sense of difference from other
films in order to excite potential viewers. These two requirements are met
within the narrative image by a fine balancing act: intertextual references
work to inform the audience that some of the film's enjoyment rests on the
viewer's familiarity with other cinema experiences, and these combine
with a new set of enigmas. The narrative image acts, as Ellis argues, as the
film text's 'promise'(p. 31). The resolutions to the enigmas generated by
the advertising strategies are to be found by viewing the text itself.
     Ellis's ideas about the way in which the narrative image works to
construct simultaneously a blend of both the familiar and the unknown

can be seen in, for example, the poster for the film *The Piano* (1993), directed by Jane Campion. The visual image which occupies one half of the poster is of a woman standing next to a stool and a grand piano, on which a young girl sits. Both wear historical dress, reminiscent of the latter part of the 1800s. The image's most startling aspect is the setting: for this small group of people and objects are on a beach. The backdrop is a dramatic landscape.

In order to make sense of this image, the reader may draw on a number of intertextual references, depending on personal viewing experiences. One possible reading therefore might be made up of a number of different references. Because a woman is centred by the image, the poster implies that she will be the focal point of the narrative. That information alone provides clues about the genre; the film is likely to be a 'women's' picture, it might be a melodrama, or possibly a romance. The period costume generates other associations: both the plain black dress and bonnet worn by the central character and the piano, a valuable instrument, suggest she may be middle class and somewhat out of place in the bleak setting. The ideas generated by the film poster, that the central character is educated (a pianist at least), has arrived somewhere or is yet to travel and therefore has a measure of independence, is evocative of other narratives either written or set in the period – for example, the Brontë novels. These kinds of literary association would not be at all alien to the kind of educated middle-class audience *The Piano* was marketed at, as this film first appeared in independent, art-house cinemas before being launched into mainstream venues.

Yet despite the possibilities for familiar associations, the poster image also creates intrigue. Why are this woman, a small girl and some of their belongings on a beach? Are they waiting to travel, and if so where and why? Are they waiting to be met, and if so by whom? If this woman is not a governess and the child is her daughter, where is the rest of the family unit? If the film is about women in the 1900s, what kinds of constraint will structure their lives? And, finally, what will this woman's personal story be and what changes will her life undergo? The answers to these questions and suppositions can only be gained by the purchase of a cinema ticket, or the purchase or hire of *The Piano* on video.

Structuralism and narrative theory

During the 1960s and 1970s the import of a theoretical movement radically changed some of the fundamental assumptions critics and scholars made about the function of the arts. New ideas from what seemed to be remote disciplines, namely anthropology, linguistics and literary studies, combined to form structuralism, a turn of thought that was to have a significant impact on criticism, particularly within the humanities. However, it

may not be entirely appropriate, as Strinati argues, to speak of structuralism as though it were a past influence, since it is still used as a means of
thinking about cultural representations today (1995, p. 88).

As a theoretical framework, structuralism makes broad claims about
the structures which underlie social phenomena. In this sense structuralism is relevant to the humanities and social sciences generally. Anthro-
pologist Claude Lévi-Strauss, whose ideas were deeply influential on
structuralist thought, argued that deep structures underpinned all social
activities, since a universal tendency for the human mind to classify,
organize and literally structure all cultural artefacts was seen to operate
in every human culture that he studied. For humanities critics, the structuralist notion that common, even universal, structures might underpin all
cultural products, offered ways of questioning some of the fundamental
assumptions held about the arts. For critics interested in narrative, structuralism offered the possibility that some narrative elements were the
result of what Andrew Tolson has described as a 'universal human inherit-
ance, which would operate across cultures as well as within them' (1996,
p. 39). Before going on to examine the impact of structuralist thought on
film studies, it is to the thinkers who most influenced structuralist criticism that we now turn.

Saussure's structural linguistics

Saussure's premise that language is a science of signs is very important
to the emergence of structuralist thought. In Saussure's conception of
language a distinction exists between what he called *langue* and *parole*.
Langue is the structural system of language, governed by a set of rules.
Parole is the linguistic act or speech utterance, selected (often unconsciously by the user) from the system of *langue*. *Parole* is therefore wholly
reliant on, and determined by *langue*. What *parole* often reveals for lin-
guists, is the underlying structural mechanism of *langue*, since *langue*
ultimately governs the form *parole* can adopt.

Saussure also argued that, instead of language offering a transparent
correspondence with external reality, language terms have an entirely
arbitrary connection to the referents they signify; meaning does not reside
in the world, waiting to be expressed through language. Rather, language
terms are differential and meaning arises in and through the relationship
between them. Language users deal in the currency of the system rather
than being the originators of 'natural' meaning; they are conversant with
a self-sufficient, rule-governed and systematic structure which operates
independently of the 'real' world. Language, according to Saussure's
conception, is a cognitive process which language users have to encode
their world.

One of the conclusions drawn from Saussure's ideas was the notion that if language could be theorized in this way, so too could other cultural systems. According to structural linguistics, and to structuralism more generally, the products of a culture could only be understood as systems with their own inner logic, which can only make meaning, and therefore be understood in relational terms. (For further details on Saussure's thinking, see the section 'Semiotic Analysis' in chapter 2.)

Lévi-Strauss

The importance of Saussure's work is brought more sharply into focus when the main principles of Lévi-Strauss's contribution to structuralism are considered. Working after the Second World War, Lévi-Strauss studied a number of tribal cultures, mainly in North and South America. His contribution to structuralism comes from revealing universal structural elements beneath the rituals, kinship laws and the stories or myths in circulation within pre-industrial societies. For him, these common structures were manifest, despite cultural difference or historical contingency. It was Lévi-Strauss's contention that the human mind's natural, but unconscious tendency to structure lay beneath all a society's cultural output. This universal, underlying structure can be likened to Saussure's conception of *langue*; its products or individual utterances are directly comparable to *parole*. Like language, whose users obey its rules unconsciously, the unobservable yet governing structural system acts unbeknown to those it organizes. Since human subjects were unaware of its central organizing influence, and the rules with which it governed, they were hardly reliable sources for research. Structuralist thinkers therefore recognized that it was their task to uncover the model underlying human societies. And, as Strinati argues, structuralists believed that such a structure held the key to what they thought of as 'an underlying reality' governing all cultures (1995, p. 96). The meaning of the elements of the structure were, like language, organized relationally – so that meaning emanated from their difference from one another in the system. What Lévi-Strauss realized from his knowledge of structural linguistics was that a clear understanding of this 'underlying reality' lay in studying the logic of its workings. This meant constructing a grand chart of its structural unity. Lévi-Strauss's conception of a grand universal structure began with a table of binary oppositions – black/white, light/dark, night/day and so on – since for him all meaning emanates from difference. What Lévi-Strauss argued was that all cultural forms have their roots in this table of logical combinations or relational patterns, but that out of them only a limited amount of combinations were possible. As Strinati sums up, Lévi-Strauss was arguing that all cultures and their forms 'represent the logical transformation of the fundamental workings of the structure of oppositions inherent in the human mind' (1995, p. 97).

One of the cultural forms that Lévi-Strauss researched were the narratives, or myths, produced by ancient and so-called 'primitive' cultures. He found the symbolic imagery of the myths to be wildly different, and, given the enormous cultural and historical differences between the myths, such differences were to be expected. Yet while they were different, he found that they were all commonly marked by their function, which was symbolically to transform the binary oppositions he had identified as being central to his model of a universal underlying structure common to all cultures. Myths, according to Lévi-Strauss, enabled people symbolically to reconcile the cruelties, inequalities and contradictions they faced in the real world. Myths had the social role of explaining away unfathomable cultural contradictions as naturally inevitable. Following on from this, narrative as 'sense-making device' can be traced back to early myths.

Lévi-Strauss's idea that binary oppositions exist in the process of narratives can be seen at work in the ways in which mainstream film texts are structured, for example. Although Lévi-Strauss studied ancient and pre-industrialized cultures and their mythologies, his ideas about the operation of narrative can be seen at work in post-industrial cultural forms. Most genre films can be broken down into structured oppositions: in the horror film it is good / evil or innocent, unsuspecting public / murderous monster; in the western it is settlers / native Americans, and so on. What the text must somehow do is to resolve them. It might do so in a number of ways: affirming one side of the opposition is one possibility, or perhaps ensuring that the central character of the film resolves them. In his book *Film as Social Practice* (1988) Graeme Turner discusses *Desperately Seeking Susan* (1985) as an example of a film in which 'the conflict is resolved by the main character repudiating one side of the opposition and opting for the alternative' (p. 76). In his reading of the film he identifies a number of oppositions: Roberta / Susan, conventional / unconventional, bourgeois / anti-bourgeois, suburban / urban. Roberta's (Rosanna Arquette) rejection of her position at the film's outset is manifest in her obsession with Susan (Madonna), whose life she would like to emulate. As a result, Turner argues, the negative oppositions disintegrate, allowing the film to become a powerful critique of bourgeois marriage.

In the Hollywood romantic comedy *The Truth about Cats and Dogs* (1996) binary oppositions can also be identified, but this narrative is resolved rather differently. A tale of mistaken identity, Brian (Ben Chaplin) falls in love with the voice of Dr Abby (Janeane Garofalo), veterinary radio hostess. Mistaking her for her beautiful flatmate Noelle (Uma Thurman), the romantic hero is left to ponder the stark difference between the intelligent voice (Garofalo) and the person he dates (Thurman). The narrative is constructed around the oppositions embodied by the two female characters: Abby / Noelle, plain / beautiful, intelligent / dumb.

During the course of the narrative the romantic hero stands between the narrative's oppositions because he loves both characters: Abby for her intelligent personality; Noelle for her beauty. However, it is what the female characters find out about themselves that results in a dissolution of the oppositions, and finally a narrative resolution. Abby learns that conventional beauty does not guarantee love and that she can be loved despite her plainness. Noelle learns to value herself for the person she is, as opposed to the person others want her to be. As a result, she learns to value female friendship. In resolving those central oppositions, the film is critical of the consumer values of Western society which emphasize the value of appearance over personal qualities.

Propp

Russian folklorist Vladimir Propp was another key thinker whose text *Morphology of the Folktale*, first published in English in 1968, was to have an enormous impact on structuralist ideas about narrative. Dissatisfied with existing work on folktales in the 1920s, Propp originally set out to provide a new methodological system for classifying them. Instead of ordering them in terms of their themes, as previous critics had, Propp analysed the tales according to their structural form. This kind of approach, which attempted to understand the internal logic of narratives as forms in their own right, was to mark a significant departure from previous studies. Whereas Lévi-Strauss's work had concluded that narratives served a universal social function, Propp's findings suggested that narratives themselves have a universal structure.

Propp studied about a hundred folktales and set about breaking each one down into its fundamental parts, which he called 'functions'. According to his model, each function was not defined as a specific event in the story; instead, he analysed the purpose it played in the overall tale. For example, particular events from different tales might seem radically dissimilar on the surface, yet serve the same function for each. Propp argued that there were thirty-one functions in his basic universal narrative structure. Perhaps not all tales would include every single function, he argued, but all tales would be composed from his thirty-one functions and the sequence of events would always be exactly the same. Moreover, he found that certain functions always occurred at particular points in the narrative. For example, it was always at the end that 'the hero is married and crowned'.

In similar vein, the characters in Propp's model were not classified in terms of the personal qualities that made them three-dimensional; rather they were classified according to the 'sphere of action' or set role they played within the narrative framework. Propp outlined seven 'spheres of action' – the villain, the donor (provider), the helper, the princess and her father, the dispatcher, the hero or victim and the false hero. These 'spheres' were not to be confused with characters, since one character could be involved in several spheres of action during the course of the narrative.

While it might be argued that a large gap lies between folktales and the commercial narratives produced by media industries in today's post-industrial world, Propp's model has been successfully applied to a number of narratives. John L. Fell (1977) found that *Kiss Me Deadly* (1955) conformed with Propp's contention that an underlying schema was common to many narratives (see also Erens's (1977) account of *Sunset Boulevard* (1950) and Wollen's (1976) morphological reading of *North by North-West* (1959)). Other critics outside film studies, notably John Fiske (1987), have been startled by the similarity between media products such as the television series and Propp's model. Analysing *The A-Team* and *The Bionic Woman*, Fiske remarks that the conformity to Propp's functions and spheres of action 'is astonishing in its precision' (1987, p. 137).

Todorov

In *The Poetics of Prose* (1977), Tzvetan Todorov suggests that narratives begin with a state of equilibrium, or 'plenitude', where the social state is satisfactory, stable and harmonious. This plenitude is then overturned or disrupted by a villainous force. The course of the narrative then charts the disequilibrium that ensues. The disequilibrium is finally challenged and ultimately resolved by a positive counterforce, which then returns the situation to a second, slightly altered state of equilibrium.

Fiske (1987) argues that Todorov's narrative model is distinctive because it privileges the social effects of narrative action above the individual forces that shape it. Indeed, Todorov's model is useful for questioning the ideological implications of narratives that conform to this schema. For Fiske, the model poses two important considerations: 'the first is the comparison of the opening and closing states of equilibrium, and the second is in identifying what constitutes a force of disruption, and what a force of stability' (1987, p. 139). Todorov's model can suitably be applied to non-fiction as well as to fiction media products.

Todorov's model can be seen to structure almost all news stories; indeed, disruption itself might almost be described as a criterion upon which an event qualifies as newsworthy. The disruptive force and state of disequilibrium are the points in Todorov's model where ideological work is most clearly in operation. As Fiske argues, it is conventional that news products retain and perpetuate reactionary values. Therefore the villains or causes of disruption are often trade-union members, left-wing social activists or social-issue demonstrators. By contrast, the heroes who restore narrative stability in the form of new equilibrium are usually servants of the state, the army, judiciary or the police force.

The impact of structuralism on film studies

In the 1960s some British critics identified structuralism as a method that might offer a break from auteurism. Critics in *Cahiers du Cinema*, for example, looked to structuralism as a potential Marxist tool with which they could sharpen their critiques of the ideological role Hollywood cinema played in society. In Britain, the journal *Screen* embraced the ideas of structuralism, and launched an attack on the textual analysis appropriated for auteur criticism then practised in journals like *Movie*. For film studies, a discipline that had struggled to attain kudos within the academy, structuralism at least seemed to offer a degree of theoretical rigour. The use of structuralist ideas to critique the work of known and celebrated directors working in Hollywood marked a period where two theoretical movements partially merged, in what became known as auteur-structuralism.

While auteur-structuralism held on to the practice of examining championed directors, structuralism's theoretical premises fundamentally undermined the auteurist premise of the director as individual genius. The ideas of Lévi-Strauss and Propp had suggested that there were predetermined narrative structures which cultural forms in all societies, throughout history, had unknowingly perpetuated. The contradiction between the privileging of the director in auteurism and the emphasis on unconscious underlying structures in structuralism was also affirmed by Barthes's work. In 'The Death of the Author' Barthes argued that structuralism's account of meaning as the effect of a differential system had displaced the author altogether. Together with Saussure's ideas that language is not an agency which can simply record the world being described, but is a system which encodes the external world, the idea of artist/director as originator of artistic meaning was undermined, as Helen Stoddart argues:

> how could a critic hope to elucidate the precise and intended meaning of an auteur when all the terms (visual or linguistic) used by the artist only obtain meaning through their relation to a whole system of other terms and, equally, when each speech act must be suspected of having been interrupted by the unconscious or the unintentional? (1995, p. 45)

The British critic Peter Wollen is one of the best-known auteur-structuralists from the 1960s and 1970s. For him, drawing on the work of both Propp and Lévi-Strauss, structuralist practice consisted of identifying the structural oppositions across the work of championed directors (see Wollen, 1976). His method of applying structuralist ideas to the oeuvres of great authors was contradictory, his insistence on applying its principles to the work of Hawks, Hitchcock and Ford lay awkwardly alongside the structuralist overthrow of authorial presence and intent.

Will Wright's book *Sixguns and Society* (1975) marked one of the first attempts to apply the work of Lévi-Strauss to a large body of work within

a generic category, the western, as opposed to individual texts or direc-
torial oeuvres. Wright examined the correlation between changes in the
US social, economic and political climate and the western genre across a
forty-year period. He concluded that the western functioned as myth in
much the same way as Lévi-Strauss had argued that stories had been
used in primitive societies. He argued that westerns acted as reactionary
catalysts, working to reinforce and perpetuate conservative values, which
in turn kept intact the status quo.

The problems with structuralist narrative models

So far, our discussion of structuralist narrative models has dealt with their
ability to 'fit' a number of media examples. However, not all critics and
commentators agree that they can be applied to any example with total
confidence. Therefore, the possibility that they might have universal
relevance has been somewhat undermined. Some critics have questioned
the kinds of example the models have been mapped on to. In her discussion of the analysts who have found a high level of compliance between
Propp's model and film texts, Sheila Johnston asks, 'Can this compatibility
be attributed to the skilful and selective choice of test cases? Or to ingeni-
ous distortions of the narratives to force them into the mould?' (1987,
p. 235) Adding weight to her argument, she cites John Fell's conclusions,
who, after successfully applying the schema to Aldrich's *Kiss Me Deadly*
(1955), also found large inconsistencies between Propp's schema and the
work of Sternberg and Hawks. To extend the point, one might also ask
how far structuralist models can be applied across mediums. While
Todorov's model might enlighten the analysis of news texts, as well as a
range of other media products such as the television police series or
television and magazine advertising, it blatantly cannot fit a number of
other examples, such as avant-garde films, whose narrative organization
eludes the stages of narrative structure suggested by Todorov.

Structuralism has also been attacked, as a critical method, for its for-
malism, or its preoccupation with the structural organization of media
forms, at the expense of other important questions and considerations. Maltby and Craven argue that while auteur-structuralism added an
important critical dimension to film studies, as an approach it can only
provide 'very partial answers to the historical and ideological questions
of the cinema's relation to the culture within which it is produced and to
which it is addressed' (1995, pp. 424–5). If we are to reach an understanding of the meaning and role of cinema, these wider, contextual questions
must be asked. This takes us back to Kozloff's observation that narrative
models need to be combined with other theoretical approaches if those
wider contextual issues are to be fully explored. Indeed, Kozloff takes her

critique of what she terms the 'large voids' that narrative theories leave behind even further:

> Because narrative theory concentrates on the text itself, it leaves to other critical methods questions about where the story comes from (for instance, the history, organization, and regulation of the broadcast industry, the influence of networks, or the contributions of individual professionals) and the myriad effects (psychological or sociological) that the text has upon its audience. (1992, p. 68)

Suggestions for further work

Visit a multiplex cinema. List the various ways in which the 'narrative image' of a new film is on display. What purpose do you think this is serving?

Look at a contemporary popular film. Create a list of oppositions that structure its narrative. Do you think they are a useful way of exploring such media texts?

Further reading

Cook, Pam (ed.) 1987: *The Cinema Book*. London: British Film Institute.
Ellis, John 1992: *Visible Fictions: Cinema: Television: Video*, 2nd edition. London: Routledge.
Stam, Robert et al. 1992: *New Vocabularies in Film Semiotics: Structuralism, Post-structuralism and Beyond*. London: Routledge.
Wright, Will 1975: *Sixguns and Society*. Berkeley: University of California Press.

7
Intertextuality

Intertextuality is an idea that has in recent times become much more relevant when analysing the media. Much of the increased usage of the term has been due to the influence of theories of postmodernism on the thinking about, and the analysis of, contemporary media products. However, not all the approaches that utilize the notion of intertextuality reside within the framework of postmodernism. This section will therefore offer a number of definitions of intertextuality before going on to introduce and explore the idea of postmodernism. It will also consider the usefulness of these ideas and approaches when analysing media texts. It will then go on to discuss the idea of intertextuality in relation to a number of examples from different media: advertising, pop videos and contemporary Hollywood films.

Definitions

In *Television Culture* (1987) John Fiske devotes a whole chapter to intertextuality, clearly indicating that for him this is an important area. Fiske's view of intertextuality relates closely to the field of semiotics, and he identifies it as a major contributor to the ways in which media texts make meaning culturally. He argues that texts relate to other texts both similar and different, and in doing so make meaning for audiences. He goes on to state that in his view intertextuality operates on two dimensions – what he terms the horizontal and the vertical.

On the horizontal dimension intertextuality operates through factors such as genre, character and content. Here the link with other texts is explicit. For example, an audience's understanding of products such as the horror film relates to their knowledge and understanding of other products of a similar type. In much the same way characters such as

Batman, who have appeared in films, on television and in comics, as well as appearing in a variety of other media such as computer games, create meaning across the texts they inhabit. In a case such as Batman, each manifestation of the character potentially has an effect on the meaning available from others. Fiske goes on to incorporate Raymond Williams's argument that television is made up of a 'flow' of sounds and images into his definition of horizontal intertextuality, when he states that 'the meaning of a traditional western is intertextually inflected by its juxtaposition with a news item about American Indians protesting their place in a white-dominated society. Adventure films taking place in unspecified Third World countries run by corrupt regimes relate all too readily with news reports from Africa or Latin America' (1987, p. 109). The meaning of the images and sounds that make up television programmes is therefore created not in isolation, but in relation to a whole host of other media texts.

Fiske's other dimension of intertextuality is the vertical. Vertical intertextuality refers to the ways in which texts refer specifically to others. He places the notion of intertextuality into an economic context by arguing that vertical intertextuality is most clearly present when one text explicitly promotes another. Examples of this include the publicity material that surrounds the release of a new feature film. In this case, secondary texts such as advertisements, posters and journalistic reviews work to mobilize and promote the preferred meaning of the primary text. This version of intertextuality theorizes it as operating in a similar way to Altman's view of genre, to support the dominant ideology (see chapter 5). It is able to do this because the secondary texts work to narrow the potential meanings available from the text they are promoting. Intertextuality assists in privileging certain positions and readings above others, inviting the audience to read texts in a particular way.

Postmodernism and intertextuality

Theories of postmodernism also engage with the notion of intertextuality. However, they move away from and expand the version offered by Fiske, theorizing the continual referencing of other texts as something which reflects wider social and cultural changes taking place in the late twentieth century. Here, intertextuality has the potential to challenge semiotics and its assumptions about meaning. As Angela McRobbie argues, 'postmodernism considers images as they relate to and across each other. Postmodernism deflects attention away from the singular scrutinising gaze of the semiologist, and asks that this be replaced by a multiplicity of fragmented and frequently interrupted looks' (1994, p. 13). The idea here is that postmodernism reflects a perceived fragmentation of contemporary Western society. When used to think about the media this leads to a consideration of the ways in which postmodern media images can be considered intertextual, or, as McRobbie puts it, 'relate to and across each other' (p. 13), reflecting inwards upon themselves. Jean Baudrillard, another important postmodern thinker, refers to this process as 'implosion', suggesting that postmodern images look in on themselves and similar texts, at the expense of engaging with an outside world which is itself, according to Baudrillard, illusory.

Italian theorist and novelist Umberto Eco identifies this inward-looking trait when he analyses Italian television of the mid-1980s. He labels it 'Neo-TV', and argues that it continually 'talks about itself and about the contacts it establishes with its own public ... Neo-TV in order to survive, seeks to hold the viewer by saying to him: I am here, it's me, I am you' (1984, p. 19). This inward-looking perspective can be observed in other television productions from outside Italy. The Emmy award-winning American situation comedy of the early 1990s, *Evening Shade*, is a useful example. Within the 'world' of the programme (which combines both the fictional world of the programme's setting and the actual world of the viewer), the audience is continually invited to bring its knowledge of other images of the show's stars to bear on its understanding of the fictional action. This is especially true with regard to the show's central star Burt Reynolds. In his case, the audience's knowledge and awareness of both his career and private life were essential if they were to understand many of the jokes presented. The intertextuality of *Evening Shade* invites the audience into the inward-looking perspective of contemporary television as outlined by Eco. For example, in one episode the characters discuss watching one of Reynolds's most popular and favourite films *The Longest Yard* (1974, UK title *The Mean Machine*) on television. In another episode a fictional character attempted to acquire actress Loni Anderson's 'phone number from someone who had recently, in the situation comedy, visited Hollywood. As Anderson was at that time married to Reynolds, this incident led to a series of knowing glances between regular characters, which the audience is invited to be part of as they share the required knowledge of Reynolds's private life. The 'real' world and the world of the television programme cease to be different, as an inward, intertextual world is created by both the text and audience. The constructed star image of the performers becomes a concrete part of the actual outside world for programmes such as *Evening Shade*. In this way, the intertextuality that is central to them assists in the creation of a continually introspective world that has the media at its centre rather than any social or political reality. The warm glow of the fictitious place called *Evening Shade* is made more attractive and seductive to the viewer than a harsh and tough contemporary America, with all its social and political problems. This perceived lack of political engagement has caused some critics to be negative about this tendency within contemporary media culture, arguing that it does little more than assist in the maintenance and reproduction of the capitalist social order. However, as we show later, not all manifestations of intertextuality need be considered reactionary.

Intertextuality and advertising

Some of the clearest examples of intertextuality within the media can be found within advertising. For example, many high-profile advertising campaigns clearly make reference to films and other forms of popular culture such as music and television. This can often be at the level of imagery. The post-apocalyptic world of the *Mad Max* series of films (*Mad Max*, 1979; *Mad Max 2*, 1981; *Mad Max Beyond Thunderdome*, 1985) is used as the setting for the series of promotional adverts for Foster's lager that follow the adventures of two survivors as they seek out the remaining 'amber nectar'. These advertisements clearly draw on the search for gasoline present in the *Mad Max* films. This example is also useful when considering Fredric Jameson's idea that all this process of textual referencing of other texts does is create what he calls a pastiche (1985, p. 114). Jameson argues that pastiche is a 'stylistic mask' which he says is often confused with parody, but which in fact lacks the latter's mocking criticism. He argues that pastiche exists in a world where 'stylistic innovation is no longer possible', and that 'all that is left is to imitate dead styles, to speak through the masks and with the voices of the styles in an imaginary museum' (p. 115). Arguably, there is no deeper meaning to the Foster's *Mad Max* adverts, apart from selling the product, than the fact that they seek to entertain in an intertextual way, and do so by using imagery and ideas in an empty, surface way. They are clearly referring to other popular texts, but not in a way that seeks to 'comment' upon them, or the society that produced them. The sole purpose of the campaign, it may be argued, is to deliver consumers for the product and increase the profits of the company producing the alcoholic drink.

However, the intertextuality of advertising campaigns such as this one may also offer audiences enormous pleasure because they allow them to celebrate and share their cultural knowledge. This point may be extended, since the intertextuality of advertising not only involves an audience's recognition of references drawn from popular culture, but also what may be labelled high culture, as some campaigns use images from fine art, opera and classical theatre. These may be moments of classical music, references to artwork such as the Mona Lisa, or characters from Shakespeare's plays. Whatever the cultural source of the intertextuality present in many advertisements, it undoubtedly offers audiences a range of pleasures, and in doing so creates meaning in a number of ways. It may be argued, therefore, that the intertextual referencing in so much contemporary advertising potentially empowers consumers, as it allows them to exchange their knowledge of other cultural references in a social context such as the workplace, when discussing the previous evening's television viewing.

Referencing other texts is not the only way in which contemporary advertisements may be thought of as intertextual. Certainly, in the mid-1990s there were a number of advertising campaigns that built upon and used audience knowledge, not only of the product being advertised but also the past campaigns employed to promote it. In these campaigns characters reappeared and events unfolded across a number of linked adverts. For example, the characters of Papa and Nicole were successfully used to promote the Renault Clio car on a number of occasions. In each case the audience built upon its knowledge of the characters and brought this knowledge to bear upon its reading of each new advert. Another example is Gold Blend coffee, which was successfully promoted through an ongoing series of advertisements that developed a romantic love triangle in the style of a mini soap opera, each one employing a cliff-hanger ending to ensure that audiences sought out the next instalment. Other products have been promoted in the same successful way over an even longer period of time. The best example of this form of advertising intertext-uality is the PG Tips chimpanzees, which have appeared in a number of promotional campaigns for tea since the 1960s. In all these cases the prior and ongoing knowledge and awareness of the consumer is central to the construction and success of each advertisement and the campaign as a whole. It is also possible to argue that the ability of an audience to read intertextually is a prerequisite to their understanding of these types of campaign, and pays testament to the sophistication of the contemporary consumer's ability to operate across Fiske's horizontal dimension when reading advertisements.

Intertextuality, politics and popular music

As we have argued, postmodern media images may be considered inter-textual because they continually reference other texts and images. Using this definition of intertextuality, we now wish to turn our attention to popular music. Meaning does not simply reside within the sound of a piece of popular music. It creates meaning through the forms in which recorded music is distributed (LP, CD or MC), the television and magazine images that help promote it, and the references to other music and media that performers include in their work. It is the increasing level of reference to other performers and texts, its intertextuality, that has led some critics to the conclusion that the contemporary music scene is postmodern. This is supported by the fact that so much of the promotional work undertaken in the music industry continually talks about, or pays homage to, earlier popular cultural images. For example, the arrival of 'Brit Pop' in the mid-1990s was accompanied by a great number of journalistic articles that claimed Blur were the new Kinks or that Oasis were the new Beatles. This reference to the past was not just present in the music press; it seemed to be something that was consciously being promoted by the bands themselves. For example, Blur included pastiches of the early 1970s film *A Clockwork Orange* (1971) in their videos.

Such popular cultural references can be found in many other pop videos by artists not associated with Brit Pop. Rapper 2Pac, for example, accompanied his single *California Love* (1996) with a promotional video that, in a similar way to the Fosters adverts discussed earlier, was clearly modelled on the *Mad Max* series of films. The settings, props, lighting, costume and make-up for the video are all clearly drawn from the *mise-en-scène* of the Australian films. This brings us back to Jameson's argument that all postmodern texts do is superficially reproduce earlier images and ideas. His general criticism seems particularly suited to the case of Blur and their aping of *A Clockwork Orange*, which carries none of the attempts to grapple with issues of social violence that are present, however unsuccessfully, in Stanley Kubrick's film. Blur merely celebrate the images of *A Clockwork Orange*, whilst steadfastly ignoring the film's attempts at social commentary. The case of the 2Pac's *California Love* video, however, offers a more complex set of issues. Whilst clearly referencing the *Mad Max* films, as we have observed, it also invites the viewer to identify the performers as outsiders. Like the film's characters, they are presented as survivors in a post-apocalyptic world. Given the oppressed position many African Americans occupy in contemporary US society, it becomes possible to read the appropriation of such images of survival as significant, and potentially carrying a political message. The *California Love* video becomes more than simply a jokey, empty pastiche as it offers images of survival for the young African-American audience consuming it. The fictional world created by the video is exclusively inhabited by black characters, and this works to heighten the possibilities that the video might be read as a political statement which consciously chooses to use particular popular cultural references as part of its vocabulary. The choice of images from popular cinema is important, because they are likely to constitute a significant part of the cultural knowledge of contemporary black American urban youth.

Intertextuality and film genre

Jim Collins, writing about genre and film in the 1990s, identifies that there are two co-existent but divergent manifestations of genre within contemporary Hollywood film-making: what he calls an 'eclectic irony' and a 'new sincerity' (1993, p. 242). Films that fall into the former category, he argues, combine very traditional elements of genre within a context where they would not normally be found. He cites as an example of this trend *Back to the Future III* (1990), which he argues is a hybrid of the traditional western and the science-fiction film. In this case the manifestation of genre is shot through with a strong sense of irony, which is reflected by such knowing moments as Marty McFly citing contemporary western icons such as Clint Eastwood in his dialogue, and his time-machine being chased in the same way as the stagecoach in Ford's 1939 eponymous film. The second trend identified by Collins is epitomized by the film *Dances with Wolves* (1990). In this case, however, he claims that there is a striving for a 'new sincerity', which is almost an attempt to rediscover a lost generic purity. These films lack eclectic irony and take themselves very seriously. He cites both *Field of Dreams* (1989) and *Hook* (1991) as further examples of this trend.

Both of the tendencies identified by Collins within contemporary Hollywood film-making firmly acknowledge the intertextual knowledge of today's audiences. In the case of those that present an 'eclectic irony' there seems to be a need for audiences to share, at least some of, the intertextual knowledge referenced by the films in order to gain maximum pleasure from them. In those texts that display the 'new sincerity' Collins talks of, there is a sense that audiences share with the film-makers a desire to return to a purer version of genre. This must be dependent upon them sharing a knowledge of what cinema has gone before if they are to understand what makes a 'purer', more authentic genre film. So, whatever the tendency, there is a strong awareness that the contemporary consumer has a great deal of cinematic knowledge to bring to bear on their reading of new film texts. Much of this is due to the prevalence of new technologies which allow viewers to watch and re-watch older generic films at times of their choice. The reappearance of older generic films, many of which are now seen as classics, on TV, video and laser disc has meant that audiences have much more opportunity to view the history of cinema. This, in turn, allows them to view across genres at their leisure. It is therefore possible to argue that these contemporary genre films help to create a cinematic culture that is as introspective as the world of Italian television described by Eco as 'Neo-TV'.

Increasingly, it is the case that both film-makers and critics are interested in the reactivation of older styles and genres. This in turn contributes to the creation of a self-reflective tendency within contemporary Hollywood film-making. Examples of this are the renewed interest in *film noir* and so called 'neo-*noir*' shown by critics and film-makers in the late 1990s, and the acceptance of a new level of cultural capital for the western which is reflected by the Oscars awarded to *Dances with Wolves* (1990) and Clint Eastwood's genre-conscious *Unforgiven* (1992). However, in this intertextual media world it is fair to say that both films and television, as well as other media, cannot be media specific with their inward-looking gaze; it is cast across different media, with films referencing television and television referencing film. But, as Eco argues, this creates an unbroken circle between the media and excludes the outside, 'real' world. Films such as *Street Fighter* (1994), *Super Mario Bros* (1993) and *Mortal Kombat* (1995) are examples of this multi-media intertextuality. They depend upon other media forms such as the computer game, the comic book and the animated cartoon for their source, and this informs the ways in which they are read by audiences. However, this manifestation of intertextuality can be examined and analysed outside the realm of the text, which is something that Eco does not do. The inward-looking reality of such intertextuality in fact lies in the economics of the contemporary media world. However 'unreal' this world may seem, it does exist within an economic reality based upon the profit motive of large media conglomerates. To understand fully media texts like *Street Fighter* (1994) we need to acknowledge the enormous influence of the industrial context of production upon them. Whilst critics may sneer at the perceived lack of originality in films which began as computer games, such as *Street Fighter* (1994) and *Mortal Kombat* (1995), their intertextuality in part depends upon the fact that profit can be made from the intertextual knowledge of the consumer. Whilst that knowledge is clearly present in the consumer marketplace, films will be made from sources such as computer games, comics will be developed that draw on films and television, and cartoons will be made from popular comic books.

Suggestions for further work

Identify a range of advertisements which reference other media texts. Why do you think advertisers are increasingly reliant on such intertextuality?

In light of the amount of referencing of other mediums that are present in contemporary media texts, can textual analysis alone provide any real understanding of today's media?

Further reading

Eco, Umberto 1984: A guide to neo-television of the 1980s. *Framework*, 25, 18–27.
Fiske, John 1987: *Television Culture*. London: Methuen.
Strinati, Dominic 1995: *An Introduction to Theories of Popular Culture*. London: Routledge.

Part II
Institutions

8
Approaches to Media Institutions

So far this book has been concerned with texts. The preceding chapters have introduced a variety of textual theories and conceptual approaches for analysing the meanings which reside in print, television, magazines and other media. Yet textual analysis alone can provide only a partial perspective for media study. A purely textual approach excludes a number of factors which are crucial for contextualizing the meaning processes of texts. For example: who has produced the text? what other representational devices did the producers have at their disposal when constructing the text and why were they excluded? what other processes, for example, matters of legality or regulation, worked to shape the text and with what results? and what other industrial influences and constraints, which are not revealed by the text, had a part to play in its production? The answers to these institutional questions provide a wider contextual picture for the study of media texts. Indeed, they may cast the theoretical conclusions that might be reached about texts into new light once the broader institutional framework is revealed. By opening up the processes of production and circulation which all texts are subject to, other meanings emanate – meanings or processes that the institution itself might have sought to repress.

What is a media institution?

There are two ways in which institutions can be conceptualized. First, they can be regarded as industries or businesses which produce media commodities in a capitalist society. Institutions in this sense of the word are contingent upon the economic climate in which they operate, so media industries can be temporary in that they come and go, or their popularity can rise and wane. Second, and in a broader sense, institutions can be seen as the large organizing bodies or structures of any society. These broader, interconnecting institutions, such as the family, the Church, the judiciary, the monarchy, education and the institution of concern here, the media, play some part in regulating the cultural values and beliefs in circulation in society. Institutions in this latter sense are more permanent and enduring. However, these two definitions are not mutually exclusive; indeed, each definition applies to a different aspect of media institutions more generally.

Regarding institutions as industry involves placing them foremost into their economic contexts. Within this definition, media products are just that: commodities which must fulfil a number of criteria in the name of making maximum profits. If profit is ever threatened by less marketable textual content, changes to a product's make-up are inevitable. The owner-ship of the media industries is highly concentrated, and only a few people have access to the means of production. As owners of the production and distribution of media artefacts, these people have access to a great deal of power. Most media artefacts are mass-produced, most often in the private, but sometimes in the public sector within an industrial, hier-archical system where there is a division of labour. Any examination of the media industries should therefore involve an investigation of the power relations in play in the context of the production of media texts. Media workers in these industries must adopt professional codes of practice in the workplace, the adoption of a newspaper 'house style' for example, which might have ideological consequences for the product. As businesses, the media industries must compete to make a profit, or even to stay afloat. In order to keep their industries profitable they must be entirely convinced that their product has a market. Audience research has a key role here as the testing ground for the viability of the product, a product which is at the mercy of markets, and indeed is, as we have argued, subject to alteration to serve those markets. The BBC is an example of an institution that must be seen in its industrial context which ultim-ately ensures it operates as a business venture. While the BBC is publicly funded through the television licensing fee, it must still compete within a broader marketplace. When examined in the light of these contextual factors, what comes to the fore is the fact that it is the media text's success as an economic object that keeps afloat its institutional parent. Each of the factors above plays some part in impinging on the final meaning of the media product; they provide the causal reasons for some textual meanings.

The media as a broader social institution or collection of institutional bodies interlocking with others, such as the family and the state, differs from the idea of institution as industry. Institutions, in this sense, form the fabric of our wider culture in a more permanent way. Sometimes they are buildings we see and use in our everyday lives, yet at the same time they seem almost to form part of 'us' in a more personal sense because they embody and co-ordinate social values. No social institution can be seen to operate independently of others; instead, they mutually support and uphold a dominant social framework. The media, as one institution among a range of others, can be seen as a body which shares and reinforces similar values to those exercised and upheld by other institutions operating simultaneously, values which confirm dominant ideas about our social relations – ideas about class and gender, for example. While institutions in this sense of the term must still be seen as operating in a capitalist economic framework, in this definition they are regarded as major power arbiters because they play such a key role in the co-ordination of social and cultural values. Yet just as industrial organizations come and go in the ruthless context of the business world, institutions in this broader sense, as well as the social and cultural values they represent, are subject to historical change. The BBC is an example of an institution representative of broader cultural values, which has been modified at different historical moments. In the 1930s, the first Director-General of the BBC Sir John Reith believed that the role of radio broadcasting should be to 'educate, entertain and inform'. At that time the BBC was a monopoly, carefully regulated by the state. By the 1950s, however, the introduction of commercial television meant that the position of the BBC as an institution was forced to change (see illustration 8.1). While it managed to retain its commitment to public service broadcasting, much of its programming became more popular in a bid to compete with its new competitors. The BBC might seem like a timeless monolith, but its ethos as an institution has been, and still is, evolving (see chapter 9).

It might be argued that as the place where media artefacts are produced and regulated, media institutions should form the primary source of investigation in media studies. However, there are issues that need to be considered before institutions are made the chief organizing force behind how sense is made of the media. One is the question of determinism. How far can institutions be regarded as the sole determining principle behind media output? How far do media owners control the values of their products, thereby ensuring the domination of their own ruling-class position, rather than encouraging a more democratic social consensus? In *Media, Communication, Culture: A Global Approach* (1995) James Lull argues that institutions can never wholly dominate media texts to produce singular meanings: 'No single institution can ever articulate but one ideology. Certainly no media institution can. In fact, diversity and contradiction are fundamental themes that emerge when we closely examine what is presented on the mass media throughout the world' (p. 122). Even less likely, for Lull, is the idea that owners can have a singular and controlling force over what a culture chooses to make of textual meanings: 'culture, ultimately, can never be fully managed by any society's political-economic power brokers, including its mass media image brokers.

Illustration 8.1   Granada Television, based in Manchester, is an example of a
commercial station.
Source: The authors.

Articulations of official or dominant ideologies do not determine culture.
Under certain circumstances, dominant ideological expressions can even
inspire violent resistance' (p. 114).

Critical approaches to media institutions

In this section we explore a range of critical approaches to media institutions, before going on to consider how useful each approach is for
assessing contemporary media institutions in both national and global
contexts.

The Frankfurt School and its critique of the culture industries

Herbert Marcuse, Theodor Adorno and Max Horkheimer are the best
known of the German Marxist scholars, collectively named the Frankfurt
School. They were to be deeply influential on debates about the status of
mass culture, and the role the 'culture industries' played as the producers

of popular culture. The Frankfurt critics' ideas were influenced by their experience of the failure of socialist revolution and the rise of fascism in Europe between the wars. After they were forced to leave Germany and relocate to the United States they were also deeply concerned with the changes taking place in American culture.

'The culture industry: enlightenment as mass deception' (in 1979) by Horkheimer and Adorno lays out some of the key principles of the Frankfurt critics' gravely pessimistic views on mass culture. They lamented that the Enlightenment project, a period characterized by a belief that old modes of thought were to be replaced by new, more liberating forms of rationality, was never to be accomplished. Instead, new scientific rationality operating in what they saw as the degenerate context of a capitalist economy meant that people in the West were to be subject to a new and potentially terrifying type of domination. The culture industries, the mechanized producers of popular forms, which they theorized as the organizers of social relations, were to act as an arm of society's control mechanism. New technologies, they argued, operating under the yoke of scientific rationality, seeped into every aspect of peoples' lives, dominating them and ultimately rendering them open to total manipulation. For the Frankfurt critics, the last force of hope for proletarian revolution – the working class – had its critical faculties nulled by the products of the culture industries. As a result they had become an amorphous 'mass' which could no longer think critically. Indeed, they argued, it was the formation of the 'mass' that had created conducive conditions for the fascist dictatorship in Germany during the 1930s. American society, as they saw it, was doomed to suffer a similar political fate.

The Frankfurt School argued that the culture industries were no different from any other capitalist industry: their sole purpose was to make a profit. As a result, culture itself had become a commodity, mass-reproduced and mass-distributed. The marketing strategies which sold products based on supposed difference were capitalist lies, since all products were standardized and were all ultimately the same. The Frankfurt School despised the popular forms produced by the culture industries; it thought that popular films, magazines and mediums such as television were utterly vile and barbaric. It saw them as instruments of capitalist manipulation, as tools with which the masses could be conditioned to conform. For the Frankfurt critics, popular forms – most particularly the media – played a key role in paving the way for totalitarian societies.

While the Frankfurt School's conception of the culture industries was rather crude and simplistic, it proved to be a highly influential model on audience effects research in the 1940s and 1950s. It paved the way for what is sometimes termed the 'hypodermic' model of media effects – that is, that media texts have a uniform effect on all audience members and that they induce changed 'copy-cat' audience attitudes and behaviour (see 'The historical development of the effects tradition' in chapter 13). While the hypodermic model has been criticized for its naivety, it is still an approach which holds some common currency about the media today. In the early 1990s, for example, violent television and video 'nasties' were seen as key perpetrators in incidents such as the James Bulger murder. Similarly, pornography is argued by some feminists to be the cause of rape – see, for example, Andrea Dworkin (1981). Audiences, according to this model, are gullible, unthinking, uncritical automatons. Yet there are millions of consumers who do not act out the behaviour of the fictional characters they view on television, nor do all the men who consume pornography commit rape. In addition, and perhaps in a more insidious way, the Frankfurt School's view that the culture industries are inherently geared to reproducing dominant ideologies and economic domination had an effect on some leftist media critics' views about popular media culture. For them, there can be no good or worthwhile media product, since they are all geared to reducing the critical viewer to a mindless consumer. What their position fails to recognize is that there are a great number of popular texts which actively critique the capitalist society out of which they were produced.

There are other problems with the Frankfurt School's conception of the culture industries. One of the most significant, as Joanne Hollows argues, was the sheer abstraction of the theoretical framework proposed by Horkheimer and Adorno to understand mass culture across societies as large and as complex as the United States (Hollows, 1995, p. 20). Moreover, their critique of the culture industries is a total one: it theorizes the industries as a seamless monolith, an all-encompassing system which exerts complete power across the entire communication process from production to consumption. Yet there are many stages within the production process which work against, contradict or even resist capitalism. Not all workers within the industry necessarily embrace the values of capitalism, and their work might well reflect their sentiments. James Lull argues that in most media industries, be they totalitarian, capitalist or communist, there are workers whose aims consistently undermine total ideological control. He uses the work of American sociologist Herbert Gans to argue that workers in the media industries in the United States have always fiercely fought to express their own values, 'to be free from control by the audience and media executives' (Gans, quoted in Lull, 1995, p. 122). Lull found that in his own study of the People's Republic of China (a context in which he acknowledges media industries operate differently) both before and after the Tiananmen Square protests, the ideology of programme content was 'discontinuous and discordant'. This, he argues, came about partly because of 'the diversity of perspectives held by influential workers in the media industries' (p. 123).

The ownership and control approach

Graham Murdock's article 'Large corporations and the control of the communications industries' (1982) makes a distinction between what he terms the 'structure/determination' and 'action/power' approaches to the control of large corporations. The structure/determination approach is concerned with the structural factors that constrain corporate controllers. Structural analyses examine how far the economic and cultural climate in which industries operate either create or delimit opportunities for industry owners. The action/power approach, on the other hand, focuses on the question of who controls the corporation. Taking the individual or collective power of the people who control the organization as its central focus, this approach examines how far those people are able to persuade or force others to comply with their wishes about the future of the corporation. Some action analyses also examine how far those owners have successfully managed to advance their own ideas and interests through the running of the organization, and via its media output.

Some media commentators, using the action/power analyses outlined by Murdock, prioritize ownership as one of the most important factors for understanding the media industries. In *Media Moguls* (1991), for example, Jeremy Tunstall and Michael Palmer use the argument that in the context of increased deregulation a select group of tremendously powerful media owners, or 'moguls', largely determined the direction of the media industries in Europe in the 1980s. The chapters on moguls, which form the second half of the book, outline the careers of British moguls such as Lew Grade, Robert Maxwell and Rupert Murdoch, as well as a number of European moguls such as Robert Hersant, Axel Springer and Silvio Berlusconi. In charting the careers of moguls like Maxwell and Murdoch, the writers are provided with a vehicle through which to describe the business trends and strategies which the industries required in order to stay afloat in a competitive world market. For example, Maxwell's 'phases of innovation' are detailed. In 1980, Maxwell took over the British Printing Company. Since it was financially bankrupt, Maxwell was able to buy the company cheaply. By cutting overheads and drastically cutting back on the workforce, he returned the company to large profits. He then replicated his success at BPC in his acquisition of the magazine company Odhams, which again made him very large profits. Tunstall and Palmer argue that Maxwell's skill at confronting and negotiating deals with trade unions ultimately served his own interests and formed a large part of his success as an entrepreneur. It was this kind of skill that Tunstall and Palmer argue marked Maxwell out as innovative, and in ways which moguls like Rupert Murdoch were to learn from. Tunstall and Palmer's argument demonstrates how key decisions have had a significant impact on both the organization and the output of the moguls.

Tunstall and Palmer point out in their opening paragraph that 'media moguldom is only one important aspect of a European media industry of almost endless complexity' (1991, p. 1). In their introduction to the book, they explore some of the changes in the media industries which led to the rise of the 'classical' or 'pure' media mogul. For example, they outline the way in which media lobbying has been used by some of the moguls to lift the legislative restrictions on ownership monopolies: 'the greatest individual exponent … has been the Italian media mogul Silvio Berlusconi' (p. 7). What Tunstall and Palmer point out is that moguls have exceptional personal skills which enable them to override industrial constraints. The mogul, they argue, is an individual with the skills to master the socio-economic challenges that building a media empire presents. As a result of this line of argument, the writers cannot avoid seeming to celebrate the moguls they describe, without providing any sustained analysis of the structural constraints that formed the wider context for their working practices.

While this kind of text provides some fascinating material about the individuals who have wielded enormous amounts of power in the European media industries, it only highlights one side of the picture for understanding corporate control. While it is important to analyse the decision-making processes of key media owners and the consequences of them for media industries, the action/power approach alone can only provide a partial analysis. A more usefully rounded analysis, as Murdock argues, requires both action and structural analyses: 'A structural analysis is necessary to map the range of options open to allocative controllers and the pressures operating upon them. It specifies the limit points to feasible action' (1982, p. 124). A structural approach allows the decision-making of key media personnel to be placed into an economic and political context.

In *Power Without Responsibility* (Curran and Seaton, 1991) James Curran uses the ownership and control framework to examine the part the press barons played in the historical development of the British press in the 1920s–40s. He argues that the barons did exert forceful control over their papers in some respects. However, his perspective is also characterized by a Marxist approach and the idea that the competitive capitalist context in which owners had to operate was inherently unstable, as a result of which they had to react to market constraints.

Curran argues that there were moments when the barons did play an active and determining role with regard to the content of their papers. In his discussion of the proprietorial styles of press barons Northcliffe and Beaverbrook, Curran details the extent to which they ensured domineering control over their favourite papers. In terms of their day-to-day working practices they exercised ruthless control: Beaverbrook sent 147 instructions to the *Express* in one day, and Northcliffe had a brusque way of firing employees: '"Who is that?" Northcliffe said on the phone.

"Editor, *Weekly Despatch*, Chief," came the reply. "You were the editor," responded Northcliffe' (quoted in Curran and Seaton, 1991, p. 53). Curran also claims that both men shaped the entire content of those papers, including their layouts. They also influenced the news items and features that appeared, 'thereby helping to form what are now the news values of the national press' (p. 55).

Yet there are also key social, political and economic features surrounding the involvement of the press barons in the newspaper industry which were beyond their control, factors which worked to alter significantly the direction the development of the press was to take. As capitalists, the barons were under constant pressure to make profits, which meant seeking ever larger circulation figures. Fierce competition in the late 1920s forced the barons into promoting their products as a way of securing sales. Some papers offered their readers insurance schemes, others hired teams of canvassers who visited households offering free gifts in exchange for signing a newspaper subscription. Indeed, Curran argues that sales pressure became so great that by 1937 the average daily newspaper employed five times as many canvassers as editorial staff. Since the cost of promotion placed even greater pressure on newspapers to make more sales, publishers had to ensure that their papers met the needs and desires of their audiences. Market research, which newspapers began to commission in the 1930s, revealed that most people preferred to read human interest stories rather than 'hard' news such as politics and current affairs. Pressure to maximize audiences meant that newspapers could only respond by providing what the results of audience research had shown. As a result, political coverage declined dramatically in popular newspapers, and this trend set the tone for the historical development of the popular press. This kind of analysis shows that while owners made decisions to use promotion strategies and to conduct audience research, they had done so as a reaction to the changing socio-economic factors of the day. In the case of Curran's work, action analyses are harnessed by structural analyses. Curran's chapter on the era of the press barons examines the complex relationship between owner action and the wider determining factors at each level of newspaper production.

The political economy of the media and cultural industries

The primary focus of the contemporary political economy approach is the industrialization of the culture industries. In this way writers such as Nicholas Garnham, and others who have appropriated this type of analysis in order to investigate particular aspects of the media and entertainment industries, can be seen to carry through one of the key features of the work of the Frankfurt School. However, while recent political economy work can be seen to have built on the model developed by the Frankfurt critics, it offers a far more intricate analysis of the contemporary media and communication industries.

Garnham argues in the opening chapter of *Capitalism and Communication: Global Culture and the Economics of Information* (1990) that media and cultural studies have tended to confine their analysis to the ideological meaning of texts. The dominance of textual analysis, he claims, has its roots in the influence of the Marxist Louis Althusser, who argued that the ideological realm or the superstructure has a degree of relative autonomy from the economic base. Althusser argued that ideological state apparatuses – the judiciary, the monarchy, the family, the media – all act to secure the reproduction of the relations of production. As a result, media theorists confined their study to the ideological work of the media as maintainer of capitalist social relations. What was crucially missing from their analysis, argues Garnham, was attention to the determining role of the economic base. For him, the economic relations of production play a central role in governing the structural power relations with which the media industries must contend: 'a political economy ... rests upon ultimate determination by the economic' (1990, p. 30).

Out of this context, political economy insists that as large-scale economic enterprises the culture industries must be analysed within the capitalist economy of which they form a part. Media products must be analysed in the context of the cultural industries in which they are produced and distributed. Their industrial processes of production and their deployment of cultural workers must also be considered in any analysis of cultural production. And the economic factors which determine why and how certain products are distributed in order to reach particular audiences also need to be considered, suggests Garnham. It is through an analysis of these economic structures that one can determine 'who can say what to whom within the process of cultural production' (1990, p. 10). The economics of the industry, according to this approach, has a direct effect on how the content of media texts is manifested and, ultimately, on whether or not they are produced: 'A newspaper article or tv programme is the way it is ... because of the way in which production is organised. To put it crudely, the budget available and the given structure of the division of labour affect what you can say and how you can say it' (p. 15).

Garnham argues that the cultural industries share particular working practices. They utilize capital-intensive, technological means of production and distribution. Cultural workers are hierarchically organized in a highly developed division of labour within a 'professional' managerial structure. Finally, the industries work towards a central aim: to maximize profit (1990, p. 156). However, Garnham is careful to point out that while the cultural industries share certain characteristics, they also require historically specific analysis. In Britain, not all media industries are capitalist and privately owned; some industries are publicly funded and controlled by the state. However, despite those differences, both public and privately owned institutions operate within a capitalist framework and therefore both must compete. As a consequence, actions within one sector impact on the other. One key example of this is the competition between ITV and the BBC. The recent pressure on the ITV network to extend its broadcasting times has placed greater demand on the BBC. ITV, as a result of its assured advertising revenue, was able to respond to public demand. If the BBC extends its hours, it would be at greater cost because it is unable to secure revenue from advertisers. It has, however, been forced to spend more money on broadcasting so as to compete with ITV for audiences (Garnham, 1990, p. 160). It is through analysing the specific economic problems encountered by the culture industries that we are in a better position to understand them.

There are other problems with which the culture industries must contend, Garnham argues. Some of those problems emanate from the difficulties that the cultural goods themselves present. Consumers have limited time to spend on cultural goods. As a result, Garnham argues that the industries have sought ways of emphasizing the domestic uses of cultural goods (1990, p. 159). It has also meant that the industries are in fierce competition to win the limited time audiences have at their disposal. Another feature of cultural commodities that has vexed these industries is the difficulty in fixing their 'use-value'. As a direct result, it is difficult to predict a market for them, making them highly risky goods in the marketplace. In order to build a relationship with potential markets, producers create what Garnham calls 'cultural repertoires'. Instead of producing single cultural commodities, the industry produces a range of related goods, so that the risks can be spread. Out of that repertoire, only a small minority of goods will make profits, but they recover the losses of the other products in the repertoire (1990, p. 162).

But it is in distribution, rather than production, Garnham argues, where the potential for real power and profit lies. The power over access to distribution results in the ability to reach audience sections in a dispersed culture such as our own. Moreover, once the channels are in place for transmission or exhibition, distribution is far less expensive than production. As a result, distributors are the real power-brokers in the industry. For example, Channel Four is effectively a distribution agent: it commissions its output from independent production companies. Ultimately, Channel Four has the final say over what kind of products it is prepared to distribute, and it stands to make far more profit than the production company whose production costs far outweigh exhibition costs. Distributors also stand to reap success in the marketplace because, as Garnham argues, accurate product placement and the generation of audiences is far more important than the quality of the cultural commodity itself. In the case of the highly successful British film *The Full Monty* (1997), for example, the strategy enacted by the distributors proved enormously profitable, especially since the film was relatively cheap to produce. By offering free screenings of the film in certain venues, the distributors were able to generate a positive word-of-mouth popular review of the film which contributed towards creating a huge audience. There is now a whole section of media workers devoted to the task of matching a cultural repertoire to the right audience, having ensured that the repertoire's cost will be met by the amount the audience is likely to spend. Workers performing these tasks, people like publishers or television distributors, are, for Garnham, one of the most vital and creative components in the industrial process (1990, p. 162).

Garnham's political economy approach enables us to understand the development of the media industries and to recognize contemporary trends as being the result of their historical development. He argues that the nature of the cultural commodity itself shapes the wider strategies that the industries have to adopt in order to find markets. As a commodity with an ambiguous use-value, which is not devoured or destroyed by consumption, the industries have been forced to find ever wider audiences for their goods. Because media products are costly to produce but cheap to reproduce, the industries have tended to try to increase audiences for reproduced products so as fully to exploit their initial investments. This has encouraged the industries to drive towards audience maximization 'as the preferred profit maximization strategy' (Garnham, 1990, p. 160). In turn, this has led to three dominant structural trends in the cultural industries: concentration of ownership, internationalization and diversification or cross-media ownership. The ownership of the contemporary media industries is concentrated into relatively few hands, as a small number of conglomerates control the entire industry. This allows owners a relatively free hand at maximizing audiences for their products, because they can work towards vertically integrating their operations. As a result, they own the means of production and distribution, therefore giving them control across the whole communications process as well as access to audiences. The drive towards internationalization has meant that media industry empires are no longer merely national; audiences are now sought right across the globe. Many cultural industries have become global enterprises in their search for profits. Cross-media ownership has allowed the industries to reproduce the same product across a variety of media so as to elongate the exposure of one product concept for maximum profits. This strategy is another way in which risks can be spread across different forms of the product – the film, the book – while simultaneously offering the audience a choice of different cultural products.

A number of critics have analysed the political economies of particular aspects of the culture industries, using Garnham's framework. For example, in 'Structural change in the cultural industries: British magazine publishing in the 1980s' (1993), Stephen Driver and Andrew Gillespie argue that the quest for audiences and the spreading of risk shaped the development of the magazine industry in the 1980s. As a result of these two driving forces, they found that the industry developed in line with the structural changes outlined by Garnham: the market is dominated by a smattering of owners who have the power to launch, advertise and sustain new titles; and publishers have sought audiences and acquired new media interests internationally. Magazine publishing has become, like other cultural industries, 'much more part of an integrated and international media economy' (Driver and Gillespie, 1993, p. 198).

A political economy approach to the media is a necessary mode of analysis if, as Garnham argues, we are 'to understand why our dominant cultural processes and their modes of organization are the way they are' (1990, p. 162). It enables us to comprehend why and how particular media texts are produced and distributed and how industrial processes shape their content and form. Because it is an historically specific analysis of the media industries, it offers a way of understanding the power relations of media production and consumption. Garnham's analysis has been accused of reducing an understanding of the media industries down to simplistic economic terms. Yet a political economy approach helps us to understand the industrial and economic context out of which media texts are produced. And to analyse the text in isolation is to choose to ignore the contextual reasons why they are the carriers of dominant ideas and meanings.

Media institutions in the context of globalization

Recent debates about the media have increasingly examined media institutions in the context of a new global society. If we pause to examine some of the characteristics which shape our contemporary world, there are a number of changes which for some have signalled the end of a conception of the world as a set of separate national entities or cultures. Indeed, because some global connections are so straightforward they seem local, leading some commentators to describe the planet as a '"shrinking" world' (McGrew, in Hall et al., 1992, p. 63). A whole set of changes seems to give the impression that the world we inhabit is a much smaller entity. The national boundaries that once divided our world have effectually dissolved and become transnational, and technological changes have created a whole network of global interconnections. Indeed, there is a whole range of activities in contemporary everyday life which McGrew argues can only be understood in the context of a global conception of the world:

> The dynamics of the global financial system; the tremendous expansion of transnational corporate activity; the existence of global communications and media networks; the global production and dissemination of knowledge,

combined with (amongst other factors) the escalating significance of transnational religious and ethnic ties; the enormous flows of peoples across
national boundaries; and the emerging authority of institutions and communities above the nation-state. (Hall et al., 1992, p. 63)

All these changes, McGrew argues, point to a new conception of the
globalized world as a singular entity, or 'world society'.

Broadly, critics' views about globalization have been divided. Some
have embraced the concept as an historical moment with almost utopian
possibilities, where humankind can at last come together as a singular
community. Others have been more cynical. They have argued that
globalization is actually the next logical step in a world already dominated
by Western society. For them, it merely marks the extension and further
empowerment of existing structures such as capitalism and industrialism.

Several studies have attempted to assess the main thrusts behind globalization. For example, Wallerstein (1991) argues that the capitalist world
economy is the central drive towards a global society. Within the logic
of late capitalism, he argues, is an inevitable drive to seek worldwide
markets. The development of global systems such as financial and communications networks has occurred as a result of an expanding capitalist
market. Other critics, for example Rosenau (1990), place technological
progress in a post-industrial society as the main causal factor behind the
move towards global interconnections in the contemporary world. Other
critics have been less content with pinpointing singular reasons for globalization. Giddens (1990), for instance, argues that globalization has occurred
at a number of specific yet interlocking dimensions – for example, capitalism, industrialism, militarism and the 'inter-state system'. Each of the
dimensions is governed by its own internal institutional forces, for
example the growth of world capitalism affects the expansion of economic
globalization. Yet changes in one dimension impact on the others and by
examining a range of factors in the drive towards globalization, Giddens
emphasizes the connections between each of the dimensions. In his account,
globalization is an uneven, sometimes contradictory, complex process.

There is a growing body of work in media studies which regards
globalization as central to an understanding of the changes currently
taking place in the cultural industries. Robert Burnett, in his book *The
Global Jukebox: The International Music Industry* (1996), argues that the
organization, distribution and consumption of popular music is carried
out on a global scale. As a product, he argues, popular music is particularly suited to a global market because it acts almost as the 'lingua franca
for a large segment of the world's youth population' (p. 1). As one of the
first culture industries to take on a truly global reach, Burnett argues that
it has provided the global foundations for transnational entertainment
and communications conglomerates.

Burnett adopts a political economy approach to the popular music industries. As an analysis, it recognizes the historical contingency of the political economy of the media, and takes globalization into account as a radical shift around which the cultural industries must reorganize. Burnett stresses the emphasis in the music industry on evading risks in the marketplace; as a result, the industry has broadly followed the three structural developments outlined by Garnham. However, the 'Big Six' major corporations who own the music industry, BMG, Sony, Warner, Polygram, EMI and MCA, have been at pains to stress their global product ethos since the late 1980s. The global significance of popular music, together with related communications and entertainment merchandise, is absolutely central to each project from the outset. Indeed, popular music itself is only one product in a string of other concept-related products that make up the 'cultural repertoire' which are marketed and sold globally. From the outset, music companies are looking for ways in which the music star or band can be exposed across a wide range of other media products as a means of minimizing risks in the global marketplace. This strategy is called 'media synergy' and is about maximizing the potential of star packages across the diversified technological and entertainment interests the big corporations own.

The term globalization has been coined in utopian ways by music producers. As Keith Negus argues in his book about the music industry, 'It has been variously employed to describe the homogenisation of tastes, "cultural interconnectedness", the globalisation of markets, capital and the communications media, as a prefix to ecological problems such as global warming, and more generally to the ways in which the world might be becoming "united"' (Negus, 1992, p. 6). Yet overwhelmingly, as he suggests, globalization is about finding new markets. It is about a change in the direction of thinking about how the culture industries are to produce and distribute their products now and in the future (p. 6). It involves dissolving national geographical boundaries to make them trans-national; it also means thinking creatively about how products can be culturally and socially homogenized to appeal to global markets. Music products by artists like Madonna and Michael Jackson have already achieved what Negus calls the 'dream of media synergy' because they do appeal across the globe. Yet there are also resistances to global products, as some regions retreat back to local forms of music culture as a reaction against the 'synthetic' feel of global products. The attempt to achieve a more even dispersal of global products is the present challenge facing culture industries like the music business.

Suggestions for further work

List as many 'media moguls' as you can. Alongside these names identify as many of their media interests as you can. What conclusions can you draw from this information about their national and international power?

Look at a variety of tabloid newspapers. Does the argument that the popular press carries little political content still hold true today? Why do you think this might be the case?

What do you understand by the term 'cultural repertoire'? Why is this idea so important within the media industries, and does the idea of 'cultural repertoire' become more or less important when the media are considered in a global context?

Further reading

Garnham, Nicholas 1990: *Capitalism and Communication: Global Culture and the Economics of Information*. London: Sage.

Horkheimer, Max and Adorno, Theodor 1979: *The Dialectic of Enlightenment*. London: Verso.

Lull, James 1995: *Media, Communication, Culture: A Global Approach*. Cambridge: Polity Press.

Tunstall, Jeremy and Palmer, Michael 1991: *Media Moguls*. London: Routledge.

9

Public Service Broadcasting and the Market

The idea of public service broadcasting has been a major influence on the development of television and radio in Great Britain. For this reason it is worthy of detailed consideration in this section of the book. However, as is the case with so many of the central concepts within media studies, public service broadcasting defies a simple, clear-cut definition. The claim to being a 'public service broadcaster' is something that a variety of different interest groups have sought to make. A straightforward definition of public service broadcasting is also difficult when one considers that the potential meaning of the term has also undergone some significant historical changes since its earliest manifestation in relation to the BBC. Paddy Scannell (1990) acknowledges this difficulty, and argues that an important distinction should be borne in mind when considering the idea of public service broadcasting. He suggests that it is essential to distinguish between 'Public service as a responsibility delegated to broadcasting authorities by the state, and the manner in which the broadcasting authorities have interpreted that responsibility and tried to discharge it' (1990, p. 11). This raises, and makes central, the question of interpretation. The concept of public service broadcasting has been interpreted in a variety of ways, each drawing out slightly different perspectives at different historical moments. What, then, is public service broadcasting?

The development of broadcasting in Britain

In Britain, broadcasting has developed in a particular way. It is important to remember that whenever decisions are made with regard to something like broadcasting policy a range of other alternative possibilities is always available, and an investigation of the reasons why certain choices are made must form a part of any analysis. In light of this, the role of the government in the establishment of broadcasting in Britain was vital, because they made many of the most important and influential decisions. The other potential possibilities can be seen through the example of the USA, where, from the outset, profit was a central concern, and broadcasting took a very different direction to the path followed in Britain. From its earliest history in the USA broadcasting was organized in order to deliver profits to owners. According to William Boddy, as early as 1927 the giant CBS was 'the first radio network explicitly organized to earn a profit from the sale of advertising time' (Boddy, 1990, p. 64).

In Britain, the authorities saw broadcasting as something with a vast potential to inform and influence the populace. For this reason, it was decided that it was too significant to be left in the hands of private enterprise. As Scannell observes, the state was therefore reluctant simply to hand over the control of broadcasting to private ownership. The Sykes Committee of 1923 stated that 'the control of such potential power over public opinion and the life of the nation ought to remain with the state' (quoted in Scannell, 1990, p. 13). This, however, did not mean direct control. A licence, issued through the post office, was established, which held the broadcasters responsible to the state for their actions.

Broadcasting in Britain was thus conceived as another public utility. As such, it joined the ranks of other services controlled by the state and operated, supposedly, for the public good. Again, one must bear in mind, as Scannell argues, that we have to ask more than who controlled broadcasting in these early days, and in addition seek to understand how they interpreted their responsibility as public service broadcasters and in whose interests they acted. In order to undertake this it is also essential to consider the interpretation of the 'public interest' in the early days of British broadcasting.

Kevin Robins and Frank Webster (1990) see the state's maintenance of control over broadcasting as exactly that: a controlling influence rather than a transparent entity which unquestionably operated for the public good. They argue that the idea of the 'public good' is a highly political one. For them, the state wanted to control broadcasting because it had sought to control other potentially socially challenging and dangerous leisure pursuits, arguing that in doing so it was operating in the public interest. Following their increasingly anarchic development in the nineteenth century, the leisure pursuits of the working class in Britain had systematically come under the influence of official organizing bodies. For example, football initially began as a mass participation activity, often involving hundreds of people, before it was organized into a game with leagues and a national hierarchy and organizing body. For Robins and Webster, these forms of popular pursuits were seen as a potential challenge to the growing, industrially based social order that developed in

Britain, and delivered enormous profits to a small number of owners and industrialists. In their view, many of the public institutions that were established in this era had a strong sense of organizing and rationalizing the leisure time of members of the working class, upon whom the industrialists depended for their profits. They argue that 'Sabbatarianism, temperance, public parks, mechanics' institutes, public libraries, all aimed to promote "rational recreation" and a sense of order, propriety, decorum and social discipline' (Robins and Webster, 1990, p. 137). Similarly, there was a sense that broadcasting had a moral and social role to play, and these ideals played an important part in conceptualizing it as a public service. In this manner, broadcasting was seen as a contributor to the public good and as something that, if used correctly, could work as a source of human improvement. Of course, as well as contrasting with the development of broadcasting in the United States, this conception also reveals how broadcasting, if indeed operating for the 'public good', arguably operated in the interests of certain parts, and not all, of society.

John Reith and the BBC

A key figure in the early days of British broadcasting, and central in the development and interpretation of public service broadcasting, is John Reith. His significance and influence can be deduced from the fact that he was invited to present his ideas about broadcasting in Britain, and the ways in which it might develop, to the Crawford Committee of 1925. Initially managing director of the British Broadcasting Company, Reith was given the task of leading the newly formed British Broadcasting Corporation (BBC) upon its establishment in 1927. He remained at its head until 1938, and it is possible to see him as responsible for its development in this period. Much of what went on during his tenure was a consolidation of the corporation as a public service broadcaster, as he conceived of it. At the core of this Reithian conception of public service broadcasting was the idea that it would in some way assist in raising and subsequently maintaining high standards within society. As Scannell notes, for Reith this meant that the 'service must not be used for entertainment alone' and that it should be continually striving to 'bring into the greatest possible number of homes ... all that was best in every department of human knowledge, endeavour, and achievement ... Broadcasting should give a lead to public taste rather than pander to it' (1990, p. 13). The idea of broadcasting leading public taste rather than pandering to it returns us to the question of whose interests this conception of broadcasting served. The rather paternalistic idea of providing services and amenities that are 'good' for the public and in their interest may certainly also be interpreted as a way of controlling, as well as leading, public taste. Public service broadcasting was therefore built upon the arguably problematic notion that 'betters' needed to influence and control what ordinary people consumed for their own good.

The organization of public service broadcasting

The initial institutional organization of the concept of public service broadcasting in Britain has had a long-lasting effect. Colin Seymour-Ure (1996) argues that the principal goals of public service broadcasting are reflected in the particular decisions made about the structure of the organization through which those goals will be achieved. Through his argument it is possible to begin to see how the conceptualization of public service broadcasting directly influenced the organizational structures adopted by the BBC. Seymour-Ure outlines what he considers to be the six principles upon which public service broadcasting was conceived (1996, pp. 61–3):

1   As a monopoly. Broadcasting should be run as a monopoly, and should be seen, as the Sykes report observed, as a 'valuable form of public property'.
2   As being under government control. The monopoly of broadcasting should be controlled by the government in order to regulate national and international airwaves.
3   As operating through a board of governors. The Crawford Committee established that the public monopoly of broadcasting should be run at arm's length from direct government control. In order to achieve this 'distance', a board of seven governors would be established. This supposedly meant that the government was not in direct day-to-day control of broadcasting. However, how much actual control British governments have had on public service broadcasting and the BBC has been a subject of great debate ever since. Seymour-Ure argues that the issue of influence and control is pushed into sharper focus during times of governmental crisis such as Suez in 1956. It is, of course, possible to ask the same question of governments in relation to more recent moments of crisis, such as the Falklands conflict and the Gulf War.
4   As a trustee for the national interest. As a public service broadcaster the BBC should serve the interests of all, and not any particular social group or vested interest. The governors were supposed to play a significant role here, as they were seen as representatives of a cross-section of the population and were therefore seen as its insurers.
5   As funded by a licence fee. It was established by the Sykes Committee that rather than be financed through the sale of advertising space, which was the model operating in the United States, broadcasting in Britain would be financed by the revenue drawn from a flat licence fee paid by all those taking the service.

Illustration 9.1 The BBC remains committed to regional centres as part of its public service.
Source: The authors.

6   As a universal service. The idea of 'universality of service' established the idea that everyone should be able to receive the service should they require. This reflected similar thinking about other services, which, it was argued, also operated for the good of all, such as the Royal Mail which reached all communities however isolated and remote. The broadcast signal was supposed to reach all in the same way.

Once again, these organizing principles reflect how public service broadcasting within Great Britain was modelled on, or at least was thought of as similar to, other forms of services provided for the public such as parks and gardens, public baths and libraries (see illustration 9.1).

Criticisms of Reithian public service broadcasting

Whilst the influence of Reith's version of public service broadcasting has been extensive and long-lasting it has not been without criticism. Some of the most interesting and significant critiques have been made by Stuart Hood, himself a former controller of BBC1. In his book *On Television* (1980) he argues that even though broadcasting may have been conceptualized

as a public service which operated for a supposed public good, it certainly
could not be regarded as having any connection with socialism. Rather,
he argues it served the interests of those already powerful within capitalist
society.

The idea of public service broadcasting is often used to evoke a liberal
tradition within British broadcasting and society, and many who do this
often seem to see its origins and application through rose-tinted spectacles.
Hood challenges this view, arguing that its origins lie as much in nineteenth-century conservative ideas of social duty as they do in liberal or
any other set of reformist policies. Again, as Hood argues, the acceptance
of a British Broadcasting Company based upon Reithian ideas about
public service broadcasting by politicians of all parties indicates how far
it was perceived as having a larger, more important purpose: 'Such an
organization, it seems to have been recognized on all sides of the consensus, would best further the maintenance of the established order and its
social structures' (1980, p. 55). Scannell gives further weight to this opinion
when he states that the establishment of public service broadcasting 'did
nothing to change the balance of power in society, and maintained the
dominance of the middle classes over the lower ranks' (p. 22).

Public service broadcasting post-Reith

Reith resigned as Director-General of the BBC in 1938. Whilst his vision
of public service broadcasting remained for the most part intact throughout the war years, one important development occurred. In an attempt
to boost morale during the war a light entertainment service was introduced. Reith disapproved of what he saw as a division of broadcasting
into different levels, but it was destined to stay. A more hierarchical
version of broadcasting was put forward by Sir William Haley, who was
appointed Director-General in 1948. He saw the BBC as a pyramid-like
structure with the light entertainment service at the bottom. In his view:

> [Broadcasting] rests on the conception of the community as a broadly based
> cultural pyramid slowly aspiring upwards. This pyramid is served by three
> main Programmes, differentiated but broadly overlapping in levels and
> interest, each Programme leading on to the other, the listener being induced
> through the years increasingly to discriminate in favour of those things that
> are more worthwhile. Each Programme at any given moment must be ahead
> of its public, but not so much so as to lose their confidence. The listener
> must be led from good to better by curiosity, liking, and a growth of under-
> standing. As the standards of the education and culture of the community
> rise so should the Programme pyramid. (quoted in McDonnell, 1991, p. 24)

Whilst the introduction of the Light Programme, and the subsequent
conception of broadcasting as a pyramid was slightly at odds with Reith's
vision of a single service available to all, it does clearly retain the idea of

the broadcaster as the leader and arbiter of good taste governing an institution whose role within society was to improve the cultural experiences of the masses. The main difference was that Haley's version of public service broadcasting sought to attract listeners through the Light Programme. Having caught their attention, the aim was then to educate their taste in a journey up the pyramid from the Light Programme through the Home Programme to the Third Programme at the top. In this model the broadcasters remained unchallenged in their self-conceived view that they could identify what was good for those below them in the social hierarchy, and the positive effect they saw broadcasting having on its audience. Therefore, whilst Reith may have been dismayed by the introduction of the Light Programme, in the final analysis it actually did little to dismantle the paternalistic model of public service broadcasting which he had established at the BBC.

Challenges to the BBC monopoly and the establishment of a duopoly

One of the major debates about broadcasting in the late 1940s and early 1950s was whether or not the BBC should be allowed to maintain its monopoly over broadcasting. The Beveridge Report of 1951 accepted the argument for the retention of the BBC monopoly, arguing that if 'broadcasting is to have a social purpose, competition should not be allowed to become competition for numbers of listeners ... we reject as a guiding principle in broadcasting competition for the numbers of listeners' (quoted in McDonnell, 1991, p. 28). The most notable opposition within the membership of the Beveridge Committee to the maintenance of the BBC monopoly came from Conservative MP Selwyn Lloyd. It is not surprising then that when the next Conservative government came to power its perspective on broadcasting was at odds with the findings of the Beveridge Committee. Indeed, its White Paper on broadcasting in 1952 entertained the ending of the BBC monopoly. The following year another White Paper, after extensive debate within the Conservative ranks and in the country generally, stated that if competition was established in broadcasting there would have to be a body whose remit was to ensure the commitment and maintenance of standards to public service. This led directly to the establishment of the Independent Television Authority following the Television Act of 1954. It was this Act which established commercial television as a integral part of the British broadcasting landscape and brought the years of BBC monopoly to an end.

The end of the BBC monopoly meant that the corporation had to adapt to a new broadcasting world, one which introduced direct competition for audiences. A main feature of the adaptation was a firmer commitment to popular programming in an attempt to prevent an exodus of its audience to the new channel. At the time this change was articulated as being as much a part of the corporation's commitment to public service as educational programming, because it provided programmes that were understood by, and accessible to, all. However, from that point on the issue of popular programming was to become a central part of the debate about the future of broadcasting, and in particular the direction of the potential new third television channel. The Pilkington Report published in 1962 reflected the centrality of this question. Many of the investigations undertaken by the committee were concerned with the perceived triviality of much of the output of the independent television companies. Central to this debate once again was the issue of public service broadcasting. The Pilkington Report made it clear that in its view public service could not simply be interpreted as 'giving the public what it wants'. Indeed, this position was stated unequivocally: 'the choice is not between either "giving the public what it wants" or "giving the public what someone thinks is good for it", and nothing else' (quoted in McDonnell, 1991, p. 42). The issue of what public service broadcasting may be was, as far as members of the committee were concerned, still an important, central question within British broadcasting.

The importance of public service within British broadcasting and the issue of how the new commercial and independent broadcasters understood and interpreted it, as well as the level of their commitment to it, was addressed in the Television Act of 1963. The Act clearly stated that these new broadcasters should adhere to the principles of public service. It stated that:

> It should be the duty of the (independent) Authority:
> a) to provide the television broadcasting services as a public service for disseminating information, education and entertainment;
> b) to ensure that the programmes broadcast by the Authority in each area maintain a high general standard in all respects, and in particular in respect of their content and quality, and a proper balance and wide range in their subject-matter, having regard both to the programmes as a whole and also to the days of the week on which the programmes are broadcast. (1963 Television Act, quoted in McDonnell, 1991, p. 45)

This was a clear assertion of the way in which, in the Act's view, commercial television should continually be aware of its responsibility and commitment to public service broadcasting. One of the major results of this reassertion of the public service responsibilities of commercial broadcasters, and the critique of their populist programming strategies, was the handing over of responsibility for the new third channel to the traditional public service provider, the BBC.

The decade between 1955 and 1965 was a very significant one for British broadcasting. It saw the establishment of a duopoly, and a recommitment, thanks to the recommendations of the Pilkington Report and the 1963 Television Act, to public service broadcasting. The establishment of the third channel under the tutelage of the BBC, and the criticism of the populism of independent television, meant that public service remained a central concern within British broadcasting. It may well have changed since its inception in the era of Reith, but it certainly maintained the central tenets of his vision. In particular, it represented a refusal to condone broadcasters who might simply seek to boost audiences through popular programming. It also sought to maintain the idea that broadcasting could contribute to the public good. This would remain the case until the late 1970s, when government reports and committees began to suggest another model for British broadcasting, one that was much more driven by market forces.

Challenges to public service broadcasting

By the late 1970s there was a marked shift in official attitudes to public service broadcasting and this was reflected in the Annan Report of 1977. The earlier acceptance of public service as the dominant paradigm within British broadcasting, which had marked earlier reports such as that of the Pilkington Committee, was now replaced by what Jean Seaton has labelled a 'pluralist view', which was one that argued that 'broadcasting should cater for a full range of groups and interests in society, rather than seek to offer moral leadership' (Curran and Seaton, 1991, p. 297). The Annan Report was critical of what it perceived as the comfortable set-up within British broadcasting. It saw the programming of the BBC and ITV networks as very similar, and argued that this prevented them from producing a diverse range of material. The fact that the two networks attracted comparable audience numbers also, in the committee's view, contributed to the comfortable status quo of the establishment, and was seen as a negative aspect of the structure of British broadcasting. In response to this, the Annan Report sought to encourage programming that spoke to those in society whose interests fell outside the material produced by the existing duopoly. However, whilst this may seem a laudable ideal, the opening up of the duopoly took British broadcasting in a new direction, one that in hindsight made possible the move away from the public service ideals that had been pre-eminent since the 1930s, towards a more market-driven media economy.

The fact that the Annan Report opened up the possibility of a market-driven media industry may, as Seaton observes, have been to a certain extent unintentional. The full potential of a free market media was fully realized by the Peacock Committee, whose report was published in 1986. In this instance the commitment to market forces was much more clearly articulated. As Seaton notes, the report argued 'that British Broadcasting should move towards a sophisticated market system based on consumer sovereignty' (Curran and Seaton, 1991, p. 298). One of the main arenas in which this shift could be seen was through the conflicting potential developments offered by Channel Four.

Channel Four

The introduction of a fourth channel to the British broadcasting scene has certainly been one of the most significant moments in recent media history. Like the introduction of the third channel it opened up wide-ranging debates about the direction in which British broadcasting should go. The establishment of Channel Four has had two linked and long-ranging effects. First, it re-established the idea that broadcasting institutions should provide something more than a staple diet of popular programmes. One of its clearest commitments was to provide programmes for groups in society who were either poorly provided for, or not provided for at all, by the output of the established television channels. However, the provision of these 'new' and 'different' programmes was tied to the other significant development heralded by the arrival of the new channel in November 1982. The channel was conceived as a publishing house, which meant that it would not produce its own programmes as the BBC and ITV networks did; rather, it would broadcast programmes produced by independent producers and companies.

Initially, the Annan Report had suggested that the new channel be controlled by an Open Broadcasting Authority. This was an attempt to break what the Annan Committee considered to be the consistent race for viewing figures that dominated the programme planning of the existing channels. The Labour government of the day would probably have followed through the recommendations of the committee. However, it lost the 1979 election and was replaced by a Conservative government under the premiership of Margaret Thatcher. Mrs Thatcher's years in Downing Street were to see some of the most comprehensive changes in British society since the end of World War II. The realm of broadcasting was not to be immune from these changes. The consensus of public service which had dominated the airwaves since the beginning of broadcasting in Britain found itself under threat, and the next fifteen years would mark an era of great transition. The Conservative government did not award the new channel to an Open Broadcasting Authority as the Annan Report suggested. Instead, it gave it to the existing Independent Broadcasting Authority. Channel Four as a model publishing house would mark the commitment within Conservative circles to independent production within a free market media economy, even if there was some debate over the content of much of the new channel's programming. Home Secretary William Whitelaw was a champion of the structure of the channel, if not its content, as an example of a deregulated, more pluralistic broadcasting system.

In its early days Channel Four broadcast a variety of innovative programmes, from the current affairs programme *Broadside*, which tackled issues from a female perspective, to the programmes produced by film and video workshops such as Sankofa, Chapter and Ceddo. The same may not be true, however, fifteen years later. A glance at the channel's schedule in the late 1990s reveals few of those original programmes. What has remained, and has now extended beyond Channel Four onto the other networks, is the number of programmes produced by independent production companies. This is a direct effect of the deregulation of broadcasting in Britain, dealt with more extensively below.

Deregulation and British broadcasting

As we noted earlier, the Conservative government of the 1980s was committed to an overhaul of many aspects of British society, especially those which it argued were not at that time directly affected by market forces. In the realm of television and radio, it incited some of the most extensive debates about the future of broadcasting in Britain when it published its White Paper entitled *Broadcasting in the 1990s: Competition, Choice and Quality* in November 1988. The extent of change, in line with the government's radical changes in other spheres, challenged many of the existing assumptions about the position and role of broadcasting within society. At the root of this change was a commitment to the deregulation of the media industries.

As Tim O'Sullivan has noted, the process of deregulation refers to the 'systematic restructuring of forms of public provision and controls and their replacement with those derived more directly from commercial operations' (O'Sullivan et al., 1994, p. 80). He argues that generally the 'de-' in deregulation implies freeing the perceived constrictions and constraints represented by the state's control of certain institutions such as broadcasting. Within a deregulated broadcasting system these constraints are supposedly liberated through commercial competition, which in turn makes the space available for greater choice and quality, particularly in terms of programming strategies designed for maximum audience satisfaction. The championing of deregulation has usually been associated with the political right, specifically those who champion the importance of a free market and market forces. The opposition to deregulation, usually drawn from the political left, argues that information and communications are too important a resource to be left to the uncertainties of the market. In addition, they argue that it is likely that deregulation will lead to a hierarchy of consumers, with those who can afford the broadcasters' product at the top and those who cannot at the bottom. The introduction of digital television in the late 1990s has raised similar questions and concerns.

The extent of the government's commitment to deregulation as outlined in the 1988 White Paper did not appear from nowhere. As we have noted earlier in this chapter, the Peacock Report challenged the duopoly that had dominated British broadcasting since the inception of commercial television in the 1950s. Ralph Negrine (1990) argues that other reports, notably the 1982 Information Technology Advisory Panel's *Cable Systems*

and Charles Jonscher's 1987 report *Subscription Television*, also contributed
to the gradual undermining of the existing organizational structure of the
broadcasting industry. The general argument was that the duopoly had
too tight a grip on the industry, which was causing it to operate in a
manner that was detrimental to the consumer. For those in favour of
deregulation there was only one direction in which broadcasting could
go if it was to be able to compete and therefore function properly in a
newly commercialized world, a world that was undergoing massive
structural change. As Negrine argues, this free market approach is best
characterized as:

> [a] desire to move from state control and state direction of industrial sectors
> and towards competition and market regulation, and it has given rise to
> policies of privatization (e.g. BT), of competition across many sectors (e.g.
> Mercury in telecommunications) and deregulation (e.g. in relation to cable
> systems) … Broadcasting, so the argument goes, should also 'benefit' from
> the competitive and enterprise spirit. (1990, p. 151)

A central concern of those uncertain about the drive towards deregulation was the future of public service broadcasting, and alongside that the
accountability of broadcasters. Negrine quotes an executive from ITV who
declared: 'The duopoly allowed for certain types of programmes and,
when ITV faces competition, it will have to be very different. That's all
there is to it … We are being forced to face up to what is in our commercial
interests' (1990, p. 152). The concern is that programmes that are less
profitable, such as news and current affairs, would no longer be produced,
or would find themselves moved to less prominent parts of the schedule.
Perhaps more significantly, the producers of controversial programmes
which challenge the status quo may find themselves unable to find
funding, or even if they do secure financial backing they might be unable
to screen 'controversial' work to interested audiences.

Negrine also argues that the drive to a completely market-driven, open
broadcasting industry was somewhat checked by the paternalistic side of
the Conservative outlook upon society: a totally free and unregulated
market potentially offered space for media products that were likely to
rest uncomfortably with Conservatives because of their sexual or violent
content. For this reason the government held back from a complete
liberalization of broadcasting, and introduced a Broadcasting Standards
Council whose remit was to oversee the suitability of programme content.
The government felt that its duty was to 'protect' consumers from the
wildest excesses of the market. This was certainly evident in the early
1990s with the reaction to the broadcasting of pornographic material on
channels like 'Red Hot and Dutch', which was prevented from broadcasting into British homes via satellite. So whilst the changes that occurred
in British broadcasting in the 1990s have been termed 'deregulation', it is

also possible to argue that what in fact happened was a re-regulation, one that, in reality, simply changed the source and position of those who regulated the broadcasting system. For all of the dismantling of the old regulatory structures associated with the state's influence on broadcasting put forward by the Peacock Report and the Broadcasting Act that followed the Conservative government's 1988 White Paper, the concern for consumers' welfare has in many ways protected aspects of the traditional ideas of public service. One of the changes in perspective that was heralded by the deregulation of broadcasting was the idea that information, the provision of which had previously been seen as part of the public service provided by broadcasters, was now a commodity in the market place.

Information as a commodity not a service

As Raymond Williams argued, the development of new technologies never occurs in a vacuum – it is usually linked to the interests of the rich and powerful in a society (for more details see chapter 16). Building upon Williams's perspective, Nicholas Garnham argues that the development of information technologies in the 1980s was strongly linked to the dispersal of labour-intensive manufacturing activity to the third world by transnational companies and corporations. This in turn led to an increased requirement for technologies which provided 'ever more sophisticated communications systems in order to manage what had become "dispersed" corporations' (Garnham, 1990, p. 117). For Garnham, this need for enhanced communications facilities led to the desire for the development of cable and satellite systems in the UK and their links with international and global communications networks. The deregulation of the broadcasting industries played an important role in the establishment of an environment that would suit these multi-national communications companies. In Garnham's view this was couched in terms that made it appear as a move towards more cultural freedom. Whilst deregulation was discussed as something that would free newly independent producers from the constraints and petty censorship of the public broadcasting system, opening up a new, market-driven world ruled by consumer sovereignty, critics like Garnham regarded it differently. For him, it was based upon two unsubstantiated assumptions: first, that once the frequency shortage had been addressed and solved regulation was no longer necessary; and second, that with the advent of technological advancements the market is a superior mode of cultural production. He argues that the first is simply untrue, and that the second does not necessarily guarantee any level of wider cultural choice based upon the demands of the consumer. He states that 'what we are in fact being offered is not a more socially responsive, politically accountable, diverse mode of cultural interchange in the electronic sphere, but on the contrary the expansion of price and profit, of commodity exchange, as the dominating mode of organization in yet another area of cultural production and consumption, as though this were a new phenomenon' (1990, p. 121). He sees this as part of the process referred to by Asa Briggs (1960) by which 'massive market interests have come to dominate an area of life which, until recently, was dominated by individuals themselves' (Garnham, 1990, p. 121). At this point the question of who controls what is broadcast enters the equation.

Deregulation and consumer choice

One of the most forceful arguments in favour of deregulation is that it offers consumers more choice. On the surface it would seem that this statement is irrefutable, especially when the rapid development of digital technologies and the enormous extension of channels that it makes available is put into the equation. However, the question 'choice of what?' remains vitally important. For many, the expansion of the number of channels available to consumers means greater choice in terms of which channel they choose to tune in to, but not necessarily in terms of programme content.

The perspective of many of the newer 'minority' channels needs closer examination in order to understand what they offer. Whilst a small number delivers programmes to ethnic minorities such as the Asian or Chinese communities in Britain, most focus on what might be thought of as minority or specialized interests. For example, B Sky B's development, in conjunction with Granada Television, of new satellite and cable channels in the late 1990s saw the introduction of schedules devoted to lifestyle: 'Granada Good Life'; chat and 'phone-ins: 'Granada Talk TV'; re-run programming: 'Granada Plus'; as well as a channel devoted to 'men's interests': 'Men and Motors'. So whilst it is certainly the case that these new channels offer space for more specialized programming, which is also manifest in channels such as 'The History Channel', 'Discovery Home and Leisure', and the 'Paramount Comedy Channel', this does not ensure that a range of alternative voices is heard. Rather, there is an extension of the number of mainstream voices available.

The fact that the rapid expansion of the number of channels available has been overseen by market forces has meant that those who initially may have seen these new technologies as creating the possibilities for a utopian television network that aimed to deliver everything the public wanted, have been forced to check their enthusiasm. An exploration of the cable and satellite schedules shows that far from extending the style and content of the existing provision, the newer channels simply further fragment the marketplace. Certainly, there is more choice, if the choice is to be from a staple diet of relatively conventional programming.

For example, a 'minority' channel such as 'The Sci-Fi Channel', which is broadcast on both cable and satellite technology, offers such mainstream products as *The Incredible Hulk*, *Voyage to the Bottom of the Sea*, *Tales of the Unexpected* and *The Six Million Dollar Man* – all of which, when first broadcast, formed part of the primetime schedule of a terrestrial channel. It is therefore possible to argue that the fragmentation of the market has simply allowed space for the repackaging and reselling of already existing products. In many ways this offers broadcasters nothing more than a chance to cash in on their already existing back catalogue. The new digital technologies offer those who control broadcasting similar opportunities to repackage existing goods to what the development of CD technology did for the record industry in the 1980s.

The future: responses to change

Nicholas Garnham argues that the struggle that surrounds new information technologies is 'a battle between the public service and market modes of cultural production and consumption' (1990, p. 131). He suggests that the appropriate political response to this struggle is difficult to ascertain. For him, there may well be a need for some sort of defence of the concept of public service broadcasting. However, alongside its defence it is necessary also to rethink what public service means. He claims that whilst the idea might be of great value, we should not be seduced into assuming that those institutions traditionally most associated with its provision, such as the BBC, are actually fulfilling their public service duties. He argues:

> In the battle for the hearts and minds of the public over the future of public service broadcasting it is important to stress that the historical practices of supposedly public service institutions such as the BBC do not necessarily correspond to the full potential of public service, and may indeed be actively in opposition to the developments of those potentials. (Garnham, 1990, p. 131)

Garnham therefore, and with some justification, points out that the working practices of the BBC actually do not differ greatly from any other major media company, and so questions to what extent a company operating in these market-driven ways can achieve the aims of public service broadcasting.

However, Garnham's reading of the situation and climate within British broadcasting has not been without its criticisms. In response to Garnham, Ian Connell (1983) argues that his view is 'negative and pessimistic'. Connell asserts that Garnham and the left more generally are simply afraid of a move towards the commercialization of broadcasting. In his view, the left have traditionally positioned commercial broadcasters as 'the opposite of all that responsive and accountable broadcasting should be' (Connell, 1983, p. 73). He argues that commercial broadcasting may not be as reactionary or ideological as is often assumed, and that it is certainly less monolithic than Garnham suggests. He cites the ability of commercial broadcasting to link with popular concerns, often in forms that are removed from the trappings of high culture. In turn, these forms are more ideologically ambiguous than their critics first perceive. Commercial television therefore, in Connell's view, should not merely be seen as the expression of capitalism and capitalist ideology. Similarly, the opportunities for potential competition within the popular programming of new cable and satellite channels should not be overlooked. For all the arguments about the reduction in quality programmes deregulation may herald, the opening up of the broadcasting airwaves to a range of voices is one of the possible positive changes that should not be ignored.

Suggestions for further work

How relevant is the notion of broadcasting as a public service in the late twentieth century?

In your opinion, what are the positive and negative aspects of media deregulation?

Look at a week of Channel Four's programming. How different are its programmes to those broadcast on other channels, and what 'minority' audiences does it serve?

Look at a day's satellite programming. How much choice do such channels offer consumers?

Further reading

McDonnell, James (ed.) 1991: *Public Service Broadcasting: A Reader*. London: Routledge.
Negrine, Ralph 1990: *Politics and the Mass Media in Britain*. London: Routledge.
Seymour-Ure, Colin 1996: *The British Press and Broadcasting Since 1945*, 2nd edn. Oxford: Blackwell.

10

Media Professionalism and Codes of Practice

Media practitioners, like workers in any other field, operate within a set of systems. This chapter is concerned with the ways in which those employed within the media conceive of themselves and the ways in which that conception has an impact upon the operations of the media organizations they inhabit. One clear way in which this impact can be identified is through what may be labelled 'occupational ideologies'. The influence of these ideological views of media practice within media studies will also be explored. The effect of the ways in which media professionals view themselves and their role in society has, it may be argued, an important knock-on effect on the ways in which they approach their everyday work. Therefore, the latter part of this chapter will consider the influence of ideas of professionalism on the media coverage of important issues such as the conflict in Northern Ireland.

The professional: definitions

Margaret Gallagher, in her article 'Negotiation of control in media organizations and occupations' (1982), offers three definitions of the professional which are a useful starting point: first, an 'expert' as opposed to an 'amateur'; second, as rational, bureaucratic, efficient – embodying an ethic of 'service' to a client or the public generally; and finally, someone whose work invests organizations with a set of moral values and norms. Each of these serves to highlight the fact that the idea of being a professional is often seen as a way of creating a distinction between those who are seen as 'professional' employees and those, such as cleaners and security officers, whose work is not considered to bestow the supposedly positive elements of professionalism onto their work.

However, the extent to which media professionals bring an aura of prestige to their work is debatable. Indeed, some writers have questioned the extent to which work in the media industries, which are deemed 'professional', in fact deserve the label. For example, Philip Elliot (1977) argues that claims to being professional within certain media contexts are merely claims at being competent. He sees professionalism as a way of mystifying the everyday activities of certain media roles or jobs. He suggests that the fact that many of the activities in organizations are attributed the label 'profession' does little more than bestow on them a greater level of cultural and social credibility. Elliot links the need to achieve this social status with the fact that most of those employed in roles that strive for professional status emanate from middle-class back-grounds where the social distinction of being a 'professional' is of great importance. However, as stated earlier, Elliot questions straightforward claim to professional status: 'Claims to professionalism in journalism are based on such routine competencies as factual accuracy, speed at meeting deadlines, style in presentation and a shared sense of news values' (1977, p. 149). In other words, the everyday tasks connected with the job become a set of 'professional' practices. Again, as Elliot notes, 'Professionalism in media occupations therefore is an adapting to the dilemmas of role conflict by which skill and competence in the performance of routine tasks becomes elevated to the occupational ideal' (p. 150).

This focus on the 'doing' of a job has important repercussions within the realm of the media. The concentration upon the carrying out of tasks in a particular, accepted way allows media professionals to lay claim to a certain distance from the material they are working with. This in turn leads to a concentration on questions of form, under the guise of 'how things are done', at the expense of issues of content which becomes an almost free-standing and transparent reality. Elliot goes on to argue that this leads to the idea that 'professional broadcasters may distance themselves from the content and disclaim responsibility for the message' (p. 150).

Broadcasters' sense of their own distance links strongly with an almost obsessive concern with impartiality, and the idea that the professional can guarantee, in some way, a distance from any controversial material they may have come into contact with through their work. In turn, because professionals will assert that they would not include materials that are unsuitable for public consumption, it may be argued that this keeps at bay the more conservative members of society who seek greater censor-ship of the media. The idea that something is unsuitable, and the per-ceived ability of professionals to judge what that material may be, are not necessarily self-evident; therefore their claim to be able to do so is a highly ideological one. Elliot links this with claims to moral leadership. He suggests that this involves the professional positioning him or herself as the one who knows the needs of the client or the public better than they do themselves. He argues that 'the effectiveness of professionalism as a mechanism of social control over aspects of social life involving conflict and change rests primarily on such claims' (1997, p. 152). What Elliot is suggesting is that the idea of media professionalism is strongly linked with the media's ability to present itself as an arbiter of good taste and correct behaviour. Of course, it is the distanced professionals, just doing their job to accepted standards and using accepted techniques, who would argue that this view lays too much emphasis upon them and their actions – but as 'middle-class professionals' they would say that. There exists, therefore, an uncomfortable contradiction: on the one hand, media professionals are those who simply do their job to a high standard and who are always impartial and removed from the material and issues they cover; on the other hand, media professionals are those who maintain the currency of ideas and beliefs within society through the employment of accepted standards, which themselves, it may be argued, are designed to reinforce certain values and views of the world.

Occupational ideologies

In following established and widely accepted patterns of working practices it is possible to argue that media professionals are conforming to what may be labelled occupational ideologies. Ex-Labour MP Frank Allaun has commented that this may be seen as a form of self-censorship, but that those accepting working practices often do so willingly: 'Self-censorship is not the cause of a jaundiced press; it is one of the symptoms. It does not take long to realise what the news desk is looking for and usually a journalist will supply it, even if it is just for a quiet life' (Allaun, 1988, p. 45). This willing acceptance means that the journalist enters willingly into a system that operates ideologically. As John Hartley argues, professionalism certainly plays an ideological role, functioning as it does to assist in the reproduction of social structures. He sees ideology as 'the means by which ruling economic classes generalize and extend their supremacy across a whole range of social activity, and naturalize it in the process, so that their role is accepted as natural and inevitable; and therefore legitimate and binding' (O'Sullivan et al., 1983, p. 183). If this view is accepted, the codes of practice that operate within a professional context can be articulated as a central part of the legitimization and reproduction of dominant ideas, beliefs and values in the workplace and in society more generally. Media professionals, it therefore follows, operate within these dominant ideas and in doing so are part of their dissemination and reproduction.

However, the codes and conventions of broadcasting and other media are presented in a different way. It is often argued by media professionals that they are neutral and exist in some way 'above' such concerns. Broadcasters often attempt to present themselves as empty vessels through which public opinion may be carried. Yet, as Manuel Alverado et al. argue, this is not the case:

> Paradoxically, this public persona of representing 'us' reproduces the state's own representation of itself as a neutral structure which transcends political differences between sections of society. Just as the state is above capital and labour, differences of race, gender and age, so is the professional broadcaster – whereas in fact, just like the state, broadcasting is a deeply engaged partisan. (Alverado et al., 1987, p. 89)

Certainly, broadcasters represent a set of ideas and beliefs, and to consider that they exist above ideological concerns seems somewhat absurd, particularly when one considers their implication in the overt maintenance of the state's interests at particular historical moments of social conflict. For example, during the 1926 General Strike Lord Reith assured the government that it could rely on the BBC to 'toe the line' when reporting events.

Professional practice and newsroom studies

There have been a number of influential newsroom studies that have been concerned with the ways in which working practices within the media industries, specifically news production, have impacted upon the construction of texts. Blumler (1969) used observations and interviews during an attachment to the BBC Current Affairs Group during the build-up to the 1966 general election to analyse the influences that were present upon producers' attitudes in their role of reporting election events. He concluded that whilst internal organizational factors were an influence on the daily relations between particular producers and the representatives of the political parties, the style and content of rival broadcasters' reports also played a very significant role in formulating their position. Clearly, this type of investigation reveals that the 'impartial' news gatherer is probably a thing of myth rather than reality, regardless of what the reporter may say.

Tom Burns's studies of the BBC (1972, 1977), again based on observation and detailed interviews with workers in the institution, considered the ways in which the organizational structures, the career pathways and internal politics all contributed to influence the ways in which employees undertook and approached their work in the corporation. Others have also investigated a variety of aspects of organizations and professional behaviour and assessed their influence on the construction of factual television. Roger Silverstone (1985) studied the making of the BBC's

Horizon science programme. He was allowed access to the production process by a BBC producer and was thus able to gain a clear insight into the workings of production and other staff at the corporation. Within his study Silverstone asks a central question about the production of factual television and the content of programmes: how far are programme makers influenced by the demands of television rather than by purely scientific considerations?

The question of how much influence the concerns of the television industry have upon news production forms an important part of Simon Cottle's (1993) study of regional news production. His work is focused around Central News West, the regional news programme that covered Birmingham and the West Midlands during the period of his study, and investigates the way in which this particular newsroom dealt with urban uprisings. The most relevant part of his work, for the purposes of this chapter, covers the professionalism of those involved as they sought to produce a regional news programme.

As we have noted earlier, the context of production forms a crucial part of any analysis of media texts, and news is no exception. Cottle acknowledges that the influence of deregulation on regional programming, including news, has meant that it has been forced to adopt a much more commercial edge. This, he argues, has manifested itself in such things as a greater pursuit of advertising, a keener awareness of the regional competition with the BBC over the early evening schedule, and the centrality of regional news to a regional programming strategy. Of course, this desire to reach an audience and produce programming they want to consume may sometimes clash with a professional view that there has been a 'long standing obligation placed on broadcasters to report with due impartiality and accuracy, and to demonstrate sensitivity in relation to matters of public taste and decency' (Cottle, 1993, p. 39). Indeed, Cottle goes on to argue that professional news gatherers also adopt 'a position of friendly gatekeeper, the professional news worker administers news in doses and in a form that are thought to be palatable: too much, or too unvaried a diet would, it is supposed, lead to chronic indigestion with long term repercussions on future news consumption' (p. 62). The context of production and the perceived audiences for local news services therefore have an impact and influence on how news programmes are constructed. Once again, the demands presented through the production context cannot be overlooked just because those working within these contexts assert that their professional codes of practice demand they do not. Indeed, at a local level it may be argued that the pressure on journalists working to produce bulletins and reports leads them simply to 'follow the rules' because it is the most cost-effective and time-saving way of operating.

Cottle argues that journalists have a view of themselves as simply gathering news from happenings in the 'real world'. Their belief that this is the case flies in the face of their actual daily involvement in the manufacturing process. Significantly, Cottle argues, it also ignores the fact that some of the material they acquire and include in their programmes has already been mediated by organizations such as news agencies. Again, this is an important aspect of the way in which the news worker conceptualizes him or herself as a professional. It also makes it easy to forget that in the context of the newsroom, 'incoming news has already been subjected to various bureaucratic routines, organized processes, and informed by the practices of other professionals each serving their particular goals and institutional aims' (Cottle, 1993, p. 54). In so arguing, Cottle makes a great deal of the fact that journalists working on regional news programmes are part of a wider news culture. Within this culture journalists become immersed in the world of news. In turn, this creates practitioners who are inward-looking where the process of creating and moulding stories is concerned, people who learn their trade by observing the practices and final products of others. In such an environment innovation and challenge is unlikely, as Cottle argues:

> This feature of the news operation is important because it locates the production of regional news within a wider media news environment which, though differentiated, none the less constantly affords a reference point in which the specificity of the news product produced can be situated and defined, and which furthermore ordinarily has no need of recourse to external criteria of justification or validation. (1993, p. 54)

Working practices also contribute to the production of similar and less innovative programmes across news production. Cottle observes that the flexibility of roles within regional news production contributes to this reproduction of form and content. The routines and working practices within news production therefore act to further the shared understanding of the form of news and hence also work to ensure a reproduction of both visual style and approach to content.

Within contemporary media contexts, however, the idea of the distanced professional, as we have discussed, needs to be challenged. The commercial concerns of television companies has meant that any attempt to distance news as a serious form from other less worthy popular forms of television has on one level been challenged. However, the cultural capital of news is evident in the ways that popular, regional news programmes are articulated by those who work on them, as distinct from other forms of popular television. These workers are of course professional news gatherers and as such see themselves as distinct from the makers of other popular television forms.

Whilst we have stressed the importance of codes of practice as a force against social change, it would be wrong to suggest that change and development are impossible within the newsroom. New technology ensures that the established practices of the newsroom are not static but open to change. In his study Cottle found a clear split between what he called 'the "old school" of regional news journalists who were allied to the old style popular "magazine" news programme, and the new school of journalists who declared themselves keen to firm up the programme and establish a respectable journalistic, hard news programme' (Cottle, 1993, p. 63). The struggle within the regional newsroom for an identity within wider news culture is therefore also a force for potential change. However, it would be wrong to suggest that the idea of the professional within the realm of hard news is any more likely to produce transparent news stories. In fact, it would be possible to argue the opposite.

Professionalism and political conflict

The assertion by broadcasters that their professional perspective on events, along with broadcasting's rational and 'democratic' codes of practice, creates a distance from content is cast into some doubt when one considers some of the highly charged, ongoing political situations they are involved in. An example of such a situation might be the 'troubles' in Northern Ireland. Events and issues associated with this conflict have been reported from a variety of perspectives. However, studies of the reporting of Northern Ireland (Schlesinger et al., 1983; Curtis, 1984) have questioned the professional distance of those responsible for the coverage of events and situations. In fact, the press and broadcast media work undertaken concerning Northern Ireland, it can be argued, reveals the ideological operation of notions of professionalism within the media industries, for it is in the arena of reporting terrorism that the contradiction of impartiality is most clearly evident.

As Schlesinger et al. argue, the fact that terrorism is overtly attacking the state and threatening social order has allowed it to become a 'field of coverage where broadcast journalism cannot remain impartial' (1983, p. 35). As the reporting of events such as acts of terrorism comes under very close scrutiny from politicians, it is an arena where journalists and producers attempt to appear at their most credible. This in turn can involve them making their values echo those of the politicians as clearly and closely as possible, as they do not want to seem out of line. Broadcasters see themselves as having a high level of responsibility, which in turn assists them to 'strengthen their claims to autonomy and so forestall attempts to impose more stringent controls on their operations' (Schlesinger et al., 1983, p. 35). Hence broadcasters' desire to remain free from direct government control is what drives their reporting in a 'professional' manner, rather than any simple desire to tell the 'truth'. However, it is so far removed from the idea of the impartiality of the professional that the constraints of so-called responsible reporting provide nothing more than a form of news that is able to present itself as a straightforward, factual account of events. Schlesinger et al. contest this, arguing that in fact news tends to be presented in a way which hides the process of selection and construction which all news media go through, and that the opinions and views presented in the news are often those of representatives of the major institutions – for example, government ministers, politicians from mainstream parties, senior members of the police force, the church or the judiciary. They also argue that news coverage of Northern Ireland tends to simplify incidents and avoid any historical background to stories.

The reporting of terrorism also provides a useful way of considering wider issues that are raised by the question of professionalism and the news coverage of Northern Ireland. Schlesinger et al. go into some detail regarding the reporting of the killing of Lord Mountbatten, arguing that the reporting of events invited society as a whole to 'stand united against terrorism which is evaluated as inhuman and irrational, as the very embodiment of chaos' (1983, p. 37). Certainly at this moment it would seem that the ideals of professionalism were removed from the equation.

The restrictions on reporting around Northern Ireland are further investigated by Liz Curtis in her book *Ireland: The Propaganda War* (1984). She argues that the restrictions often placed upon journalists and other media workers were done so indirectly by the organizations they worked for. She quotes a letter from Tom Rhys, secretary of the Federation of Broadcasting Unions, who argues that: '"Checks and balances" introduced by the BBC were becoming as effective as censorship, probably more effective because they were not known outside the circles immediately involved, were superficially merely an intensification of normal safeguards, and were too vague and distant a target for public criticism' (Curtis, 1984, p. 13). Rhys went on to suggest, according to Curtis, that BBC staff at that time were starting to avoid Irish stories because they felt that they may have a detrimental effect upon their careers should they be forced into any sort of disagreement over items covering Ireland.

The clash between the idea of professionalism within the field of journalism and the ideal of impartiality, and the so-called responsible position journalists were continually being asked to pursue in relation to their reporting of Northern Ireland begins to reveal a basic contradiction: between the assertion that they are impartial and the fact that they obviously operate in the interests of the state. It is in relation to this contradiction that it is possible to see most clearly the difficulty, and almost self-delusion, of journalists who want to appear impartial professionals operating within a system where their employers are overtly or covertly a part of the state's institutions.

Whilst there were those who raised questions about the reporting policy of television and newspapers with regard to Northern Ireland, there were many who were able to use the idea of professionally getting on with their day-to-day job as an excuse to gag themselves. As Frank Allaun (1988) suggests, some journalists can quickly adapt to the needs of the institutions that employ them. Curtis observes in the conclusion of her book: 'Britain's activities in the North have been handled like guilty secrets' (1984, p. 275). Reporters, it may be argued, have been party to those guilty secrets, and many, under the label of professionalism, have contributed in their own ways to their remaining so.

Following on from Curtis, it is possible to argue that one of the most important conclusions that can be drawn from suggestions such as the one above is that the restrictions that reporters have been working under in relation to events in Ireland may be extended and developed when it comes to reporting other 'sensitive' areas. The most obvious in recent times has been the revelations about the Gulf War, and the activities of British troops during it, that have been revealed after the event but were not reported whilst it was taking place. Again, it may be argued that this was simply responsible journalism, with all that that implies.

Suggestions for further work

What impact do the idea of professionalism and working practices have on the production of television programmes?

Look at an edition of television news. What are the codes and conventions of news presentation (both with regard to presenters and reporters), and how do they limit the perspectives that might be present in news programmes?

Further reading

Cottle, Simon 1993: *TV News: Urban Conflict and the Inner City*. Leicester: Leicester University Press.

Curtis, Liz 1984: *Ireland: The Propaganda War. The British Media and the Battle for Hearts and Minds*. London: Pluto Press.

Elliot, Philip 1977: Media organizations and occupations. In James Curran et al. (eds), *Mass Communication and Society*. London: Edward Arnold.

11

Independent Media

The idea of independence has become an area of great debate within the contemporary media world. New legislation has meant that many new 'independent' media production companies have begun to seek exhibition for their products through the established broadcasting companies of the BBC and ITV networks. However, these new independent companies are not the only media organizations to lay claim to being independent, and their close relationship with mainstream broadcasters is not the only scenario within which independent media work can take place. This chapter will explore a range of different contexts within which what might be labelled independent media production, distribution and exhibition take place. It will then go on to discuss the various reasons why media organizations feel the need to claim independence, and what they want to be independent of. We will begin by addressing the central question: what is an 'independent' in today's media world? We then turn our attention to three contrasting examples of independence drawn from different media industries within Britain. First, a community radio station. Second, an independent cinema. And finally, *Undercurrents*, an alternative news production and distribution organization.

What is an independent?

A dictionary definition of the word independent suggests that this section may be straightforward: 'Not depending upon the authority of another, not in a position of subordination, not subject to external control or rule; self governing, free.' However, in relation to the media the idea of independent production presents a paradox: it is both simple and complex. On the one hand, an independent product is made by a company which is outside the major producers in its industry – for example, the major Hollywood film studios, BBC and ITV television companies, or large magazine publishers such as Emap. On the other hand, many companies which are independent in this sense have very close links to mainstream, major and often multi-national media organizations. This can perhaps be best seen within the context of the American film industry. Many production companies making films in Hollywood, such as Amblin Entertainment and Imagine, can lay claim to being independent because they produce their own films. When key figures within these two organizations are identified as Steven Spielberg and Ron Howard respectively, it is certainly possible to argue that their products, such as *Jurassic Park* (1993) or *Ransom* (1996), are completely within mainstream film production and not independent at all, even if at a basic level it is possible to put forward a case for them because they control their own interests. This leads to a situation where the context of production needs to be examined more closely in an effort to understand fully the idea of independence.

In a variety of contrasting situations the notion of independence has a certain currency. Any analysis must therefore acknowledge that there is a variety of often conflicting and contradictory notions as to what being independent in today's media actually entails. One of the initial ways in which an exploration of media independence may take place is by assessing how a company or organization has attempted, for a variety of both economic and political reasons, to remain independent within its own media industries.

Media structures

Absolute independence would mean that a media organization had control of production, distribution and exhibition. It is this level of independence that some alternative and politically radical organizations strive for. However, the extension of control that is achieved by bringing together these three spheres, or what is sometimes known as vertical integration, is very difficult to achieve. On the occasions when some semblance of it has been achieved it is usually by conglomerates with so many global companies that within their enormous portfolio of interests lay examples of all three aspects. An example of a company that has controlled production, distribution and exhibition in Britain is Cannon films.

In the 1980s Cannon expanded from a small film production company into the areas of distribution and exhibition. This was achieved by taking over the ABC chain of cinemas. Although its overall control was brief, it remains a useful example of an integrated company which had some control over production, distribution and exhibition. The fact that the company controlled these three arms meant that it could be sure of distribution and exhibition when it put Cannon films into production. This is certainly a luxury that few production companies can be totally assured of as they develop an idea and move towards production. However, the one aspect of the equation that Cannon could not totally assure was audiences, and a number of the company's films during this period failed to find large or even medium-sized audiences. The result of this under-performance at the box office was that the company struggled financially, and in the end a number of titles announced at international festivals failed to appear and the company began to sell off its assets, including film back catalogues and cinemas. Its brief moment of integration, it seems, floundered on poor financial decisions.

New Line Cinema

Another example of an independent company which saw the advantages of integrating elements of production with distribution was New Line Cinema. New Line began in the 1970s as a film distribution company specializing in low budget genre movies such as horror films for the drive-in and college circuit. A good example of the sort of product it handled at this time was the very successful horror film *Texas Chainsaw Massacre* (1974). However, as it became more successful the demand for products that it knew it could successfully distribute grew. In order to create a steady stream of suitable films New Line moved into the area of production, choosing to finance films it was confident that its own distribution wing could make a profit from. Initially, this saw New Line Pictures producing films such as *A Nightmare on Elm Street* (1984). The massive success of that film and the subsequent series of films that followed meant that the company was able to expand its production horizons in terms of both subject-matter and budget. The result of this expansion was films like *Teenage Mutant Ninja Turtles* (1990) which had larger budgets, more sophisticated special effects and which again proved successful at the worldwide box office. With this move towards larger budgets the difference between the New Line independent film product and those of the so-called major studios narrowed greatly. Indeed, the similarity between 'smaller' independent companies such as New Line and the major Hollywood studios led to the former being labelled 'mini-majors'. The similarity between the majors and the mini-major independents in terms of the films produced is further reflected by New Line's production of such so-called independent films as *Dumb and Dumber* (1994).

New Line's move towards the mainstream was, in a sense, completed when Robert Shaye, head of the company since its inception, sold his interests to Ted Turner's multi-media empire in the early 1990s. Although he remained in a prominent position, it is possible to argue that the company's independent status was lessened as it became subsumed into a larger media conglomerate. In turn, Turner found that towards the end of the 1990s his companies were sold and became part of Time-Warner's massive media multi-national stable. The era of New Line Film's status as a truly independent production company was over.

British television

When the Conservative government passed its Broadcasting Bill in the 1990s it had a great effect on the idea of independence within British broadcasting. One of the major effects of the Bill was that it instigated a quota system which meant that at least 25 per cent of materials broadcast on both BBC and ITV services had to be produced by independent companies. The concept of 'independence' had played a significant part within British broadcasting since the 1954 Television Act set up the Independent Television Authority, with a view to the establishment of a network of commercially funded, regional television companies. Within this context, these companies' independence was certainly conceived of in relation to the BBC, which at the time was the major player in the British broadcasting landscape. These new companies would also be independent of the state as a result of funding through revenue gained from advertising rather than the licence fee. The licence fee was paid by every household with a television set and the revenue gained from it went towards funding the BBC exclusively.

The independent production companies championed by the 1990s legislation were conceived as producing programmes that would be screened on the main four (now five) terrestrial channels. This in turn had a great effect on the form and content of programmes made by these independents. Whilst they are not controlled by the BBC or ITV companies, they *are* attempting to make programmes that will be broadcast on these networks. The result of this is that they aim to produce programmes that, for the most part, do not look out of place alongside programmes produced internally by these major organizations, or that are produced by other similar independent companies. For example, the visual style of a situation comedy produced by an independent company often differs very little from those produced by Yorkshire Television. Similarly, a game show produced by an independent may look and sound identical to another produced by Granada Television. In one sense, then, it is possible to argue that the aim of many of the independent companies that appeared after the 1990 Act is to produce programming that, if it was not labelled as the product of an independent production company, would not be identified as being any different from material produced by major television companies, and would fit seamlessly into their schedules. In this context, then, independent is merely an economic definition, and the success of these so-called independent companies is often totally tied in to the success of their relationship with one or more of the major companies, and their ability repeatedly to win commissions from them.

Ultimately, however much it may be possible to argue that such companies are independent, their close, mutually fulfilling relationship with major, mainstream media organizations will always leave space open for the criticism that they are in fact independent in name only. We now want to turn our attention to an exploration of media organizations that attempt to be more clearly independent from the major players in the media world, and in doing so establish a real alternative to them.

Community radio

An ideal of independence has been the driving force behind the development of the community radio movement, which has grown in the UK throughout the 1980s and 1990s. This growth, and the continuing enthusiasm for community radio, can be seen as a direct reaction against the centralizing control within the so-called independent radio sector of the mainstream radio industry in the hands of a small number of companies such as Emap, which run a nationwide network of independent stations. Within this context it is certainly possible to go further and argue that the expansion of community radio stations and the Community Radio Association (CRA) is a direct reaction against the centralization of control within the industry and the uniformity of format championed by the controlling companies through rigid elements such as the play-list. In the face of this lack of regional or local identity within the mainstream regional stations, the growth of community radio stations represents a reclamation of the label 'local' from stations that had long since joined the ranks of the establishment. Indeed, the CRA sees itself in this crusading light, its aim being to create a third sector within UK radio broadcasting, one that particularly serves the needs of local communities and is not driven by the desire for private commercial gain.

To some extent this has been achieved by the establishment of a network of local community radio stations. These were able to expand and develop by using Restricted Service Licences (RSLs), which allow broadcasters to send signals within a restricted distance on an allocated wavelength for up to twenty-eight days. Examples of the sorts of events for which licences have been granted include: Bradford's Festival Radio, which was set up to provide information and celebration throughout the city's annual arts and cultural festival; and Aberfeldy's Raft Race Radio, which, as its name suggests, was licensed to broadcast during the day of the town's traditional raft race. However, as the 1990s have progressed, more commercial organizations have seen the possible opportunities an RSL can offer them. For example, Manchester United have been able to operate a station on match days, serving supporters in the vicinity of their Old Trafford ground. Of course, it is possible to argue that such a service serves a specific community, the Manchester United football supporters, but the nature of their operation is obviously very different to that of more traditional RSL users, and the CRA's attempt to serve more traditional versions of local communities.

CRA's code of practice

The major differences between members of the CRA and operations such as Manchester United's radio station are represented by the CRA's code of practice. In fact, the association's code does emphasize how these community stations are determined to remain independent from the powerful commercial companies currently operating within the radio industry. It is therefore worth quoting, as it states that community radio stations:

1 Serve geographically recognizable communities or communities of interest.
2 Enable the development, well-being and enjoyment of their listeners through meeting information, communication or cultural needs; encourage their participation in these processes through providing them with access to training, production and transmission facilities; stimulate innovation in radio programming and technology; and seek out and involve those sections of the community under-represented in existing broadcast services.
3 Take positive action to ensure that management, programming and employment practices encourage non-sexist, non-racist attitudes and representations; for example by including such pledges in their constitutions or secondary rules and by instituting relevant training and awareness programmes.
4 Reflect the plurality and diversity of their listening community and provide a right of reply to any person or organization subject to serious misrepresentation.
5 Draw their programming from mostly regional / local sources rather than national sources.
6 Have their general management and programming policy made by a broadly based Council of Management including the producers.
7 Are legally constituted as non-profit-making trusts, co-operatives or non-profit-maximizing limited companies.
8 Are financed from more than one source, such as public and private loans, shares, advertising, listener subscriptions and public grants.
9 Have ownership solely representative of their locality or community of interest.
10 Recognize the right of paid workers to be unionized and encourage the use of volunteers.

As can be seen from this code of practice, those local community stations that operate by it are clearly committed to representing the needs of their listeners and to remaining free from the influence of the major financial players in the contemporary media world. The emphasis on the local, and the acknowledgement that different groups of listeners want different things from a station, reinforce the need for these community-based stations to be, and remain, independent. The CRA's code of practice clearly highlights its awareness that this is an issue of central importance to community radio stations, the community radio movement as a whole, and the listeners they serve.

Bradford Community Broadcasting

Bradford Community Broadcasting (BCB) is a good example of a community radio station that attempts to put the CRA's code into practice. As BCB itself put it in a programme guide leaflet, it sees itself as 'Bradford's very own community radio station ... radio as it should be – involved, opinionated and concerned, but most importantly local'. The programming strategy at BCB reflects this, and shows its attempts to give a voice to local people and local concerns. Nevertheless, with slots such as *The Asian Magazine, Discovering Bradford* and *Sports Talk* there is a marked resemblance to BBC local and regional stations which do cover some similar territories within their programming strategies. However, outside the arena of programming there is a strong sense of difference, independence and community. Access to production training and the potential involvement in the work of BCB make it a real community resource. It is this ability to take people from the community into the radio station that marks out the independence of organizations such as BCB when compared to the likes of the BBC. For example, with regard to BCB this is reflected in the work of Radio Venus. Radio Venus is Bradford Women's Community Radio Project, and it seeks to involve local women in the production of radio programmes. As with much of BCB's output, Radio Venus is promoted as a station for local people to express themselves, allowing them access to the airwaves and production skills. It is this aspect of the work of community radio stations that really challenges the mainstream and marks their independence. On the level of programming and programme content, however, the level of independence present is much more open to debate as they reflect the production values of more mainstream radio productions.

Independent cinema exhibition

As James Snead has identified in his article ' "Black independent film": Britain and America' (1994), one of the major issues surrounding independent production is the fact that 'All too often independent films are packed away for discrete presentation of elite museums, late-night educational television programmes, and infrequent, often poorly attended conferences on "independent cinema".' In Britain one of the ways that this problem of exhibition is addressed is through a network of independent cinemas and regional film theatres. These are often funded by regional arts boards and the British Film Institute, although some operate independently of such bodies.

These independent cinemas and regional film theatres often attempt to integrate the screening of new, lesser-known independent films alongside second runs of more widely distributed, commercial films, in an attempt to offset the financial risk sometimes represented by the exhibition of independent film. However, there remains a clear commitment by these cinemas to attempt to find an audience for such less obviously commercial films. Sometimes this can be done through the careful programming of less well-known titles alongside better-known films in themed seasons or retrospectives. On other occasions they may be part of a mini-festival of independent cinema. Examples of these strategies can be explored by looking at the brochures that advertise the programmes of independent cinemas and regional film theatres. For instance, Cornerhouse in Manchester hosts a well-established festival of independent American cinema called 'Mavericks in Manchester', which brings together the latest works of established names such as Jim Jarmusch, with new films from first-time American directors (see illustration 11.1). By carefully programming a mix of potentially

Illustration 11.1   Cornerhouse Cinema, Manchester. An example of an independent exhibitor.
Source: The authors.

successful films with more off-beat projects, the cinema is able to present its patrons with a wider, fuller picture of the current state of American independent cinema. Similarly, Watershed Media Centre in Bristol has been associated with the Black Pyramid Film Festival, which showcases work from throughout the African diaspora. Indeed, the commitment to independent and alternative cinema is made explicit by the aims laid out by the cinema department of the Watershed Media Centre in its mission statement. Within this document it states that its aim is to 'provide a regional facility for international cinema, including marginalised, experimental and special interest product, thereby ensuring that the region's audiences are not limited to the narrow diet of mainstream commercial cinema.' This written commitment is reflected in the cinema's programme, which has a firm commitment to screening at least 50 per cent European films, and regular programming slots such as 'The Cutting Edge', which is devoted to presenting new film and video which explore the impact of new technologies on the world of film-making. Of course, a commitment to the screening of independent and alternative films is dependent upon the patterns of distribution present in the British film industry.

Independent film distribution in the UK

It is certainly the case that much of the power in the relationship between distributors and exhibitors lies in the hands of the former. It is the distribution companies that decide what products will be available on British screens. Many of these companies are linked to the major American studios, and exist to distribute their films to cinemas. Organizations like Cornerhouse and Watershed are much more dependent upon what can be termed independent distribution. As Julian Petley argues, 'When applied to the distribution sector the word "independent" has usually been taken to denote that the distributor in question is not tied to the products of any particular Hollywood studio, but I would suggest that the definition needs to be expanded to cover the kinds of film distributed and to include a commitment to British cinema, Europe, the Third World, and left-field Hollywood as well' (1992, p. 78). However, the ways in which non-independent distribution companies are able to control the images that reach the vast majority of screens in Britain mean that the financial rewards for the sorts of independent distributor championed by Petley are small. In turn, this therefore limits the number of films they feel that they can afford to put into distribution. The logical knock-on effect is that however committed to the screening of independent and alternative products cinemas may be, if the films that their programmers see at international film festivals never reach distribution, they simply are unable to screen them.

Undercurrents

Undercurrents is an alternative news video which claims to cover key social and environmental issues that are ignored by the mainstream media. However, it is the fact that *Undercurrents* productions, as well as organizing alternative news gathering, also attempt to operate independent distribution of their product, which in turn leads to a more flexible and independent mode of exhibition and consumption, that makes them truly independent. It is their control over aspects of production, distribution and exhibition that makes them a significant example of an independent media organization.

Undercurrents is a collection of news reports drawn from sources such as community groups, activists and campaigners, often gathered on domestic video equipment. One of these sources is the Camcorder Action Network (CAN) which has activists with video production skills ready to film protests, campaigns and demonstrations wherever they occur. Originally, the network was established to provide alternative versions of events to those presented within the mainstream news media. However, on occasion the network has found that its footage, often because it is willing to film events from the protesters' side of the police lines, has been of interest to mainstream companies which have included it in their news reports or documentary features. As journalist Ted Oakes has noted, 'CAN's archive is now arguably Britain's largest library of "protest" footage which may be developed into films for UNDERCURRENTS and is available for documentary researchers and producers of broadcast productions' (1995, p. 14). Despite the mainstream interest in its footage, much of what the CAN shoots certainly finds its most natural and supportive home in products such as *Undercurrents*.

Since it was established in 1984 *Undercurrents* has produced video tape journals that have addressed a wide range of issues through their reports and features. The content of these tapes aims to challenge the dominant view of events contained in mainstream news production in an attempt to produce news coverage that is independent. For example, the first edition of *Undercurrents* contains an award-winning report that charts the progress of the campaign to stop the M11 link road, entitled 'You've got to be choking'. This was followed up by a yearly round-up of the campaign called 'You've got to be choking too' in the second edition. The titles of other reports give a flavour of the events covered, and the approach favoured by *Undercurrents*. For example, 'Street news' was a round-up of stories 'television fails to cover', 'Celtic enemy' looked at Welsh villagers and a direct action protesters' campaign against open-cast mining, and 'Welcome to the jungle' covered DIY pirate radio in the council estates of London.

The campaigning character of much of the contents of *Undercurrents* can be explained by the fact that it has been shot by activists and is edited in such a way as to reflect *their* interests and concerns rather than those of the mainstream media news. For example, in *Undercurrents 6* an item entitled 'If I had a hammer' reported the dismantling of a Hawk jet by four women at British Aerospace in Lancashire, offering the thoughts of the women and the reasons for their actions. This contextualization of the news 'event' is something that mainstream news coverage of this action sadly lacked. Indeed, it is fair to say that it is the fact that so much material is shot by activists 'on the spot' that maintains the independence of perspective so clearly present in each item present on an *Undercurrents* tape. Again as Ted Oakes suggests: 'CAN members have special access and insight into the story because of their involvement. They are therefore better placed to capture images that reflect the point of view of a community than, for instance, a BBC news crew visiting from London' (1995, p. 14).

Undercurrents's independence is also maintained by its distribution through subscription and sales in specialist book shops. According to Undercurrents Productions, it reaches around 40,000 people through community communal screenings. This distribution network means that the producers of the tapes do not have to tailor their product to the demands of mainstream distribution, and further ensures that *Undercurrents* maintains its independence of perspective and is not compromised in terms of its content. *Undercurrents 6* contains footage shot at the protest at the celebration of one hundred years of the motor car at Coventry Cathedral. A naked woman appeared at the service and shouted her opposition to the celebration and highlighted the pollution caused by cars. *Undercurrents* was free to show its footage of the woman and her painted body. Mainstream news gatherers may well have resisted the inclusion of such footage, citing decency and good taste as their 'professional' reasons.

From the footage shot by activists such as those involved in the CAN, to its editing by campaigners at the non-profit organization Undercurrents Productions, and finally through its alternative distribution network, *Undercurrents* maintains a high level of independence. This independence challenges the assumptions and production values of mainstream media production. In doing this *Undercurrents* continually reminds those who watch its tapes that alternative versions of the events that appear on the news do exist, and that other events are just overlooked by those working within the mainstream. In *Undercurrents 6* an item called 'Snodland news' lists those world events that happened on the same day over an ITN news story about a child who walked home alone from a play group. In turn, items such as this may lead to a wider reflection upon the power of those conglomerates which control much of the media's production, distribution and exhibition.

Clearly the idea of independence has a number of definitions dependent upon the context in which the work claiming the label appears. The word itself has, on occasion, been used to describe products that exist almost entirely inside the mainstream of media production. Others attempt to establish their independence through some kind of alternative practice. On occasion this may relate to the needs of a particular community which may not be adequately served by mainstream media production. In other instances it may relate to a perceived lack in the products produced by the mainstream and therefore constitute some attempt at redressing this. Whatever the reason for seeking the label 'independent', it is a term whose once radical meaning has become somewhat diluted, to the extent that it has ceased to evoke the alternative practices it once did. The term in this context therefore has become less useful. However, this does not mean that an examination of what independent means today is not without value.

Suggestions for further work

Select a television situation comedy that is produced by an independent company and another produced by the BBC. How similar are they, and do they in any way differ?

In what ways do you feel the CRA's code of practice is a challenge to the working practices of mainstream radio organizations?

Gather together the programme brochures for two or three independent cinemas. Compare and contrast their programming and assess how far they might really be considered 'independent'?

Further reading

Petley, Julian 1992: Independent distribution in the UK: problems and proposals. In Duncan Petrie (ed.), *New Questions of British Cinema*, London: British Film Institute.

Part III
Audiences

12

Conceptualizing and Measuring Media Audiences

We begin our audiences section by considering how media practitioners attempt both to conceptualize and measure media audiences. This chapter starts with a consideration of television scheduling. This is a useful way of understanding the ways in which media institutions formally and publicly, through the construction of their schedules, present a view of how they conceptualize their audiences at different points throughout the day. We then look at the actual processes used to measure audience numbers and ask why they are so important to those who run media organizations.

Conceiving the audience: television schedules

As with all media exhibitors, television companies must have a strong sense of who their audience is, or may be, and how large they are at any given moment. For commercial television stations this is linked to a need to be able to provide particular audiences with very specific profiles to advertisers. For state-run stations, such as the BBC, there is a need to be able to provide evidence that their programming is providing a service for large sections of the licence fee-paying public.

The ways in which broadcasters conceive of their audiences also link with wider issues and concerns within media studies, such as gender, race and class, because they often attempt to break down audience profiles along these lines. One of the most effective ways of considering how broadcasters regard their audience can be seen through the way in which they construct their programming schedules. Scheduling commands a great deal of time and effort and is an important part of the exhibition of the television medium. It is through the strategies employed by broadcasters that it is possible to begin to gain an understanding of how they see the make-up of their audience, and why certain types of programme appear when and where they do.

The job of scheduling is to create a strong sense of familiarity amongst viewers. It is through a consistent programming strategy that programme makers can rely on viewers returning to certain viewing slots again and again. This return is often based upon generic preferences, hence the continual programming of certain types of television on particular days and in specific time slots. For example, the BBC tends to show 'easy-going' newly produced dramas such as *Lovejoy* and *Pie in the Sky* between 8.00 and 9.00 p.m. on a Sunday evening. The potential viewer becomes familiar with this strategy, so even if the programme scheduled for that slot is unknown they may well expect a certain style and content from the product. It is the familiarity born of scheduling strategies that allows this. In a similar way the ITV network places drama serials such as *Heartbeat* and *Where The Heart Is* in the same time slot. Audiences presented with a new drama in that time slot, as they were in 1997 with *Wokenwell*, can be confident of the type of programme they are likely to experience based on their knowledge of that programming slot and the previous dramas that have occupied it. *Wokenwell's* setting in a small northern village, with its focus on the lives of its inhabitants, would therefore not have surprised them. This scheduling practice is further linked to the idea that traditionally within British culture Sunday is closely associated with the family. How true this common-sense assumption actually is may be open to question, but it certainly seems to inform the way in which broadcasters conceive of their Sunday evening viewers, tending as they do towards the programming of products they consider suitable for all the family. As Richard Paterson notes more generally about scheduling, 'a central notion in any understanding of the structures of television programming, in its aesthetic, economic or cultural modes, is that it is addressed to viewers in the home. It is a domestic medium and the space of domestic life, the family household, invokes a set of understandings which inform scheduling' (1990, p. 33).

Paterson also argues that the strategies utilized for trailing new programmes are highly dependent upon assumptions about the make-up of television audiences. Trailers are placed amongst programmes that broadcasters assume are watched by the audience groups most likely to respond positively to new programming in a similar vein. Therefore, a new family serial to be broadcast on a Sunday evening on ITV may well be trailed before or after a weekday soap that is also, in the eyes of the broadcaster, watched by a family audience. However, this new programme is unlikely to be trailed around a late night special interest programme because such a show is unlikely to attract the target family audience that the channel wants to reach.

The conception of audiences by broadcasters, which as we have argued can be identified through their scheduling strategies, clearly assists advertisers in terms of where they place their promotional material in order to reach their target audience or market. For example, the placement of television programmes designed for children, such as cartoons, in regular Saturday morning slots allows advertisers to promote products aimed at that very particular audience. These may include advertisements for soft drinks, pop music or toys, which often appear within the available slots during a typical Saturday morning output on mainstream television. On occasion, they may also include spin-off products from the cartoons themselves.

The analysis of television schedules and the ways in which they can reveal broadcasters' assumptions about their audiences can be taken a step further. By looking closely at the daytime schedule of terrestrial and satellite television it is possible to begin to construct a profile of their version of their audience. The placement of certain types of programmes at certain points in the schedule shows that broadcasters are not afraid to make enormously broad assumptions about those who choose to tune in during the day. These assumptions are often based upon common-sense ideas about who is at home during the daytime, the sorts of activities they enjoy and the interests they wish to pursue. For example, the schedule below is for Granada Television on Monday 23 March 1998:

8.50 a.m. *Lorraine Live* (GMTV)
9.25 a.m. *This Morning*
9.30 a.m. *Vanessa*
10.10 a.m. *This Morning*

Through an analysis of this schedule it is possible to begin to create a viewer profile. Certainly the structure of the schedule after 8.50 a.m. suggests that broadcasters consider the majority of their viewers to be female. GMTV shifts from its normal format of a male and female presenter to a single female, Lorraine Kelly, for its *Lorraine Live* slot, which focuses on showbiz gossip, cooking and general lifestyle concerns. The content and the way in which that content is structured suggest that the target viewer is female, probably married and may have just finished taking her children to school, and so is open to a 'relaxing' half hour of programming that is devoted to the concerns of contemporary women, before embarking on the day ahead. Of course this will not be the only viewer available at this time, but in terms of the target for the programme it is the only part of the potential market that is of concern. Indeed, this is further reflected by the appearance of advertisements for sanitary products, washing powder and shampoo during the commercial breaks. Sometimes the content of this 8.50 a.m. *Lorraine Live* slot represents features which have appeared earlier in that morning's GMTV, but here are given a 'softer' angle.

As the morning schedule progresses the initial assumptions about the audience seem to be further confirmed. This is at its clearest during a later programme, *This Morning*. Usually hosted by husband and wife team Richard Madeley and Judy Finnigan, this example of morning scheduling reveals the assumptions about audiences which inform its structure. Lasting around $2\frac{1}{2}$ hours, the programme is fragmented into shorter slots which focus on a range of subjects such as cooking, fashion and make-overs, household and garden design, as well as 'phone-ins designed to assist viewers with their medical and emotional problems. The early part of *This Morning* always carries a menu, which is continually referred to as the programme progresses. Daily, each feature is trailed on the menu with a precise timetable, which allows the viewer to plan across the programme rather than continually watch from the opening to the final credits. This type of menu assumes that the viewer will be performing other activities during its running time. Again, the features seem to assume that the typical viewer is female, because they focus, as *Lorraine Live* did, on subjects that are usually associated with female viewers. The tone of address adopted by the programme, particularly around features such as the make-over, also reinforces this reading of the programme's sense of its audience profile. The menu, broken down as it is, assumes that the viewer will be in the house for the duration of the programme, but that they may go off and pursue other tasks as it runs, returning at the allotted time for the feature that previously grabbed their attention. It is possible to take this a little further and suggest that a programme such as *This Morning* aims its content at housewives who are doing their housework during the programme and so will effectively 'graze' across the content as their work allows. Whilst, as we have argued earlier, these assumptions are based on problematic versions of the daytime viewer, they do mean that the stations broadcasting the programme can suggest that certain products, if advertised during the programme, will reach a very defined audience. If, for example, the unemployed, night and part-time workers are watching, they distort the picture broadcasters wish to paint of their daytime audience. Actual viewers and their needs therefore become of less concern to broadcasters than the creation of a schedule which suggests an audience profile which will satisfy potential paying advertisers.

However, assumptions about the make-up of media audiences are not enough simply to attract advertisers on their own – a more concrete source of information is ultimately required. This desire for information about viewers tuning into both individual programmes and channels led to the development of a variety of methods for collecting data about media audiences. The fact that broadcasters are very concerned with ratings is evident from the 'battle' for viewers that takes place around such key moments as the Christmas Day schedule. The continual struggle to be the top-rated soap opera is another example, with *Eastenders* and

Coronation Street introducing plotlines that are designed to boost viewing figures whenever ratings dip or fall too far behind their rivals. The importance of audience figures within broadcasting has been commented upon by Raymond Kent, who argues that:

> the ratings achieved by individual broadcasts, television channels or radio stations, the circulation and readerships obtained by the print media, cinema attendances and passages past outdoor commercial posters are all crucial to those involved in the industry, since such measures are the basis for determining the success or failure of media outputs, and constitute the 'currency' for negotiating advertising space or time. (1994, p. xi)

Measuring media audiences

The expansion of a deregulated television and radio service within Britain has meant more competition for advertising revenue. In turn, the result is that greater resources have been put into audience research because broadcasters and advertisers are concerned to understand fully the break-down of their audiences in terms of categories such as social class, gender and race. As Kent argues, 'audience fragmentation has meant that even the most popular programmes, newspapers and magazines have smaller audiences than they once had. The result is that market segmentation and targeting are vital. To do this, accurate and regular audience measurement data is essential' (1994, p. 4). Because of this, media organizations are willing to pump enormous resources into finding out about the profile of their audiences.

Measurement organizations

Some organizations are devoted to the measurement of media audiences, although the debate as to what methods of information-gathering are the most accurate is an ongoing one. For example, the Broadcaster's Audience Research Board (BARB) provides certain forms of information to both broadcasters and advertising companies. One of the techniques BARB uses in the collection of data on television audiences is a meter system. This process involves placing a recording device in a sample of television sets around the UK. Supposedly representative, this device simply records when the television is on and what channel is being tuned into. It is also possible to record which members of the family are present through the use of a special remote control panel. The information gathered by BARB through such methods is formulated into national viewing figures and published in a variety of sources such as the weekly rating tables that appear in the *Radio Times*.

A similar organization, known as Radio Joint Audience Research (RAJAR), operates to provide information about radio listening figures and profiles. However, measuring radio audiences throws up a number of significant issues. We now explore this aspect of audience measurement in more detail.

Measuring radio audiences

Radio as a medium presents a number of very specific issues in relation to audience measurement. As an aural medium it can often accompany other activities, such as driving, which would be inconceivable in relation to other mediums such as television or print. Tony Twyman has noted that one of the major problems faced by those undertaking audience research is the fact that when asked to recall their listening habits many people are unable to identify the station they were tuned in to. He states that: 'In some research by the Bureau of Broadcast Measurement in Canada only about 60% of those aware that the radio was switched on felt that they knew exactly what "the programme" was' (1994, p. 89). Judging by this type of statement, it is certainly possible to argue that radio listeners have a tendency to 'graze' across, and in and out of, programmes. This raises a very important issue: what constitutes 'listening' to the radio? It would seem that this is a question that those contributing to radio audience surveys have difficulty in answering; hence, they are unsure of how to respond to questions about their listening habits. It is because of issues such as these that a variety of techniques for questioning audiences about their listening habits have been developed.

Twyman, who played a leading role in the setting up of RAJAR, acknowledges that the framework for research is of paramount importance. For instance, he argues that different results are likely when audiences are prompted by lists rather than simply invited to recall their listening cold. He identifies five main techniques of data-collection employed by those gathering information about the listening practices of radio consumers. First, 'systematic recall' which, according to Twyman, involves interviewing people the day after a chosen date inviting them to identify the content and occasion of their radio listening. This technique of data-collection is known as 'day-after recall' or DAR. Second, 'diaries', which involves the respondent keeping a written record of their listening. Twyman argues that whilst this may seem a good way of collecting direct audience responses, in fact many of those who listen to a lot of radio material may be put off taking part in this form of data-collection because the amount of writing involved makes it very cumbersome and time-consuming. The third technique is known as 'general habits', and this involves asking respondents about their general listening habits. Whilst this type of approach may be very useful in relation to mediums closely associated with consumption habits, such as regularly tuning into television forms such as soaps, in the case of the more casual radio listener it is less effective. Twyman notes that 'the task for the respondent is to summarize a whole range of casual events without being provided with the context or content cues to reconstruct even a simple day. Media habit questions are generally difficult for respondents to answer, but they are especially difficult for radio' (1994, p. 92). 'Coincidental interviewing', the fourth category, attempts to ask people about their listening at the moment of consumption. In North America this technique has attempted to go so far as to ask drivers about their listening whilst they waited at traffic lights. However, this method of interviewing, as Twyman points out, is very expensive when measured against the amount and usefulness of data collected. The final method of data-extraction involves 'recording devices'. In the case of radio this is usually a meter which is placed inside listeners' machines. Whilst this technique may be well suited to television viewing, which is for the most part undertaken in a fixed venue, radio listening can be experienced in a wide variety of contexts, some of which are actually in transit. Therefore, this technique is less well suited to the collection of data concerning respondent's radio listening because it too is not very cost-effective.

UK radio research in practice

Following his outline of research techniques, Twyman goes on to explore in more detail the ways in which those potential approaches have been put into practice within the United Kingdom. Up until 1992, when it was abandoned, the BBC employed DAR to undertake around a thousand in-home interviews. However, this type of interview proved to be inadequate as more regional radio stations came into being, therefore a change of approach was needed. As Twyman notes, their appearance meant a change of focus away from the established method of data-collection, because a different set of information was required. He argues: 'the BBC local samples reflected the changing requirements away from individual programme audiences to "typical" audiences for consistently formatted programming, often with high music, news and information content' (1994, p. 99). This reflects the fact that data-collection is continually having to change and adapt. Indeed, it may be argued that the contemporary media landscape with its rapidly developing new technologies is more in need of this adaptability than ever before. The introduction of more channels has meant that audience data-collection is an ever-evolving set of techniques.

In 1973 Independent Local Radio (ILR) joined the BBC national and local stations in broadcasting radio signals to the nation. As with the BBC, and possibly more so due to their reliance on advertising revenue, local radio stations also needed to collect and reflect upon audience information (see illustration 12.1). Following a number of years of data-collection by an industry body known as JICRAR (the Joint Industry Committee for Radio Audience Research) which employed diary-keepers as its sample

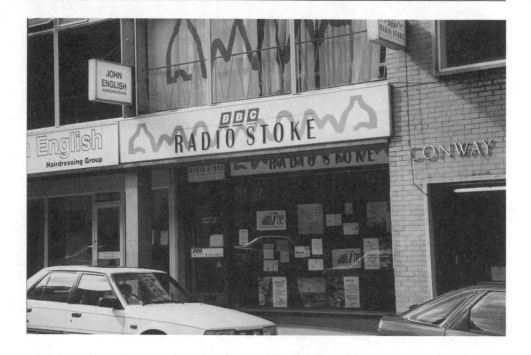

Illustration 12.1   Smaller regional radio stations, such as Radio Stoke, need to know
who is listening in order to deliver an appropriate service.
Source: The authors.

and annually calculated its results based on four-week periods, there
was a shift to a more continuous system of data-collection. These techniques, however, did not satisfy all those requesting data. Stations of
various sizes argued that they required different levels of input within
different time scales. Again as Twyman argues, any changes are not
without their problems: 'Spreading research means that it is not at the
mercy of atypical events, but assumes unchanging programme schedules
which achieve stable audiences. Concentrating research can avoid the
problem of programme schedules changing in the middle of a research
period and this strategy is more interpretable in programme terms' (1994,
p. 100). Problems therefore seem to exist in both forms of data-collection,
but the need to have some form of data that may be interpreted seems
to be the overriding factor in these cases.

In an attempt to create a system of data-collection which satisfied the
needs of large and small, national and local radio stations, RAJAR was
established in 1992. It attempted to collect data from listeners by employing a week-long diary technique that was carried out by households rather
than individuals. Named columns in the diaries included the names of
all national stations, including newer stations such as Virgin and local

ILR and BBC stations. Whilst not without problems – for example the diarists need to be able continually to identify stations when they are not always obvious – this offered a more detailed set of results.

It is important to assert that data-collection is something that is never without potential drawbacks. However, as increasingly more organizations desire ever more detailed information about the consumers of broadcasting and other media, data-collectors are likely to continue to strive for methods that will deliver the necessary information at the level of detail they require.

Suggestions for further work

Look at a day's programme output of the terrestrial television channels. Can you identify any moments in the day when clear assumptions are being made about who is watching and why?

What other forms of data collection might now be possible due to new media technologies, and how would they improve on the methods already employed by audience measurement organizations?

Further reading

Kent, Raymond (ed.) 1994: *Measuring Media Audiences*. London: Routledge.

13
The Effects of the Media on Audience Groups

What are the aims of effects research?

There is a surprisingly long tradition of effects-based audience research, and an examination of it reveals a significant body of different approaches. All have in some way sought to examine the effects of media output on their audiences and all have argued that the media influence their audiences in some way. Effects work is also characterized by its attempt to identify a particular aspect of the media as the agent of effects; it might be a particular aspect of media content or form which causes the effect, or the media technology through which media output is received. As a school of research it has often been dismissed as an overly simplistic approach to media audiences. However, some communications critics, who wish to defend contemporary effects work, argue that it is often evoked in overly simplistic ways in academic schools of thought which have an interest in privileging their own method and research findings (McLeod et al., 1991, p. 235).

The more commonly known strand of the effects tradition argues that the media have effects which in turn have the power to influence the thoughts of individual audience members to such an extent that they might 'act out' the ideas and activities the media have exposed them to. This approach is often characterized by its focus on the negative impact of the media and its potential to incite dangerous, violent or socially unacceptable forms of behaviour. In line with the effects conception of the audience as essentially malleable, the tradition argues that particular groups, for example teenagers and children, are especially vulnerable to certain kinds of media exposure. This kind of approach to media audiences has enjoyed a great deal of popularity in times of moral panic, panic which has often been incited by the media itself. As a result, effects research, some of which is more complex than the strand discussed here, has been maligned. Yet despite the obvious simplicity of dominant effects work, it still informs many of today's 'common-sense' approaches to the media in popular debates. It would be fatuous to argue that the media have absolutely no impact on their audiences, yet media and communications research as a whole have come to little agreement on the type and the extent of media effects.

The historical development of the effects tradition

McLeod et al. (1991) argue that effects research began as far back as the late nineteenth century and early twentieth century when observers of society, some of whom, out of concern about the effects of the press, drew up early plans for empirical research. They note Max Weber, Walter Lippmann and John Dewey as social reformers of this kind (1991, p. 239). However, most commentators begin their version of the effects tradition in the 1930s. In David Morley's historical account of effects research, or what he calls the 'dominant conceptual paradigm' in audience studies, he argues that it was originally formed in response to the Frankfurt School's 'pessimistic mass society thesis' (1992, p. 45). The Frankfurt School argued that new industrialized societies, dominated by capitalist scientific rationality, had created the masses: uncritical, gullible hordes who were incapable of rational critical thought. The work of the capitalist industries had made the masses vulnerable and ripe for the domination of totalitarian dictatorships as they had witnessed in Germany in the late 1920s and early 1930s. Likewise, people were vulnerable to the dangerous, pro-capitalist products of the culture industries, because the masses were likely to soak in their political sentiments. It was out of this kind of analysis of the culture industries that the effects school in the United States began to develop its conception of the media as potentially all-powerful. McQuail argues that the early history of effects theory, from the turn of the century to the end of the 1930s was dominated by a belief that the media, 'could be immensely powerful' (1994, p. 328). Experimental researchers of the time, whose surveys were heavily influenced by social psychology, worked in an atmosphere where advertising and the political propaganda that maintained the communist regime in Russia as well as the fascist states in Italy and Germany, seemed to be extremely influential. It was in this context that the 'hypodermic' model was developed, a model that marks the popular branch of the stimulus-response idea which lay beneath most of the writing on audiences during this period. This strain of effects research argued that repressive ideas and ideologies could be injected straight into the masses and that direct and even responses could be expected from all 'mass' members as they act upon those ideas.

However, American empirical researchers at work during the 1930s began, in what was to become the second phase in effects research, to conclude that the stimulus-response model was too simplistic. It proposed an overly unmediated and direct relationship between the media and their audience and its assumption that other social structures, such as the opinions of family and peer group members, had no effect on audiences was naive. Empirically driven researchers set out on a wide range of different projects which mostly assessed the effects of the content of the media on selected audience groups. For example, researchers analysed both the use of the media to persuade and propagandize and the possible destructive effects of the media for causing delinquency and violence. Alongside this there was a growth in work on the power of political campaigns to influence voting decisions (Lazarsfeld et al., 1944; Berelson et al., 1954). The growth and development of empirical research led to refinements and developments of the research methods that were used. Increasingly new and different variables were introduced into the research so that a whole range of factors was taken into account in the kinds of effects that were measured: differences in social and psychological characteristics of those tested, and types of social and environmental factors were also considered. But it was Lazarsfeld et al.'s work on the 'primary group' (1944) that eventually persuaded his body of researchers to reject the hypodermic model. In this research conducted on political campaigns it was concluded that there was scant evidence to suggest that people actually changed their views as a result of the media's influence. The opinions of the primary group, they argued, were a more influential factor on the political choices individuals made at polling times, and this group acted as a type of 'safeguard' from direct media effects. In 1955 Katz and Lazarsfeld developed the 'two-step flow' model of communication, where they demonstrated the role of 'opinion leaders' and interpersonal relationships in the mediation of media messages. No longer could the audience be seen as a mass of atomized individuals; instead, the audience consisted of social groups, the dynamic of which influenced the interpretation of media messages.

Lazarsfeld and Katz's findings also had an influence on the work of Klapper, whose 'limited effects' work is often thought of as encapsulating the mood of researchers at the end of this second phase. In *The Effects of Mass Communication* (1960) he argued that there was a series of mediating factors which impinged on media effects: selective exposure, perception and retention of media messages, as well as group processes and norms, including factors such as opinion leadership. By the end of this second phase of effects research in the late 1950s it was concluded that the media were not the sole cause of audience effects. Instead they were considered to be one factor among others to affect change amongst audience members. Klapper's conclusions seemed to sum up the shift in thinking about audience effects: 'Mass communication *ordinarily* does not serve as a necessary and sufficient cause of audience effects, but rather functions among and through a nexus of mediating factors and influences' (1960, p. 8).The media were still seen as a significant factor in shaping audience attitudes and behaviour, but their effects were limited.

Katz later began to develop an interest in another strand of audience research that was to pose a significant challenge to the effects school as a whole. He became interested in 'functionalist' approaches, which concerned themselves with the motivational reasons why individuals seek out the media and how they utilize and interpret them. We consider the model that was later to emerge, as 'uses and gratifications', and the kind of challenge it was to bring to the dominance of effects audience analysis later in this chapter.

Some critics, however, were reluctant to abandon effects research, notwithstanding the conclusions reached by researchers such as Lazarsfeld and despite the shift towards functionalism, and in the early 1960s the tradition was revived. One reason for this was the arrival of television in the late 1950s, which as a domestic medium was thought to have important and potentially worrying social implications. Some work within this period, however, did progress to some extent away from the crude stimulus-response model which had underpinned early effects research. Instead, writers introduced a larger number of variables which were geared towards understanding longer-term media effects. For example, researchers considered the social and cultural context of media use and motivation, as well as the social factors which produce group identities such as belief systems and ideologies. Researchers of this period also attempted to analyse media production; they began to consider how media institutions packaged the content of their products before exposing them to audiences.

The period is also characterized by attention to the negative effects of the media, particularly with regard to the issue of television violence and 'copy-cat' aggression. Psychological models of learning behaviour were also used in laboratory experiments in an attempt to measure effects quantitatively. The work of Bandura and Berkowitz in the 1960s (cited in Morley, 1992) was characterized by this type of approach. They attempted to analyse how far media violence incited people to imitate aggressive behaviour. There was also a spate of state-funded effects research in the United States during the mid- to late 1960s where the connections between television violence and social and racial unrest in certain states was examined. Government reports such as the *National Commission on Causes and Prevention of Violence* found only tenuous connections between television and aggressive activities. Ultimately, they were forced to conclude that the media was one factor amongst several others in causing violent unrest. Yet the government, as Morley argues about the National Commission Report, was still reluctant to dismiss the potency of the media as an overriding influence: despite this gesture to mitigating or intervening social influences, the conviction remained that a medium saturated with violence must have some direct effects' (Morley, 1992, p. 50). Indeed, the conviction that the media must have some direct effect on audiences is staunchly held both generally in contemporary debates about the media and in particular by government officials, as documents such as the 1994 Newson Report testify. The limitations of effects research are well established within academic circles, yet, to the dismay of some, more general, popular debates seem to persist in their reluctance to explore their conclusions.

The limitations of effects research

There is a range of objections to effects research. The effects school is criticized for focusing too heavily on the power of the media to persuade, thereby ignoring a host of other possible effects. There are also problems for some researchers about the conception of the audience in effects research. The effects tradition claims neutrality and scientific objectivity with regard to methodology, yet its methods are often underpinned by loaded assumptions about which groups in society are particularly at risk from the media. As Barker and Petley argue, 'Upon whom are the media supposed to have their effects? Not the "educated" and "cultured" middle classes, who either don't watch such rubbish, or else are fully able to deal with it if they do so' (1997, p. 5). In this way effects research can be seen actually to condemn individuals for their lack of education and social and cultural awareness. By atomizing individuals, effects research fails to take the power structures of society into account. One reason for this tendency might rest with the fact that effects research is often sponsored by government and state bodies, which wish to maintain the status quo. The conclusions of administrative, as opposed to academic, projects are often tied to the ideological or political objectives of such bodies, which often means leaving structural inequalities intact (Barker and Petley, 1997, p. 4). The effects perspective on audiences is also heavily criticized by cultural studies critics, who argue that the tradition ignores a number of vital factors with regard to the ways in which audiences make sense of the media. One criticism is that as a result of its focus on the variables affecting isolated individuals such research manages to divorce subjects from their cultural environments. As a result, the activities of audiences and the means by which audiences adopt strategies to decipher textual meanings are almost entirely overlooked by the objectives of effects work. And because of its research methods, which aim to produce results which describe general audience tendencies, the rich and various responses to the media that people produce tend to become homogenized. In the poorest cases, cultural studies critics claim that effects research treats audiences as passive, gullible victims, duped by media content (Hall, 1981; Nava, 1992).

The effects school is also criticized for its approach to media content. Despite the gesture made during the 'limited effects' phase to examine the production context of different types of media, such work never really established a foothold as a worthwhile avenue of exploration. As a result, the effects tradition often lacks any sense of the power structures at work in the production of media texts. Consequently, within this position textual meanings are taken as transparent, neutral 'messages' which are unproblematically quantifiable. In similar vein, cultural studies critics argue that effects research is as reductive about media content as it is about audiences. By focusing exclusively on quantitative results based on studies measuring manifest content, it ignores the qualitative meaning-making aspects of media content to which audiences also respond.

An early challenge to the effects tradition: uses and gratifications

While 'limited effects' marked a swing away from the traditional effects school of research in the 1950s, the 'uses and gratifications' model posed the most lasting challenge to effects dominance. Katz laid some early foundations for this approach and the influence of Klapper's work on audience selection can also be seen to play a part. In 1959 in 'Mass communication research and popular culture' Katz argued that there was a need, when thinking about effects, to consider why audiences selected particular aspects of the media. People, he argued, as a result of their psychological disposition and their social surroundings, have particular uses for the media which are fulfilled through discerning what texts are suitable for satisfying their needs. Katz's findings were later to reappear in the form of the 'uses and gratifications' approach.

The central premise of the uses and gratifications model is the idea that when media consumers read advertisements, watch videos or read newspapers, they are actually gratifying already existing needs. If a media consumer wishes to find out the weather forecast, for example, by finding weather information on television teletext they have actually satisfied their need for knowledge about the day's weather.

Building on the early 'uses and gratifications' model, McQuail et al. in *Sociology of Mass Communications* (1972) suggest a number of particular audience needs which different media gratify. For example: forms of media entertainment might offer the individual audience member the opportunity to find a 'diversion' from the monotony of everyday activities such as work or household domestic tasks, thereby satisfying the individual's need for relaxation; similarly, news media might gratify the individual's desire to glean and 'survey' information about the society in which they live. McQuail's extension of the basic model shows the ways in which individual audience members use varying aspects of the media to satisfy a range of different needs.

The model marked an important shift in thinking about audiences because it reversed one of the basic premises of the effects tradition. As

Halloran argued, it prompted researchers to move 'away from the habit of thinking in terms of what the media do to people, and substitute for it the idea of what people do with the media' (quoted in Morley, 1992, p. 51). Uses and gratifications marked a realization that audiences were not empty vessels waiting to be filled with media messages. Instead, audiences selected what they wanted to see and hear because the media served a function for them and their selections gratified their needs for information. In this way the model was the first to acknowledge the idea that audiences could be active. The audience, for the first time, was seen to choose, reject and assimilate aspects of the media. Instead of being at the mercy of the messages media producers beamed down at them, audiences could overlook them. Not only that, the approach also introduced the idea that according to the different needs their psychological make-up or individual background produced, the audience could assimilate and construct meaning from the media in different ways. Indeed at this point, at face value the uses and gratifications approach seems to concur with the Birmingham Centre for Contemporary Cultural Studies (BCCCS) approach, which emphasized audience activity (see chapter 14). However, an exploration of some of the limitations of the model serves to highlight the important differences between the two approaches.

The limitations of the uses and gratifications model

The model has been criticized for not taking the content of media texts into account in its assessment of audience uses and gratifications. For example, since some media texts are structured in ways which produce preferred readings, the text's role in positioning the reader might to some extent impinge upon the gratification of audience needs. For example, does audience gratification depend upon the adoption of preferred reading oppositions, or does the resistance of certain positions produce satisfaction of audience needs? The lack of attention to media content has meant that the issue of how far media messages themselves might produce certain forms of audience activity has been neglected. The model also, as Elliot argues, assumes a straightforward, unproblematic notion of audience selection and gratification (1973, p. 21). It might be that audiences select certain media forms as a result of their comfortable knowledge of certain genres rather than as a result of selecting texts in total congruence to their 'needs' as perceived by the model. The assumption that uses are somehow evenly balanced by gratifications is therefore fundamentally flawed because the model pays insufficient attention to the complex reasons why audiences choose particular media forms.

The uses and gratifications approach has also been criticized for its 'insufficiently sociological nature' (Morley, 1992, p. 53). As an approach which focuses wholly on the personal uses and gratifications of individuals, it tends to produce a psychologistic model of human behaviour in relation to media consumption. This tends to divorce media consumers from their socio-historical context, therefore ruling out the possibility of considering how audience needs and gratifications are socially and historically produced. Its overemphasis on individuals, rather than on characteristics within and between social groups, means that the model fails to recognize the power relations which structure different types of media consumption. In this way individual activities remain atomized 'individual' responses which cannot be understood within the framework that group studies potentially provide. It is in this respect that the uses and gratifications approach differs widely from the audience research undertaken at BCCCS. As Shaun Moores argues in *Interpreting Audiences*, 'Whereas Morley, Hall and others at BCCCS were working towards a sociologically grounded semiotics of the text-reader dialogue, gratifications researchers concerned themselves with how individuals use the media as resources "to satisfy their needs and achieve their goals"' (1994, p. 7). Whereas the BCCCS work attempted to theorize how sense is made of media texts socially within the context of power relations, by analysing audience responses within social groups, gratifications researchers looked narrowly at the confines of how the media function for the individual human personality.

The dominance of effects research in the 1990s

Evidence in the late 1990s in popular debates about the media shows that overwhelmingly the effects tradition is the preferred way of conceptualizing how audiences make sense of media texts. Barker and Petley in *Ill Effects: The Media/Violence Debate* (1997) announce in their introduction that the aim of the book is to challenge the dominance of the effects tradition in late twentieth-century debates about the media. The book was compiled in response to the 1994 Newson Report, the subsequent Alton Bill, and the support for the assumptions both made about media audiences in the media's treatment of the issues surrounding their publication. The Newson Report was commissioned in response to the murder of James Bulger in 1993. At the trial the judge speculated about whether or not violent videos might have influenced the children who murdered James Bulger. In response to this the press suggested that the film *Child's Play III* had acted as a trigger, despite the lack of evidence to support their claim. Only weeks later the Alton Amendment was passed in the House of Commons, and in response to it the Criminal Justice Bill was amended to ensure that the British Board of Film Classification assessed more stringently the kind of material that was to be released on video. The Newson Report argued that the 1990s had seen a new kind of video available to young people on the market, and that such videos contained more violent and sadistic 'messages' than they had before, encouraged identification with the perpetrators of violence, and were likely to worsen because the makers of new technologies had a vested interest in profiting from them. The report also claimed that a staggering body of effects research supported current claims that heavy viewing increased aggressive behaviour, confirming the link between violence in the media and violent behaviour amongst viewers.

In the opening chapter of *Ill Effects*, 'The Newson Report: a case study in "common sense"', Barker sets out to refute the key claims of the Newson Report (Barker and Petley, 1997). He argues that when examined closely its terms are actually irrational. However, they do provide an 'easy' solution for explaining why horrific crimes occur in society. In his assessment of the assumptions that underpin the report, Barker implicitly offers a wider critique of the particular strain of the effects argument which so often manifests itself in the debates within the media at moments of moral panic.

Barker begins by questioning Newson's definition of a media text's harmful message. The report contains reference to *Child's Play III* as an example of the 'bad materials' available for the young. Yet, as Barker argues, close textual reading of the film reveals that it is actually a very moral story. The film's narrative is based around a maligned teenager who decides to devote himself to fighting the evil doll Chucky, and who wins a girlfriend through his dedication to that cause. Moreover, the film also contains liberal political sentiments because it portrays big business and its approach towards children as cynical and self-serving. In actual fact, he concludes, the claims in Newson's Report are based on inaccurate and insupportable evidence about the film's 'message' (Barker and Petley, 1997, p. 20).

Barker goes on to take Newson to task on a number of other key claims made in the report. For example, the claim that media violence causes violence to be acted out by audience members rests upon the notion that some viewers identify with those who perform 'evil acts'. Yet identification theories, Barker argues, remain theories because the idea that readers identify with characters in textual narratives is notoriously difficult, if not impossible, actually to prove. One reason for this is that identification cannot be accurately monitored: 'An observer can't look at someone, and say: "Look, s/he is identifying!" Still less can an observer look at four people, and see one as more prone to identification than the others' (Barker and Petley, 1997, p. 25). Barker also refers to previous media studies research concerning identification which he found lacking: either existing studies have tended to make taken-for-granted assumptions that identification takes place to such an extent that it has not seemed necessary to carry out direct tests; or when tests have been carried out they have revealed a total lack of evidence to prove their assertions. The problem with identification claims in the case of the Newson Report and with regard to effects work more generally is that they are assumed as 'givens', but never actually questioned or scrutinized.

Barker also questions the notion of how 'media violence' is defined in both the Newson Report and in debates about violent content in the media and its effects more generally. Barker contends that the term 'media violence' is applied to such a wide variety of media content that it has become an almost meaningless category:

> It is supposed to encompass anything from cartoons (ten-ton blocks dropped on Tom's head by Jerry, Wily Coyote plummeting down yet another mile-deep canyon); children's action adventure films (the dinosaurs of *Jurassic Park* alongside playground scuffles in *Grange Hill* and the last-reel shoot-outs in westerns); news footage from Rwanda and Bosnia; documentary footage showing the police attacking Rodney King in Los Angeles ... etc, etc. (Barker and Petley, 1997, p. 27)

In short, Barker labels the list of 'violent media' a 'useless conflation of wholly different things' (p. 27). For Barker, the notion that an audience might be so uncritical as to be blind to the differences between forms such as cartoons and documentary footage is an assertion not even worth attempting to challenge.

In their introduction to *Ill Effects* Barker and Petley also discuss some of the underlying motives for censorship campaigns. Using a number of historical case studies, for example the campaign against horror comics in the 1950s and Mary Whitehouse's sustained attacks on violence, sex and swearing in the media, they argue that behind them lurk 'interests' about how such groups believe society ought to be controlled. The 1950s rally against horror comics was less concerned with the horror comics themselves; rather, it amounted to a fight about protecting the meanings that existed at the time about 'Englishness' and childhood. In similar vein Barker argues that certain media texts have historically been labelled 'violent' or 'bad' by interested parties acting to erase politically embarrassing material or texts which contradict dominant political sentiments. For example, the television play *Scum* was banned in the 1970s because it was simply said to be 'violent'. Yet, as Barker argues, the play's portrayal of the treatment of young inmates actually amounts to an attack on the brutality of the borstal system. It was withdrawn, Barker argues, because it evoked uncomfortable questions for the Conservative Party which was campaigning to introduce the 'short, sharp shock' treatment for young offenders (Barker and Petley, 1997, p. 21). As Barker and Petley conclude, 'arguments about "effects" (and therefore, usually, censorship) do not exist in an ideological vacuum and generally tend to spring from deeply felt beliefs about how society should – and shouldn't – be organised and regulated. They are not simple "proofs of harm", in some para-medical sense' (1997, p. 4).

As we have argued, in public debates about the role of the media the effects model, albeit a crude representative of the effects tradition, still holds common currency. For academics such as Barker and Petley the challenge ahead is to continue the battle against what they see as the damaging aspects of effects research. They conclude their introduction to

Ill Effects (1997), by urging academics and students undertaking media studies to begin publicly contesting the tradition with the key findings of media researchers who have worked against it. Opposition from within media studies to the crude strain of the effects tradition and even to the academic effects model is under way.

Meanwhile, some communications researchers remain committed to the notion that the media effects tradition can offer new insights in audience research because they argue that the field has continued to evolve, particularly since the early 1980s. Jack McLeod et al. (1991) argue that the newer findings in effects research have been simplified and labelled pejoratively by academics in competing disciplines – cultural studies, for example. Such critics have been negative about effects because of their wish to assert other critical and theoretical perspectives on media audiences. As a result, effects work has been maligned and misunderstood.

It is worth examining briefly the kinds of development McLeod et al. (1991) suggest have taken place within the tradition, since the key thrust of their argument is that the effects tradition has taken on board the criticisms it has been subjected to. They argue that research has developed in five areas: expansion of effects, elaboration of media content, formulations of media production, conceptions of audience activity and developments in the process and levels of analysis. 'Taken together', they argue, 'they reveal an understanding of media effects as a multi-layered process connecting media production with outcomes of active reception by audiences' (p. 242). With regard to audience activity, McLeod et al. cite several factors, including gratifications, selectivity, attention and information-processing strategies, which they argue are now taken into account when measuring effects. Kosicki et al. (1987), for example, found three tendencies in information processing: selective scanning, the selection of certain material within time constraints; active processing, where individuals go beyond the material they are presented with according to their 'needs'; and reflective integration, which is the process whereby audience members retain certain elements of information and reflect on them with others. These factors were then tested out for their impact on political decision-making.

However, the additions to effects research discussed by McLeod et al. share some of the problems harboured by the uses and gratifications approach. There is still the tendency to overplay the idea of individual audience freedom in the tested areas, without reference to the socio-historical background of the audience. As a result, there remains no sense of how factors like attention, selectivity or audience selection strategies have been socially or historically constructed. Critical reference to theories which address the social positioning of audience members – theories of ideology, for example – are also missing. The factors which take audience activity into account still cannot offer any insight into how societal power relations structure different kinds of audience responses to media texts.

While the newer effects research might combine its studies with a number of other findings within mainstream communications research, it still lacks some of the basic theoretical premises addressed by other audience models explored in later chapters.

Suggestions for further work

What are the limitations of effects approaches to media audiences?

In what ways does the uses and gratifications approach address these limitations?

Can you identify any moments when the lasting influence of the effects tradition has been apparent within the popular press?

Further reading

Barker, Martin and Petley, Julian (eds) 1997: *Ill Effects: The Media/Violence Debate.* London: Routledge.
Moores, Shaun 1994: *Interpreting Audiences: The Ethnography of Media Consumption.* London: Sage.
Morley, David 1992: *Television, Audiences and Cultural Studies.* London: Routledge.

14
Contexts of Media Consumption

In chapter 13 we explored the main features and limitations of the two most dominant approaches to audiences this century: the 'hypodermic needle' model and the 'uses and gratifications' tradition. The former has a naive conception of media influence on the audience; its main focus is what the media do to audiences. According to this approach the media have powerful and direct effects upon a passive, inert audience. In line with this argument is the idea that the audience is vulnerable to media messages, to such an extent that they might even 'act out' the violence witnessed on, for example, television or video. On the other hand the uses and gratifications approach is about what people do with the media, but this approach is still problematic in its conception of audiences. It emphasizes the various meanings individual audience members glean from the media, but it suggests that those meanings arise from the personal and psychological differences of audience members. In this way, this approach denies the sociological location of audience members and tends to ignore the power relations which structure audience interpretations.

In this chapter we suggest that work which has shifted the focus towards incorporating what 'real' audiences say about the influence of the media in their lives provides a more fruitful way of conceptualizing audiences. What is known as a cultural studies perspective shifts attention away from the conception of the audience as an abstract 'given' which must take up the positions inscribed by the media text, to the idea that the meanings audiences produce become the focus of study in themselves. This approach attempts to understand how audience members, themselves positioned by class, gender, race or age, generate meaning in the context of the wider power relations at work in society. In this way, the cultural studies approach to audiences usefully departs from both the hypodermic and uses and gratifications approaches, neither of which attempted to grapple with the societal relations of power and subordination which impact on audience responses to the media. In order to build into their studies a firmer sense of the social and domestic scenario in which audiences consume media texts, some of the critics we examine draw upon ethnographic methods. This might involve interpreting personal accounts, letters or questionnaires or, in the anthropological sense in which ethnographic methods are used, observing or even sharing the living space of 'real' audiences for sustained periods of time in order to access information about their consumption habits and media preferences.

While this work has developed in several important directions, for the purposes of this chapter we examine three concerns within recent work in cultural studies: first, it has questioned the notion that the media have direct power to determine the meanings audiences receive from media messages; second, critics have grown increasingly concerned with the 'lived' cultural context in which media messages are consumed; and finally, there has been a growing interest in the cultural power dynamics of how technology is utilized in domestic contexts.

The developmental context of the cultural studies approach

In the late 1970s and early 1980s work undertaken at the Birmingham Centre for Contemporary Cultural Studies (BCCCS) provided the basis for cultural studies approaches to audiences. However, before outlining the influence of the key proponents of audience studies at Birmingham it is necessary to contextualize this work through a consideration of the other approaches to audiences prevalent at the time. In the 1970s the highly influential film journal *Screen* had a particular conception of the text–audience relationship. However, writers at Birmingham, for example Hall, Morley and Brunsdon, found the *Screen* conception of audiences inadequate.

Many of the British writers on the left who contributed to *Screen* were influenced by the Marxist thinker Althusser, and in particular by the premises laid out in his essay 'Ideology and ideological state apparatuses' (in Althusser, 1971). As we outline in chapter 3, Althusser argued that key institutions in society, for example education, the family and not least the media, work to maintain and reproduce the inequalities produced by the capitalist means of production. He argued that these institutions, or ISAs win consent ideologically rather than coercively. Althusser also argued that ideology acts as a representational device which interpellates or hails its subjects. These aspects of Althusser's work were powerfully attractive to film critics writing in *Screen*. By regarding the media as an ideological state apparatus, Althusser's theory offered a way of understanding how media texts secure the ideological acquiescence of audiences.

Furthermore, the idea that media texts actually lay out already ideologically prescribed locations for audience members as subjects made them
question the various ways in which film operated as a system to position
its readers.

Screen also had particular ideas about the relationship the audience had
with realism as a mode of representation. Writers such as Colin McCabe
(1974) regarded realism as an inherently bourgeois form which worked
to maintain the existing dominant order. The danger of realist texts,
according to McCabe, was that the transparency of the form offers an
illusion of allowing the viewer access to 'real' events. Viewers are therefore lulled into the idea that texts offer a transparent window with which
to look through onto events. Influenced by Althusserian Marxism,
McCabe argued that realist texts position the audience according to the
camera's ideological version of events. Yet if the form of realism acted to
seduce the viewer, the relationship realism encouraged between viewer
and the media message was perhaps even more worrying. According to
McCabe and others associated with Screen in the 1970s, viewers were also
duped into accepting the ideology of the media message as somehow
'real', obvious or inevitable. Audiences are 'positioned' by the realist text
and as a consequence they become stranded into accepting the ideological
version offered them by the text. The only means of countering the dangers of mainstream realist texts, Screen argued, was to champion the political radicalism of the avant-garde. In direct opposition to the mainstream,
avant-garde texts self-reflexively drew attention to their form as a means
of laying bare the ideological nature of their construction. This at least
allowed audiences the opportunity to recognize ideology at work and to
accept or reject its meanings.

Meanwhile, the media group at BCCCS was beginning to develop very
different ideas about how audiences interact with the media, and its
standpoint marked a radical departure from the Screen position. First, it
rejected the idea that mainstream texts necessarily impose blanket ideological domination over their readers. Rather, it regarded mainstream
texts or popular forms as a site of contest between dominant and subordinate groups. As a result, it was far less concerned with the stark
negative / positive divide between the reactionary mainstream and the
political progressiveness of avant-garde texts. Instead, the group was
interested in questioning the contradictions and the resistances which
inhere within the popular. Second, BCCCs researchers argued against the
Screen contention that texts create a singular, already inscribed position
for the passive reader to adopt. Indeed, they went so far as to argue that
it was simply impossible to predict the ideological effects of a text by
merely examining its formal characteristics. They set out to show that
readers might not necessarily accept the reader positions made available
to them within the text. The typical television viewer, for example, has
a social history and a set of attitudes and beliefs which they take with

them to the television text. While it might be possible to suggest that the programme implies a particular reading for the viewer to accept, the actual audience member is not obliged to take it up, indeed they might accept it, they may be able to substantiate part of it or they may well refute it altogether. Audience members, according to this conception, were not passive recipients of textual meaning; they were, instead, active decipherers who might produce a range of different interpretations in their consumption of the media. Critics like Brunsdon and Morley (1978) insisted that the context of consumption, the socio-economic circumstances of the 'active' reader, their education, class position and occupation as well as their cultural competencies, needed to be assessed in relation to the meanings they gleaned from texts. The cultural studies approach therefore represented a far more dynamic way of thinking about the relationship between media texts and the socially located active decoders who consume them.

The cultural studies challenge to the power of the text

Hall's encoding/decoding model

Stuart Hall's article 'Encoding/decoding' (1980) was important for two reasons: it provided the critical foundation for the BCCCS critique of the *Screen* model of text/reader relations and it formed the basis of the empirical audience studies that other researchers at Birmingham were to undertake. In his essay Hall sets out to account for the communication process in its entirety, from the moment texts are encoded in the context of industrial production, through to the consumption of texts by their audiences where they are decoded. Hall argues that media texts develop out of a range of institutional constraints, for example professional codes of practice and technological conventions which work to construct the meaning of the media text. At the opposite end of the communicative process audiences are also engaged in semiotic 'work' as they interpret the texts they receive. But as Hall suggests, the two processes are not necessarily congruent. The texts produced by the media industries are not necessarily consigned to one possible reading; rather, they are polysemic and therefore open to a host of available meanings. However, Hall stresses that a text cannot mean absolutely anything the reader wishes it to mean. Instead, he argues that the notion of polysemy must be tied to the sociological context in which texts are consumed, the power relations of which act to hone down the range of possible meanings one might produce from the text, so that readings relate back to the '"structure of dominance" in a culture' (1980, p. 134). However, Hall suggests there are other reasons why encoding and decoding cannot be seen as processes working in direct parallel. Each reader brings his or her own social history, attitudes and beliefs to bear on the reading of a text, so that the encoded meanings might well either be accepted, refuted or partly qualified, but, crucially, the reader can decode in ways that the media institution had not anticipated. Hall is careful to warn against the idea that readers read differently as a result of individual preferences. Rather, the cultural competencies and creative resources they might draw upon in order to arrive at possible readings are socially and culturally produced. Sociological factors, one's class position, gender, race, age, and so on shape the textual reading the reader might make.

Hall argues that there are three decodings or possible positions that readers might produce: dominant, negotiated and oppositional. The dominant or preferred reading is the position which accepts the encoding inscribed by the media. People who make oppositional readings directly contest the text's message, recognizing, for example, 'every mention of the "national interest" as "class interest"' (Hall, 1980, p. 138). The negotiated reading, however, which Hall claims is the most frequently taken up by audience members, lies somewhere between the dominant and the oppositional positions. Readers who make negotiated readings don't merely accept dominant readings, but nor do they completely reject them either. They might, for example, find that the dominant version does not concur with their own experiences. Hall uses the example of the worker who might accept the message from government and factory owner to 'tighten the nation's belt', but who at the local level still strikes for the right to more pay. What was so important about Hall's contribution to audience studies in 'Encoding / decoding' was the shift he generated from the analysis of the text to the more complex, more dynamic relationship between text and reader: meaning can never reside in the text alone; rather, it lies in the interchange between reader and text and the negotiated readings that result. However, Hall's three positions were 'hypothetical' because they were drawn up without recourse to any kind of empirical evidence. The premises of his essay therefore cried out for empirical grounding. The *Nationwide* projects (Brunsdon and Morley, 1978; Morley, 1980a) which were later undertaken at Birmingham attempted to test out the three positions using textual studies of television and actual responses from its viewers.

The Nationwide *studies*

The first research project which attempted to flesh out the encoding / decoding model was Charlotte Brunsdon and David Morley's monograph *Everyday Television: Nationwide* (1978). The book was largely given over to semiotic analysis of the current affairs programme *Nationwide*. It investigated areas such as the structure and arrangement of interviews and the presentation of current affairs topics. Yet for Brunsdon and Morley textual analysis only acted as a yardstick against which audience responses were to be measured; their semiotic findings, they argued, would later be modified in the light of audience responses to the programme. The first *Nationwide* project, then, clearly indicated the shift of critical attention from text to audiences. This first monograph, however, really anticipated the need for a larger audience study, which was to be conducted by Morley in *The Nationwide Audience* (1980a).

This next project signalled the shift to investigating the decodings audiences produced from their viewing of *Nationwide*. Morley's main objective was to test out how far audience members accepted *Nationwide's* preferred reading position. However, there were questions which underpinned his prime aim: Morley wanted to find out if there would be a link between the readings audience members produced and their socio-economic background; he was also interested in asking how far cultural factors such as class, gender and race impacted on consumption practices.

Morley convened twenty-nine audience groups of managers, students and trade-union members who were tested collectively so that he could examine the consensus response of, for example, trade-unionists. The groups saw editions of *Nationwide*, some of which had already been subject to analysis in *Everyday Television*. Respondents were then asked to share their reactions. Morley analysed the data he had managed to glean from the group interviews, dividing the material by probing respondents' views of the ideological stance of the programme as well as the style in which current affairs were being presented.

Perhaps the most important aspect of Morley's findings was the discovery that the socio-economic background of the respondent did not necessarily determine their readings. In fact, respondents who shared similar backgrounds sometimes produced different responses. He also found that other cultural frameworks and institutions, for example affiliation to institutions such as trade unions as well as the impact of informational sources such as the press, worked to shape audience responses to the text. For example, he found that the three reading positions simply couldn't accommodate the black students he interviewed. These students found very little in *Nationwide* to engage with; in fact, they declined to respond at all to the text and as a result their responses fell outside the three dominant positions. But that wasn't the only limitation Morley found in the reading positions laid out in the encoding/decoding model. He also found that while the managers broadly affirmed the ideological sentiments of *Nationwide*, they were disparaging about the populist presentational style of the programme. The shop stewards he interviewed, however, were comfortable with the programme's populist production values, but voiced dissatisfaction with what they saw as its favourable treatment of management. As Shaun Moores argues, this type of difference between cultural ideas about taste within the groups could not be accounted for within the confines of Hall's model (1994, p. 21). Yet clearly such findings do reveal important information about the relationship between audience decoding and class habitus (see chapter 17).

Morley was conscious that the workplace and the home as audience research sites had been missing from his *The Nationwide Audience*, and he was aware that the next stage in investigating contexts of consumption must somehow focus on the lived arenas in which media texts are actually consumed. Indeed, several of the shortcomings of *The Nationwide Audience* were to indicate the need for a book like his own *Family Television* (1986). However, in the final analysis Morley's work heralded one of the first empirical studies of the dynamic, interdiscursive relationship between text and reader, at a point in time when other schools of thought still believed that a text's formal features determined meaning for the viewer. His study was also to prove foundational for other audience researchers in the field. Moreover, Morley's work did affirm Hall's chief contention that audience members are not blank tablets of stone onto which the media write their messages – in fact, quite the reverse. Morley's work established empirically that meaning can never wholly reside in texts alone; rather, meaning lies within the readings that are produced out of the negotiation that takes place between text and reader. The notion that the media have the power to determine meaning had indeed been challenged.

The cultural studies turn to 'lived' contexts of consumption

Whereas previous studies had moved from analysing wider societal class relations and their impact on both textual meaning and audience decodings, the audience research projects that were to follow shifted their central focus. Post-1980 researchers interested in investigating consumption as a cultural entity began to recognize that the analysis of media readings offered only a partial picture: cultural consumption must also be about the context within which those readings are made. Critics therefore began to develop an interest in getting as close as they possibly could to the everyday, mundane perspectives that actual viewers inhabit as they consume. Several writers drew upon ethnographic methods as a means of accessing the actual location, as well as the interpersonal relations which structure media reception. However, several of the studies, for example work by Dorothy Hobson (1980) and David Morley (1986) were still concerned with the ways in which wider power relations impacted on how audiences made sense of the media. Their work analysed the ways in which the social order impacted on the dynamics of situational, lived contexts of consumption. Work in this period was also characterized by a move away from looking only at current affairs programmes to examining the reception of popular fictional programming which has, on the whole, traditionally attracted female audiences. This came partly as a response to feminist protest against the concept of the 'public sphere', which tends to conceive the personal and domestic as private issues which should be privately resolved (see chapter 18). Feminists, however, had vested interests in making the personal political. It is not surprising, therefore, that some of the work characterizing this period was informed by feminist concerns.

Another of the early ethnographies of domestic television consumption was 'The social uses of television' (1980) by James Lull. With his team of researchers, Lull observed more than two hundred American families and their day-to-day use of television across a three-year time span. His data enabled him to compile an inventory of the different ways television was utilized by his participants: it provided background companionship while family members did household tasks; its programming schedule acted as a structuring principle around which to organize the domestic routine; its use was recognized as a way of diverting family members, such as grandparents and children, when participants preferred to do other activities; and it also became the catalyst for interpersonal battles over who would control it – it was often the father. (Interestingly, in Lull's later study, *Inside Family Viewing: Ethnographic Research on Television's Audiences* (1990), he found that children often held the seat of power when it came to programme choices.) One of the weaknesses of this project, however, was that it lacked the theoretical underpinning provided by the Marxist and feminist approaches which informed the cultural studies work at Birmingham. Unfortunately, Lull's conclusions therefore lack any theoretical connection to the structural power relations that frame his findings.

Dorothy Hobson's ethnographic study 'Housewives and the mass media' (1980) set out to explore what the media meant for working-class women situated in a domestic context as housewives. Hobson, like Brunsdon and Morley, had also been a postgraduate student at Birmingham, but she had studied as part of its 'Women's Studies Group'. As a feminist, she theorized the family as an oppressive institution for women. Within the working-class home, women are chiefly responsible for unpaid labour such as childcare and housework, forms of labour which are often not even recognized as constituting 'real' work. For the women Hobson studied, the home was primarily defined as a sphere of work, where they frequently felt a sense of loneliness and isolation.

Hobson visited several housewives' homes, and recorded the conversations she had with the women about the role of both radio and television in their lives. The radio acted as an accompaniment to housework. Housework is often described as cyclical, ongoing and never finally accomplished, so for these women the radio gave structure to a formless day: 'In terms of the "structurelessness" of the experience of housework, the time boundaries provided by radio are important in the women's own division of their time' (Hobson, 1980, p. 105). Radio One was particularly popular amongst the women Hobson studied and the disc jockeys (DJs) played an important role as company in the context of a lonely day. But more than that, they often provided the women with a male voice that they utilized in other ways, seen here in this response by one of the women: 'I like Radio 1. Tony Blackburn. I think he's corny but I think he's good. Dave Lee Travis I like and Noel Edmonds. Noel Edmonds, I think he's absolutely fantastic' (quoted in Hobson, 1980, p. 106). As Hobson argues, 'my *reading* of the role of the DJs is that they play the role of a safe, though definitely sexually attractive man, in the lives of the women' (p. 107). The radio therefore provided the women with strategies for coping with the isolation of their positions as housewives.

Hobson's article is attentive to the text as well as to the ways audiences use them. She points to the way in which Radio One operated ideologically to affirm the women's roles as housewives, thereby affirming their collective role in isolation. The DJs play a part in this ideological work through their 'reinforcement of the dominant ideology of domesticity' (p. 108). One of the ways in which they are able to do this is through the talk between the music. The political perspective of Tony Blackburn, for example, is, for Hobson, blatantly conservative:

> if by chance they happen to hear what Tony Blackburn has to say, they will be subjected to an onslaught of chatter which definitely reinforces the ideology of the sexual division of labour and places women firmly in their 'correct' place – in the home … The 'working man', strikers, punk rockers, women involved in divorce actions (in the wake of his recent divorce) all warrant criticism from him. Women who are playing their traditional role as housewives and mothers constantly earn praise from him. (1980, p. 108)

It was fortunate, therefore, Hobson asserts, that the women did not concentrate fully on the DJs: the radio acted only as a background to other household activities.

In her work on television consumption, Hobson found among the women she interviewed that they had particular taste preferences, which manifested themselves along generic lines. The women enjoyed fictional programmes which dealt with the emotional or which were dramatized in contexts with which they felt they could relate, such as the home, for instance soap operas; or they enjoyed programmes which were based on fantasy where they felt they might escape their daily routines. Conversely, they often expressed dislike for programmes that they defined as masculine, such as current affairs programmes, the news or documentaries.

Unlike Lull, whose work is open to the criticism that it lacks a theoretical underpinning, Hobson's work was firmly situated in the critical frameworks established at Birmingham. These women's uses of the media, Hobson argues, are not made by free-standing individuals; rather, they must be understood in the context of their social location as gendered subjects who live in particular circumstances because of their class position. The lived contexts in which they utilize their meaning are embedded within the wider ideologies at large in society.

Yet while Hobson's work might be seen to have revealed compliant female subjects in the home, other ethnographic studies have found acts of resistance in the consumption of popular forms. Janice Radway's book *Reading the Romance: Women, Patriarchy and Popular Literature* (1987) about women's consumption of romantic fiction in the home is worth mentioning here. Radway used ethnography in order to research the consumption patterns of a female reading group from Smithton, Ohio. While Radway interviewed her sample group with the view to investigating their textual preferences, she found that it was the act of reading itself which was so significant for them. The context of the home was precisely that in which the pressures of family and domestic life were most urgent, yet Radway found that the activity of reading within this context acted as a type of resistance. She quotes the thoughts of Dot, the local bookstore owner and resident expert adviser to the 'Smithton women': '"Hey" they say, "this is what I want to do and I'm gonna do it. This is for me. I'm doing for you all the time. Now leave me, just leave me alone. Let me have my time, my space. Let me do what I want to do."' Radway's findings brought her to conclude that a text-based approach would miss the fact that romance reading can be a resistant activity. As she argues, 'the significance of the act of reading itself might, under some conditions, contradict, undercut, or qualify the significance of producing a particular kind of story' (1987, p. 210).

The work of both Hobson and Radway anticipates to a certain extent some of the themes of Morley's book *Family Television* (1986), for which he individually interviewed each member of eighteen white, working-class to lower-middle-class families. But whereas in *The Nationwide Audience* (1980a) he had analysed the different decodings of programme contents, his focus shifted now to a consideration of the domestic context as the framework of study and to the various uses of television within the power relations of the family. Morley found that no matter what the ideological content of programmes, watching television is embedded within the power relations of the domestic context and gives rise to a number of different activities, all of which involve television, though not always directly. Indeed, television was used in a variety of ways: as a means of generating discussion about television topics and characters both at home and in the workplace; as a way of structuring time; as a conflict deflector; or as a bartering device for a parent to use with a child. In these ways his findings relate to Radway's Smithton women who read their novels more as a means of giving time to themselves as opposed to reading them for their love of romance fiction. Like the Smithton women, the family members Morley studied selected programmes based on the activities which took place as a result of the power relations in the home. As a consequence, programme selection in many cases did not relate to the ideological sentiments of a programme, nor did it depend on the enjoyment of certain programmes. In many cases, watching took place as a result of the familial circumstances and power play within the domestic context. The responses Morley received about gender and viewing styles illustrates his point.

Morley foregrounds his chapter 'Television and gender' with the assertion that the different forms of gendered behaviour he found in relation to television are the result of social construction, rather than of essential biological differences. As a result of societal conventions about gender, Morley argues that men and women define the home differently: men regard home as a place of relaxation and leisure, women see it, even if in full time paid work outside it, as a second workplace where housework is done. These different conceptions of the home impact directly on the viewing practices of men and women: 'men state a clear preference for viewing attentively, in silence, without interruption, "in order not to miss anything" … many women feel that just to watch television without doing anything else at the same time would be an indefensible waste of time, given their sense of their domestic obligations' (1986, p. 150). For men, keeping an attentive gaze was something they felt able to do, whereas women's watching practices were far more partial and distracted. This example illustrates that the link between the text and how audiences consume cannot be divorced from a consideration of how audiences are positioned within the domestic context.

However, there are potential problems with *Family Television*. As Mark Jancovich argues, while Morley is right to claim that the meaning of television viewing cannot merely be reduced to their decodings as a result of focusing wholly on the domestic context as a framework, he is guilty of ignoring textual decoding altogether. As a consequence, 'Morley tends to lose sight of the textual processes through which television establishes social, cultural and political agendas' (Jancovich, 1992, p. 136). As a result of not testing out the decodings family members might have made of particular programmes, Morley is unable to investigate the ways in which family roles are constructed by particular media texts. Furthermore, in ruling out the part media institutions play in their production of media texts, he neglects the wider framework of domination which in some way must also impact on how audiences make sense of media texts within the domestic context.

The power relations of media reception and technology

Woman: …I don't get the chance to use the automatic control. I leave that to him. It is aggravating, because I can be watching something and all of a sudden he turns it over to get the football result.

Daughter: The control's always next to Dad's chair. It doesn't come away when Dad's here. It stays right there. (Morley, 1986, p. 149)

Since *Family Television* a number of ethnographers have examined the power dynamics of how technology is used in lived cultural contexts. Where technology is concerned, issues of class, age and gender are factors which inevitably impinge on the different interpretations and uses of technology. Morley's *Family Television*, for example, touches on the power relations of who commands authority of the television remote control. In most situations the father claimed ownership to this, and some of the women's and children's responses mentioned above testify to the frustration this can create in the home. Shaun Moores's oral history study of the introduction of radio into the domestic environment during the 1920s and 1930s charts the historical evolution of the insertion of broadcasting technology within domestic power relations. In this sense, his material acts as an interesting precursor for later work. As Moores argues, 'Broadcasting's entry into the home appears to have been marked by quite deep social divisions between household members' (1994, p. 77). Moores found that it was mostly young men who built radio transmitters out of do-it-yourself kits and male household members tended to dominate the process of listening too. Early radios, as Moores describes, were not advanced enough to transmit clearly to a collective group. Instead, headphones were used by a single receiver, usually male. As a result, female partners often found themselves out in the cold, as this response testifies:

Question: Did the set have headphones?
  Answer: Oh yes, only one person could listen at a time.
Question: Who had first choice?
  Answer: My father of course. I remember he used to listen to the news with the earphones on. I don't think we ever heard the news – my father always got the earphones. Well, he was in charge, you see. What he said went. (Moores, 1993, p. 79)

As Moores argues, his findings historically anticipate the power plays over media technologies found by Morley in *Family Television* as well as those found in studies by writers such as Anne Gray, to whom we now turn. In each instance the arrival of the new technology is subject to the gendered power relations already embedded within the domestic context.

In *Video Playtime* (1992) Anne Gray explores women's perceptions of the role of the VCR in their domestic lives in terms both of the use of video technology and of the programmes and films they gained access to as a result. Gray interviewed a sample of thirty women from mixed class backgrounds in the mid-1980s. She found that the women she interviewed regarded, sometimes quite unconsciously, the technology in their homes as gender-divided. For example, when Gray asked her interviewees to colour-code the tasks, as well as the technology required to fulfil them, from blue to pink she found quite substantial evidence to suggest that technology was gender-patterned: certain gadgets were blue, some were lilac and others firmly pink. In a particular respondent's case only one item in the kitchen qualified as blue: '"I suppose that mostly it's [kitchen] pink ... I mean he would work the dishwasher and the washing machine, but I'd have to give him specific instructions. The coffee percolator can be blue – he'll often make the coffee after a meal"' (quoted in Gray, 1992, p. 47). Yet the gendered meanings of domestic technology, which Gray found extended to media technology such as the VCR, were intimately connected to the gendered technical competencies which made men feel more comfortable in handling 'blue' objects, and vice versa. With regard to the VCR, many of the women Gray interviewed admitted only a partial knowledge about how to operate it, preferring instead to leave working the video timer to their male partners.

What is interesting about Gray's findings are the ways in which different technological competencies are clearly valued by the women. For example, most of the women she interviewed had an intimate knowledge of working out the complexities of white goods, such as washing machines and sewing machines. However, these kinds of goods were not classified by the women as constituting what they would define as technology. Instead they regarded the knowledgeable use of blue goods as more intelligent, and since they themselves in several cases couldn't work aspects of the video, saw themselves as unintelligent or inadequate. Yet conversely, when the men in the households were unable to operate white goods the women chose not to categorize them as stupid or incompetent. One woman, for example, excused her husband for not being able to operate the washing machine, arguing that he didn't have the time.

Gray is at pains to stress that no technology is either essentially masculine or feminine; rather, technologies become gendered through their social and cultural uses. However, not all the women Gray interviewed could be categorized as ideologically complicit. Often, their disinclination to learn how to operate blue goods was a carefully calculated response. Indeed some of the women deliberately harboured a lack of enthusiasm about learning how to operate the video timer, precisely as an act of resistance against taking on more household chores. As two of her '"calculated ignorance" strategists' remarked: '"I really don't want to be taught how to do it, really deep down, I know that, because if so it will be my job to deal with it ... that's the truth" ... "No I'm not going to try. No. Once I learned how to put a plug on, now there's nobody else puts a plug on in this house but me ... so (laugh) there's method in my madness, oh yes"' (Gray, 1992, p. 168). Yet despite these pockets of resistance, Gray concludes that it was women who lived in working-class households who experienced the most marked gendered power imbalances within the home.

Cultural studies and consumption

Cultural studies work on audiences usefully challenges a number of previously held assumptions about the relationship audiences have with the media. The idea that the readings audiences made of texts could be arrived at by analysing their formal features was rejected as over-deterministic. Further, cultural studies critics recognized that the role of the media could not be wholly understood without some investigation into the lived household contexts in which consumption takes place. And finally, cultural studies researchers found that the dynamics of inter-personal media reception had a profound effect on how technology was consumed in the home. Since the mid-1980s, however, the move towards the relative autonomy of audiences to determine meaning in cultural studies has spawned a large proliferation of ethnographic studies (see, for example, Nava and Nava, 1992; Willis, 1990; Seiter et al., 1989; Gillespie, 1995). These studies foreground the critical and creative potential of 'ordinary' audiences. For example in 'Discriminating or duped? Young people as consumers of advertising/art' (1992) Mica Nava and Orson Nava argue that young people, far from being the mindless dupes media representations would have us believe, often make sophisticated, complex readings of the aesthetic dimension of today's television advertising. Indeed, they argue, young people often disregard the marketing function of advertisements, choosing instead to focus only on the pleasure-giving aesthetic dimension of advertising images. Far from being duped by capitalism, then, young people come to view adverts in much the same way as they would any other cultural product. This study, and others like it, challenge the damaging pessimism of the Frankfurt School which saw audiences, often comprised of ordinary consumers, as being duped by a capitalist media. As such, the political importance of these studies cannot be underestimated because they foreground the critical and dis-criminating voices of groups which are so often marginalized in public life – women, young working-class people and people of black and Asian descent. They challenge the idea that those who consume are necessarily duped by the media, and they reveal the often quite sophisticated critical responses audiences make of media texts. They also counter the negative idea that consumption, so often conceived as a female activity, is a trivial, naive cultural practice.

However, ethnographic audience studies have also been attacked, in the main by political economy critics. One of the arguments levelled against such work is that audience studies play into the hands of the media industries by providing them with invaluable market research – they might even be accused of colluding with the capitalist media. Aligned to this point, political economists argue that there is a tendency within such studies to celebrate and overread elements of resistance in consumption. The search for progressive reading practices tends to offer the impression that there are no problems with the relationship between the capitalist media and their audiences because 'critical consumers' are catered for by media texts which serve their tastes and preferences. The problem is that the structures of domination, both political and economic, which mould how the media serve their citizens are therefore left intact by the findings of cultural studies audience research. Indeed, the focus on the attempt to find authenticity and resistance in 'real audiences' has deflected attention away from the material, economic factors which serve to oppress the groups under study. In short, political economists argue that audience research privileges consumption at the expense of production. As a result, the political and economic factors which shape the institutional and structural context in which the cultural practices of consumption take place are neglected. As Graham Murdock argues:

> cultural studies has made a substantial contribution to research on practices of consumption … The problem is that these practices – of sense making, interpretation and expression – are seen as embedded in and sustained by the immediate contexts of action. There is no account of how localized situations are themselves shaped in fundamental but particular ways, by broader, underlying, social and economic dynamics. (Murdock, 1997, p. 90)

In similar vein, Jim McGuigan in *Cultural Populism* (1992) offers a critique of Nava and Nava's article 'Discriminating or duped'. While McGuigan concedes that Nava and Nava are right to challenge a 'purely manipulative theory of advertising', their study is ultimately one-dimensional, since it ignores, 'the circulation of commodities, their sensuous aspects and historical contexts, mediated by advertising and marketing' (McGuigan, 1992, p. 122). For McGuigan, the lack of attention to the economic practices which frame and organize the advertising industry makes this kind of analysis at best partial and at worst inadequate.

Ellen Seiter argues that the mistake made by the political economy approach in its assessment of audience ethnographies is that it fails to recognize their importance. As a result, political economists privilege production at the expense of consumption, thereby ignoring a whole dimension of cultural life. Seiter also objects to the 'masculinist orientation' of political economy work, which tends to keep intact the idea that 'consumption is feminine and bad, production is masculine and good' (Seiter et al., 1989, p. 8). Instead, Seiter calls for a dissolution of the staunch production / consumption divide. One way forward is surely to place audience studies within a political economy framework, thereby advocating a multi-dimensional method of analysis.

Suggestions for further work

List the ways in which a cultural studies approach to audiences may differ from earlier models of media analysis.

Note down Hall's three reader positions outlined in the encoding/decoding model. Watch an edition of your local television news, consider each report in turn and note if your viewer position shifts at any point.

Further reading

Gray, Anne 1992: *Video Playtime: The Gendering of a Leisure Technology*. London: Routledge.

Hall, Stuart 1980: Encoding/decoding in the television discourse. In Stuart Hall et al. (eds), *Culture, Media, Language*. London: Hutchinson.

Lull, James 1990: *Inside Family Viewing*. London: Routledge.

Morley, David 1980a: *The Nationwide Audience*. London: British Film Institute.

Morley, David 1986: *Family Television*. London: Comedia.

15
Minority Audiences and the Media

This chapter explores what is meant by the term minority and discusses the ways in which a variety of minority audiences interact with the media. We consider how minority or marginalized groups use, in particular, mainstream media texts, and how these audiences have found potentially positive images within the most unlikely contexts. The work we draw upon considers black women, gay men and lesbians as minority consumers of the media. Alongside this we argue that fans as consumers of media texts may also be labelled minority.

What do we mean by minority?

As Danny Saunders warns (in O'Sullivan et al., 1994), it can be very misleading simply to identify minorities numerically. He argues that a minority is 'a group that is associated with a lack of power' (1994, p. 182). In relation to the media this manifests itself in a number of significant ways. For example, the lack of opportunities for members of minorities to gain employment within the media industries. Also, and arguably linked to the previous point, the inability of minorities to control or influence images of themselves produced and circulated by the media. More recently, however, minority groups have been seen to consume the media produced by others in alternative or challenging ways.

In relation to these definitions, it is also possible to consider that numerically large groups of media consumers, such as women, constitute a minority due to their lack of social power. The focus of this chapter is a consideration of how minority consumption of the media has been investigated and theorized within media and cultural studies. In relation to this work it is important to remember that media texts are polysemic, which means that they are capable of signifying a variety of meanings. With this fact in mind it is possible to argue that minority audiences can therefore, on occasion and in specific circumstances, decode media texts in a variety of different ways due to their economic, social and cultural positions within society.

Black women as cultural readers

The sub-title for this section is taken from an influential article by Jacqueline Bobo, 'The Color Purple: black women as cultural readers' (1988). In this piece Bobo reveals how a specific text, Steven Spielberg's film of Alice Walker's novel The Color Purple, has been read differently by various sections of the American black community. She outlines the mainly negative responses the film elicited from some journalists and critics, detailing that many argued that the film failed to examine the question of class; that it portrayed black men as harsh and brutal; and that it represented black people as sexually wanton and irresponsible. This negative response to the film, she explains, culminated in the black activist group, the Coalition Against Black Exploitation picketing its première in Los Angeles. Bobo argues that even though there had been such a visible negative reaction to the film, her own research found that it elicited positive reactions from many black women. The main aim of her article is to show how 'a specific audience creates meaning from a mainstream text and uses the reconstructed meaning from a mainstream text to empower themselves and their social group' (p. 93). Bobo evokes the encoding / decoding model developed by Stuart Hall (1980) which was closely associated with some of the most influential work undertaken at the Birmingham Centre for Contemporary Cultural Studies (BCCCS). Bobo argues that black women's reading of the film The Color Purple is, due to the cultural experiences and knowledge they bring to the text, oppositional. She argues that:

> An audience member from a marginalized group (people of color, the poor and so on) has an oppositional stance as they participate in mainstream media. The motivation for this counter-reception is that we understand that mainstream media has never rendered our segment of the population faithfully ... as readers of mainstream texts, we have learned to ferret out the beneficial and put up blinders against the rest. (1988, p. 96)

In doing this it is possible to argue that viewers therefore read 'against the grain' of mainstream texts, manipulating through their reading the possible meanings that best reflect their own interests. This, in turn, highlights the fact that the meanings of texts cannot simply be read off from an analysis of their formal features, without any consideration of the decoding process undertaken by an audience.

Bobo claims that black women, because of their historical and cultural background and experiences, have a different perspective from other viewers of the film. She argues that this is highlighted by the different responses she received, when undertaking research into this area, from black women in relation to *The Color Purple* compared to the negative reactions of predominantly male critics. Bobo clearly links this response to what she terms the cultural competences of black women readers, connecting their response to the film with their consumption of other texts which focus on the experiences of black women, such as those by writers Terry McMillan, Toni Morrison and Alice Walker. As cultural consumers, they are receptive to works such as these because they allow them to engage positively with examples of work 'more in keeping with their experiences' (Bobo, 1988, p. 103). This type of analysis is marked by its focus on the value of the reader's response rather than any inherent cultural value within the text. Here, the context in which consumption takes place clearly influences the responses a text draws from a reader which are based on their actual life experiences.

Elsewhere, and in a similar vein, Bobo has argued more generally that black audiences tend to seek out the elements of mainstream texts that link with their own lives (1992). When this happens the audience does not wholeheartedly take on the values of the text they are viewing; rather, they use aspects of the text that relate to their own needs and desires. She argues that the resistance black people have to make against the attraction of mainstream texts reflects wider struggles they have in society:

> For black audiences the struggle to resist the pull of certain works is the same struggle waged against domination and oppression in everyday life. Their work of resistance involves acknowledging that mainstream works will at some point present caricatures of Black people's lives and balancing that knowledge with their more personal responses to the parts of the films that resonate with other elements of their lives. (1992, p. 70)

It is therefore possible to argue that the readings certain social groups make of texts are informed or shaped by their 'history, both media and cultural, and by the individuals' social affiliations such as race, class, gender and so on' (Bobo, 1988, p. 103). The desire in minority audiences to find texts that show or reflect their experiences in some way can lead them to read media products in ways that are at odds with the way they are decoded and understood by other groups. Of course, this may occur for a wide range of marginalized groups within any society. For example, in the context of Britain, Ashwari Sharma makes similar observations about his family's experiences of watching British television programmes set in India, such as *The Jewel in the Crown*: 'Our identification is with the Asian characters and environment, and not with the main white stars: a form of oppositional reading' (1990, p. 64). Clearly, these sorts of responses to mainstream texts show that it is dangerous ever to suppose that there is one simple interpretation. Indeed, fully to comprehend textual meaning, some sort of engagement with audiences and their position within society must be utilized.

Sexual minorities and the media

The definition of 'minority', as we have already indicated, is neither simple nor straightforward. Larry Gross (1989) makes a strong distinction between sexual minorities (lesbians and gay men) and what he terms 'traditional' racial and ethnic minorities (p. 130). He argues that his distinction is based on two important factors: first, members of sexual minorities are self-identified and, second, members of sexual minorities are not automatically easily identified by others. Significantly, Gross argues that lesbians and gay men are often perceived as a threat to the 'natural order' of things and the so-called normality of mainstream society. This conception of sexual minorities as a threat, according to Gross, in turn means that they are represented within the media in particular ways. These representations have significant effects on the way both society at large thinks about these groups and the ways in which members of minority groups think about themselves. According to Gross, most representations of gay people within mainstream texts are not constructed to be consumed by gay audiences; rather, they are constructed in ways which serve mainstream heterosexual audiences. This impacts upon the types of images used, for example, in the Hollywood movie *JFK* (1991): the conspirators who plotted to kill Kennedy are clearly visually encoded as gay, whilst justice is personified by the clearly heterosexual Jim Garrison (Kevin Costner). This type of representation reflects Gross's argument that such images position audiences to feel a degree of negativity towards these minority groups, and that this leads to what he terms 'symbolic annihilation'. The lack of everyday and ordinary images of gay people within the media means that non-gay audiences receive images that continually reinforce many of the negative ideas and beliefs that are in circulation within society. In this way, any positivity mainstream audiences may have is systematically destroyed through a continual bombardment of negative media representations.

Related to these points, Gross also argues that, as a self-identifying minority, media images are of vital importance to gay men and lesbians. They work to socialize the members of a society with regard to their sexuality and what the perceived normalcy of that society is. As Gross puts it: 'In the absence of adequate information in their immediate environment, most people, gay or straight, have little choice other than to accept the narrow and negative stereotypes they encounter as being representative of gay people' (1989, p. 135). He goes on to argue that the 'normal' gay character is something that is generally missing from mainstream media texts. For him, if gay characters are present they are most likely to appear as a plot device designed to allow space for an exploration of their supposed deviance and threat to the moral order. Any positivity that may be connected to an exploration of these issues is usually countered by these characters being the subject of ridicule or the victims of physical violence. Here, Gross touches on a very important point. If certain social groups are continually represented in a negative way, does this have a significant effect on the way that that group sees itself and the way that others see it? For Gross, the continually negative representations of gay people in the media is due to the fact that positive and 'normal' images may offer challenges to generally held assumptions about people's sexuality. Non-stereotypical images may prove a threat to the mainstream because they undermine 'the unquestioned normalcy of the status quo' (1989, p. 137) and in turn throw open alternatives to those members of society who had previously never considered the choices that may be open to them.

However, the idea that seemingly negative images are always interpreted in that way by gay members of an audience can be challenged. Gay film critic Robin Wood, in his article 'The Incoherent Text: Narrative in the '70s' (1981), points out that the films *American Gigolo* (1980) and *Cruising* (1980) both played in the same Toronto cinema complex, but that only the latter was the object of protests by gay activists. However, he argues that for him *American Gigolo* was by far the more offensive. In the film:

> gayness appears peripheral, the film's homophobia being so muted as to have passed largely unnoticed ... Nonetheless, homophobia is central to *American Gigolo*. It was playing without protest in the same Toronto theatre complex where gay activists were picketing *Cruising*. I find it incomparably the more offensive of the two films, and would argue that its social effect is probably far more harmful, being covert and insidious. The entire progress of the protagonist, Julian (Richard Gere), is posited on the simple identification of gayness with degradation. (1981, p. 36)

Interestingly, whilst Wood's comments about *American Gigolo* echo some of Gross's argument about the impact of negative images of gay people, he goes on to suggest that *Cruising*, a film roundly condemned by many gay activists as negatively representing gay lifestyles, may in fact be read as more challenging. Indeed, he claims that *Cruising* is 'radical and subversive' (1981, p. 38), basing his argument upon the fact that the narrative is incoherent, therefore it cannot be seen simply to carry negative meanings; rather, it allows a more radical interpretation. This point of view again draws us back to the argument that whilst texts on one level create certain meanings for some members of the audience, it does not follow that everyone's interpretation will be uniform. In the case of *Cruising* divergent readings were clearly being made by those gay activists protesting against the film being shown and by the gay critic Wood, who championed the film's radical potential.

Star images and gay men

Richard Dyer's influential chapter on Judy Garland in his book *Heavenly Bodies* (1986) offers an analysis of the ways in which the image and persona of film star Judy Garland have been appropriated and read in particular ways by gay audiences. These readings are different from those made by mainstream audiences and, arguably, the intentions of those involved in the industries that produce those images. Dyer's argument begins by stating that his attempts at interpreting Garland's star image and its meanings for male gay audiences are historically and (sub)culturally specific. This is reflected by the fact that he, for the most part, concentrates on reading Garland post-1950 when she was sacked by the Hollywood studio Metro Goldwyn Mayer. Dyer argues that the fact that she was sacked, combined with her much publicized suicide attempt, made possible 'a reading of Garland as having a special relationship to suffering, ordinariness, normality, and it is this relationship that structures much of the gay reading of Garland' (p. 143). Garland's actual links with gay audiences are noted by Dyer as a way for gay men openly to identify or display their sexuality. He argues that many accounts of Garland's stage performances in the post-1950 period mention the fact that gay men were openly present in the audience. It was this attachment to the Garland image that for many 'constituted a kind of going public or coming out before the emergence of gay liberationist politics' (p. 145). Dyer quotes from a letter he received from a man who attended a Garland concert in Nottingham which reflects this point: 'the fact that we had gathered to see Garland gave us permission to be gay in public for once' (p. 145).

Responses such as these reveal how marginalized groups are able to use the images created in sources such as the media for their own needs. The fact that the image of a performer can come to mean different things for different members of an audience demonstrates the polysemic nature of any film star's persona and the images of them in circulation. It is certainly true to say that not all of Garland's 1950s audiences would have been using her persona in the way outlined by Dyer, thus creating a number of different and competing interpretations and uses of the Judy Garland image.

The importance of historical specificity to any reading of the media is further explored by Dyer who details the ways in which the interpretations and uses that gay men have made of Garland's star image have undergone change over time. He notes a shift from what he terms a reading of Garland as a 'loser fighting back' towards an admiration for her 'indomitable spirit, not her self-destructive tendencies' (p. 148). This, he suggests, reflects a change in the possible ways in which gay men see themselves, partly due to the positive influence of the gay liberation movement on their self-confidence, and how they then interpreted the Garland image.

So why are images of Garland and her star persona important within gay men's culture? Dyer identifies three elements which answer this question. First, the idea of ordinariness; this is an important touchstone because gay men are brought up within mainstream culture to be ordinary, within a society where being gay is not seen as being ordinary. Dyer sees the later Garland persona as a shift away from her girl-next-door image that pervaded her early screen performances. The fact that she is presented as an ordinary girl in her early image but in later years becomes something far from ordinary is of vital importance: 'To turn out not-ordinary after being saturated with the values of ordinariness structures Garland's career and the standard gay biography alike' (Dyer, 1986, p. 159). It is significant that Garland's image is constructed around an idea of authentic ordinariness, based as it was around a lack of the glamour so much a part of the image and persona of other female Hollywood stars of the era. Even when she played characters in films set in large metropolitan cities, they were originally from small towns. Garland therefore portrayed the values associated with the American small town in these films, representing a figure who was an outsider within the mainstream metropolitan environment, which provided a point of contact with gay men in the audience.

The second aspect within gay culture that Dyer argues is of key importance in understanding the significance of Garland's image is androgyny. Throughout her career her image is androgynous. Dyer cites examples of the characters she plays appearing in men's suits, dungarees and sailor suits, and focuses on the famous image of her performance of 'Get Happy' in the film *Easter Parade* (1948), which he argues creates a 'stylish androgyny'. During this number Garland becomes 'one of the boys' as she performs with the male dancers.

The final aspect of male gay culture that links with Garland's image, according to Dyer, is the fact that she is camp. Camp is 'a characteristically gay way of handling the values, images and products of the dominant culture through irony, exaggeration, trivialisation, theatricalisation and an ambivalent making fun of and out of the serious and respectable' (Dyer, 1986, p. 178) Part of Garland's campness is the way in which she seems to reflect back knowingly 'on her own image in the film or vehicle in which she has been placed'. This knowingness is central to reading Garland as camp, and it is also reflected in the awareness she displayed about her gay following and her personal ease in their milieu. It is also Garland's knowingness that created her special relationship with gay audiences. For Dyer this awareness leads him to argue that Garland herself *is* camp rather than her image being made camp by fans.

Richard Dyer's analysis of Judy Garland clearly shows how the star persona and the films of Hollywood stars are open to a number of different readings. These in turn allow particular interest groups or minorities to appropriate and interpret these images in ways that are in opposition to dominant readings of mainstream audiences. The fact that minority audiences are able to read against the mainstream intentions of texts also shows that the intentions of those involved in production are not always able to control the textual meanings they construct.

Reading against the grain can take place in relation to any media text, and is often sparked by the knowledge the reader already has about the subject-matter represented. When one has knowledge or experience of a group or situation that is represented in the media, critical or counter readings of those representations are certainly more likely. When one has little or no experience of the issues or people at hand, the media representations can become more seductively realistic and truthful. For members of minority groups the continual battle with media representations of their own experiences is likely to create more resistant consumers. This is precisely because these groups are made continually aware of the media's process of selection and construction in relation to images of themselves. They are therefore more generally aware of the media's ability to create problematic images of others.

Fans and fan culture

Another, increasingly visible 'minority' audience for popular media texts are fans. For John Fiske, the fan can be seen as part of a culture that resists the mainstream meanings of their chosen media texts. Clearly, this type of definition links with some of the work which we have already explored in this chapter. However, not all of those investigating fans see them as a resistant, subcultural group. Fiske, however, argues that 'fandom is typically associated with cultural forms that the dominant value system denigrates – pop music, romance novels, comics, Hollywood mass-appeal stars' (1992, p. 30). He asserts that the fan enters into a process of creation, distribution and circulation that places them outside the normal, everyday systems of production, distribution and consumption (see illustration 15.1.) Importantly, for Fiske, fan culture has 'its own systems of production and distribution that forms what I shall call a "shadow cultural economy" that lies outside that of the cultural industries yet shares features with them which more normal popular culture lacks' (p. 30). Fiske sees the ways in which fans collect, distribute and communicate as ultimately short-circuiting the usual process of capitalism. Indeed, he quotes his correspondence with Henry Jenkins which suggests that fans who make money out of their fandom are seen to be 'hucksters' (p. 40). An important exception to this are fan artists who are able to sell their paintings of, for example, main

Illustration 15.1   Fan groups often consume in specialist shops such as this one in
Stoke-on-Trent.
Source: The authors.

characters in television shows such as *Xena: Warrior Princess* for hundreds
of dollars without being seen in a negative light by other members of fan
groupings. This suggests that within fan cultures there are certain modes
of behaviour that are acceptable and some that are not. For Fiske, the
activities that are not acceptable are more clearly linked with the operations of dominant capitalist society, making those that are more symbolically resistant.

Other writers who have investigated fan cultures see them as more
linked to the dominant political economy of the media. Henry Jenkins
argues that fans can be seen as either lacking control over or having power
over the object of their fandom, which he suggests is controlled by more
powerful media institutions: 'No account of fan culture makes sense
unless it is seen as responsive to a situation in which fans make strong
emotional investments in programmes and yet have no direct control over
network decision-making' (1991, p. 92). Jenkins's work investigates the
ways in which fans and fan culture operate. He acknowledges that fans
are making enormous investments, both in terms of time and money, in
their chosen media product. Significantly, the interpretation of fans and
their actions provided by the likes of Jenkins is not always seen as

oppositional and providing a symbolic challenge to the status quo. As Hollows and Jancovich note of Jenkins:

> one of the advances made by this work is the way it acknowledges that audiences have profound investments in certain texts or groups of texts. This doesn't mean that they necessarily make oppositional readings but neither does their investment render them passive – for example, in fanzines and on the Internet, fans actively exchange responses to their favourite texts. (Hollows and Jancovich, 1995, p. 11)

So whilst some critics have attempted to represent the fan as one who is resistant to the dominant meanings of popular texts, this view must be set against those fans who, whilst enthusiastically following a programme, star or film series, do not seem to resist anything.

Of course, the variety of uses to which texts can be put means that one cannot easily dismiss the argument that some fans use their chosen texts to construct alternative visions of the world and that they can be seen symbolically to resist its dominant systems and power relations. Minority audiences therefore are often marked by their willingness to work against the dominant meanings of media texts, instead choosing to select the elements of the media that reflect their outlook and experiences. In doing so, they assist a rejection of the idea that media texts can simply position and influence those who consume them.

Suggestions for further work

In what ways might fans be considered different from other minority audiences discussed in the chapter?

Why is it important to consider the ways in which texts may be 'read' in a variety of ways?

Further reading

Dent, Gina (ed.) 1992: *Black Popular Culture*. Seattle: Bay Press.
Dyer, Richard 1986: *Heavenly Bodies*. London: British Film Institute / Macmillan.
Dyer, Richard 1990: *Now You See It: Studies on Lesbian and Gay Film*. London: Routledge.
Jenkins, Henry 1992: *Textual Poachers*. London: Routledge.

16
New Technologies and Media Audiences

The central focus of this chapter is the ways in which new media technologies impact upon audiences, potentially changing their relationship to the products they consume. The increasingly rapid introduction of new technologies in the media means that any analysis must in some way acknowledge that a perspective or approach to technology must underpin any attempt to understand both the implementation of new technology within society and the effect this has on the ways in which products reach and are consumed by audiences. This chapter begins by considering the work of Raymond Williams, who offers a useful perspective on technology and society. It then examines the implications of the various ways in which the history of technology has been written and conceived. Finally, it considers the changing relationship between technology and media audiences.

Technology and society

In *Television: Technology and Cultural Form* (1974) Raymond Williams argues that the influence and impact of new technologies is often presented as a mere 'given' within society. Thus, the world simply changed enormously when the wheel, the steam engine or the telephone were invented. Written into this approach is the idea that the impact of these technologies upon society does not require analysis – rather, their effects are self-evident. Williams argues that the emphasis on effects meant that other central questions about the relationship between technology and the society which produces it were masked. For him, the link between technology and its social uses must be examined alongside the institutions that exert an influence over their development and application. It is only when these questions are addressed that it is possible to reveal the real impact technology has on the everyday life of a society. It is the practical application of technologies in specific cultural contexts which must be addressed if an overall understanding of the actual effect that technology has on society is to be achieved.

Williams identifies two dominant ways in which technology has been theorized. First, 'technological determinism', which he argues sees technology as creating the conditions for human development and progress: 'New technologies are discovered, by an essentially internal process of research and development, which then sets the conditions for social change and progress. Progress, in particular, is the history of these inventions, which created the modern world' (1974, p. 13). Second, 'symptomatic technology', which for Williams is less determinist. This version suggests that technology is the result of a wider desire and thrust for change within society: 'Any particular technology is then as it were a by-product of a social process that is otherwise determined. It only acquires effective status when it is used for purposes which are already contained in this known process' (p. 13).

Williams goes on to argue that these two positions form the basis of much of the debate about technology. Central to the position of the technological determinists is that technological change is self-generating. For those who argue from a position of 'symptomatic technology', it is seen as self-generating, but dependent upon others 'picking it up' and using it. Within both of these positions technology is seen as a 'self-acting force' (p. 14), an entity that happens and then either leads society to change or provides the conditions that enable change to take place. Both positions, according to Williams, make a central assumption: that technology is created in isolation. Using television as his case study, Williams argues that this central assumption must be challenged and alternative versions of technological development sought. For him, it was vital to 'restore intention to the process of research and development. The technology would be seen, that is to say, as being looked for and developed with certain purposes and practices in mind ... known social needs, purposes and practices to which the technology is not marginal but central' (p. 17). The significance of Williams's argument is that it suggests that institutional interests, and the uses to which these institutions will put new technologies, have impacted enormously on the ways in which new technologies have been 'discovered'. Within this view experiments regarding new technologies are carried out seeking particular results and with certain potential applications in mind. This view clearly challenges at a fundamental level the idea that technologies are self-generating in any way, and so marks a break from the dominant positions outlined by Williams.

Williams goes on to consider the actual uses to which technology has been put. He links the development of new technologies with the needs of those who have a controlling interest in society. He argues that technological development is dependent upon the economic position and power of those who desire it within the social formation, arguing that 'A need which corresponds with the priorities of the real decision-making groups will, obviously, more quickly attract the investment of resources and the official permission, approval or encouragement on which working technology ... depends' (1974, p. 19). The connection between economic power and the ability to develop technologies is central to Williams's argument. Technologies only develop quickly if they assist the interests of the economically powerful in society. Hence, some very important technological innovations have been developed to assist industrial or military needs. For example, the Internet was developed initially for use by military personnel. For Williams, these considerations should centrally inform any analysis of technological development.

Williams argues that the development of television needs to be understood alongside wider social change. It could be seen as a form of social control because it was developed as a form of communication which was harnessed to the domestic. In so being it worked to atomize a population which had previously taken part in social gatherings such as mass political meetings and rallies, and which had constituted members of mass organizations, such as trade unions, that met on a regular basis. In a sense, then, the implementation of the technologies of television can be seen to have served the political interests of those with power within capitalism. In Williams's view it was the focus back onto the domestic that prevented mass responses to pressing political questions and issues. Alongside this it is important to assess who controlled such technological developments. Williams argues, with regard to television, 'The history ... is of EMI, RCA and a score of other similar companies and corporations' (1974, p. 25). The idea that the history of technologies is linked to wider economic interests has been argued by others interested in fully understanding why technologies appear when they do, and in the forms that they do. One such writer is Edward Buscombe. In his consideration of the development of colour cinema Buscombe (1985) echoes a number of points made by Williams.

The development of colour cinema

It is impossible to understand fully the place of colour film or cinematography within the Hollywood film industry without acknowledging the influence of a particular company, Technicolor. This company had a virtual monopoly over the development and application of colour technology up until 1948. Initially, in the 1920s, Technicolor had developed a two-colour process, and in the 1930s it developed another, more sophisticated, three-colour process. Its control over these developments was also linked to a series of agreements made with the film stock company

Eastman Kodak. In *Hollywood Cinema: An Introduction* (1995), Richard Maltby and Ian Craven argue that Technicolor was able to maintain its dominance for a number of important reasons: first, the colour process required special cameras that the Hollywood studios could only hire from Technicolor; second, it also controlled the supply and processing of film stock; third, the studios had to hire camera operators and colour consultants from Technicolor to ensure the technology was operated properly; and finally, due to their control over the technology, Technicolor was able strongly to influence the number of colour films that were allowed to go into production (Maltby and Craven, 1995, pp. 157–8). Maltby and Craven argue that these aspects of control had an impact upon the aesthetic uses to which colour was put. For example, the heavy and cumbersome size of the cameras needed to produce colour films meant that it was less easy for directors to incorporate camera movement into shots. This in turn forced technical staff to shoot films in a much more straightforward way, making it possible to argue that one technological innovation, colour, may have limited the experiments conducted in relation to other aspects of film production.

Edward Buscombe (1985) also clearly links technological innovation within cinema with economic concerns, but significantly suggests that the application of technology also has an ideological aspect. He states:

> economic theories can only partially explain technological innovations, since economics cannot say why innovations take the form they do, only why they are an essential part of the system ... No new technology can be introduced unless the economic system requires it ... But a new technology cannot be successful unless it fulfils some kind of need. The specific form of this need will be ideologically determined; in the case of cinema the ideological determinant most frequently identified has been realism. (p. 87)

For Buscombe, colour provides an interesting test case. He argues that colour did not connote 'reality' but the opposite: it was seen as fantastical and unreal. This, he believes, explains why it took so long to take hold within Hollywood film production, particularly when compared to other new technologies which were quickly assimilated by the industry such as sound. Colour, unlike sound, could not be instantly accommodated into the realist aesthetic. Buscombe goes on to argue that colour's 'unreality' is linked to the uses to which it was put. This, he says, was closely linked to a particular hierarchy of genres that operated in Hollywood at the time, one which ranked them according to 'the extent to which the world they portray, fictional or not, is close to what the audience believes the world to be like. Thus at one end of the scale we find newsreels, documentaries, war films, crime films, etc. and at the other cartoons, musicals, westerns, costume romances, fantasies and comedies' (1985, p. 89). The former was associated more with realism, the latter with a lack of realism.

Indeed, Buscombe quotes from a film industry handbook *Elements of Color in Professional Motion Pictures* (1957) which reflects this line of thought: 'Musicals and fantasy pictures are open to unlimited opportunities in the creative use of color. Here we are not held down by reality, past or present, and our imaginations can soar' (1985, p. 89).

Buscombe adds significantly to the argument about why technologies are applied at particular historical moments. He links the economic concerns highlighted by Williams to more ideological matters, placing the need to fit an already existing notion of realism as a central reason for the length of time it took for colour to become commonplace within the cinema. However, whilst the views of writers such as Buscombe provide useful insights into the reasons for the application of certain technologies in certain industrial contexts, they do not address the technologies that are developed as ways of consuming media products, such as cinema projectors. It is important to see the history of any new technology as written from a particular perspective, and in turn that perspective informs the way in which its history is written.

In his article 'Color and cinema: problems in the writing of cinema' (1985) Edward Branigan's aim is to 'expose the assumptions (framework, theory) which a historian uses to generate a history – all of which is normally obscured beneath apparently neutral and unassuming titles, such as "The Development of Color Cinematography" or "Refinements in Technique"' (p. 122). He argues that history is written from a particular perspective which may be theoretical, practical or industrial, and that it is dangerous to conceive of these perspectives as simply neutral. His article is therefore an attempt to show how historians' perspectives directly inform the ways in which they approach their subject.

What Branigan suggests about the history of cinema and the development of colour technology can be applied to a range of other technologies and other mediums. Historians of those developments are also working from a particular perspective selecting certain events that are then simply re-presented as 'history'. Branigan's critique of those who write the history of technologies, in order to expose their underlying perspectives, can also be applied to those we have already discussed such as Williams and Buscombe. In many ways it is the task of the media studies student to reveal the underlying positions of those they read.

Branigan identifies four angles from which the history of cinema has been approached: 'Adventure', 'Technology', 'Industrial Management' and 'Ideology'. He argues that one is able to identify which angle a history is written from by asking a number of crucial questions of the work (1985, p. 122). These are focused around three criteria. First, 'cause', the way in which the historian presents the things that they argue caused change to happen: 'by cause I mean a historian's reasoning about the determinants or conditions of a state'. Second, 'change', the ways in which change is explained and the way in which the historian articulates the change from one state to another, 'that logic may appear in innumerable guises; for instance, change may be characterized in terms of a transition, evolution, progression (progress), regression, transformation, mutation'. The historian's choice of perspective gives a strong indication of how they view the material they are writing about. Third, 'subject', which focuses on the way the historian presents the individual and their contribution to the historical process: 'that role may run a spectrum from the individual as a psychological agent to the individual as one constructed (placed, positioned) by large-scale forces'. By which he means that individual actions are dictated by larger forces such as capitalism or class. It is the way that a writer uses or presents these criteria that enables Branigan to understand the perspective of their work and place it into one of his already identified positions. Branigan's work is significant because it removes the 'common-sense' idea that history just happens and that historians merely record it. What should never be overlooked is that the history of the media, and of media technologies, reflects the position and outlook of the writer.

Media technology and the individual

In *Dynamics of Modern Communication* (1995) Patrice Flichy discusses the importance of the domestic to the development of new technologies. She argues that it is possible to see the development of the theatre box as a way of extending the private, the drawing room, into a public space, the theatre. She notes that 'The theatre box constituted a new mode of articulation between the private and public spheres. It was the first attempt at "privatizing" the theatre' (p. 154). The theatre therefore marked an important shift towards the domestic consumption of leisure. Clearly the technologies of both radio and television allowed this shift to become more marked. Radio, which was enormously popular in the 1920s, is often presented as a family medium, one that was listened to and enjoyed by all the family members together. It is certainly possible to find many promotional images for radio showing a family gathered around the set listening as a group (the actual reality of this image has been challenged by writers such as Shaun Moores, whose view is discussed in chapter 14). As Williams observed, the mass communication of radio was to a fragmented audience gathered in the private space of the home. In a similar way, the decline in cinema-going after the Second World War is often linked with the rise of television, another medium which is consumed within the private space of the home.

Flichy argues that as other media technologies developed, such as the transistor radio and the record-player, they further fragmented the groups consuming them, thus creating a more individualistic mode of consumption. The result was to turn an already inward-looking unit even further inwards. Flichy also notes that such music technologies developed alongside the rise of the teenager, and the changes that this brought to family life:

> When they were launched, the transistor and long-playing record benefited not only from a new form of music (rock) but also from a profound change in private life. The family did not disappear but it was transformed; the home was maintained but as a place in which individual practices were juxtaposed. Music was particularly well adapted to this new 'juxtaposed home'. Family members could all listen to the music they wanted in their rooms. (Flichy, 1995, p. 164)

The shift towards individual consumption via new media technologies has continued and the development of the Walkman, mobile telephones, pagers and even video recorders has all contributed in various ways to this shift. Once again it is possible to argue that this fragmentation and individualization works to further prevent collective responses to media content, which in turn works to assist those in power whose interests are served by people not acting collectively. This trend is likely to continue as new technological developments are pushed towards ever more personal hardware, such as mini-televisions. These will make it possible for individuals to consume events such as football matches, which in the near past were mass events, on their own.

New technologies, media audiences and resistance

New technologies can also challenge our assumptions about the physical nature of certain mediums. Sean Cubitt goes to great lengths to ensure that his reader is aware of the differences between television and other mediums: 'Unlike cinema, the TV image is smaller, less well-defined, often watched in the light rather than the dark, and is generally a domestic or social leisure appliance, so that its messages are in competition with the rest of domestic or social life. Like that life (or those lives), it is ephemeral in its broadcast form' (1991, p. 29). Video, for Cubitt, is the technology which takes television beyond this definition. It breaks the here-and-now of television, because, 'Through video, TV can cease to be a slave to the metaphysics of presence' (p. 36). It is through the technology of video that viewers are able to time-shift – that is, record programmes off air and then watch them at a time that fits their own personal schedule. Cubitt argues that this allows an extension of the viewing day and frees audiences from what he calls 'the tyranny of the network schedules' (p. 36). He goes on to argue more forcibly that the ability of audiences to time-shift means that 'The balances of power between institutions, texts and viewers are radically unsettled' (p. 37). In Cubitt's view, the technology of video recording allows viewers to challenge the power of media institutions, creating their own viewing schedules that suit them personally and are not dictated by more powerful agencies. This leads to the suggestion that viewers are able, through their use of technology, to challenge those who control television exhibition. He states that 'video is out of control', arguing that it is a technology that empowers those previously open to the controlling forces of the television institutions. However, he does acknowledge that video technology is not totally outside the direct intervention of the state. So, whilst the domestic use of video may be seen to challenge media institutions, in passing bills such as the Video Recordings Act the state is able to legislate certain uses of that technology.

The argument put forward by Cubitt raises a number of important points regarding the potential empowering nature of new technologies. However, it must be remembered that the application of technologies, as Williams argued, is often linked to powerful economic interests. The distribution of new technologies, such as video recorders, is dominated by powerful multi-national companies such as JVC and Sony. The way in which these companies put new technological developments into mass circulation remains an important consideration when analysing the potential radical usage audiences may develop in relation to hardware.

Postmodernism, cyberspace and the media consumer

Mark Poster (1995) argues that one of the central discussions about changes in communications systems as the twentieth century draws to an end is focused on whether or not new technical innovations will change the way in which individual identities are structured. He states:

> In the twentieth century, electronic media are supporting an equally profound transformation of cultural identity. Telephone, radio, film, television, the computer and now their integration as 'multimedia' reconfigure words, sounds and images so as to cultivate new configurations of individuality. If modern society may be said to foster an individual who is rational, autonomous, centred and stable (the 'reasonable man' of the law, the educated citizen of representative democracy, the calculating 'economic man' of capitalism, the grade-defined student of public education), then perhaps a postmodern society is emerging which nurtures forms of identity different from, even opposite to those of modernity. And electronic communications technologies significantly enhance these postmodern possibilities. (p. 80)

New media technologies may therefore challenge the conceptualization of people as free-thinking individuals. The possibilities new technologies offer to create multiple realities mean that experience will no longer be the source of the 'individual', as consumers will be able to experience a range of competing realities through an engagement with new media technologies. Of course, this potentially radical view of the application of new technologies must be set against questions of institutional control, as Williams argued. The ability of multi-media corporations, such as

Microsoft, to control the points of access and the distribution of these new technologies will certainly greatly effect the potentially radical aspects of them. In this sense, Williams's assertion that the history of technology is the history of the major corporations whose interests are served by their development has enormous relevance, and that history is ongoing.

Kevin Robins (1995) has challenged the conception of cyberspace as a place that frees the individual from the shackles of reality, questioning the idea that it is a 'utopian vision for postmodern times' (p. 135). For Robins, the actual reality of people's everyday lives must not be forgotten in the creation of a mythical freedom within cyberspace. Indeed, he argues that it would be extremely dangerous to withdraw from a political and social perspective about new technologies, stating that, 'In considering the development of techno-communities, we must continue to be guided by social and political objectives', and that it 'is time to relocate virtual culture in the real world (the real world that virtual culturalists, seduced by their own metaphors, pronounce dead or dying). Through the development of new technologies, we are, indeed, more and more open to experiences of de-realization and de-localization. But we continue to have a physical and localized existence' (1995, pp. 152–3). In view of this, it is essential that any analysis of new technologies, and the implication for the societies that use them, acknowledges the economic and political interests that influence the uses to which they are put.

Suggestions for further work

Consider new media technologies, such as computer games. How relevant is it to think about these technologies in relation to the interests of large corporations?

Again, consider the development of new media technologies. How far do they extend both the domestic and individualistic tendencies of the media as identified by Patrice Flichy?

Further reading

Cubitt, Sean 1991: *Timeshift: On Video Culture*. London: Routledge.

Nichols, Bill (ed.) 1985: *Movies and Methods vol. 2*. Berkeley: University of California Press.

Williams, Raymond 1974: *Television: Technology and Cultural Form*. London: Fontana.

17

Media Consumption and Social Status

In *Keywords* (1976) Raymond Williams points out that early definitions of consumption saw it as a process whereby goods or products are used up, destroyed or devoured. Yet the act of using up goods, the process of consumption itself, often occurs through active, sometimes even creative social practices. Celia Lury describes consumption as a dual process; for her it is 'both a moment of consumption *and* production, of undoing *and* doing, of destruction *and* construction' (1996, p. 1). For example, an audience watching a film 'uses up' the text in the sense that they have witnessed it shot by shot from beginning to end. However, in order to make sense of the film the audience must engage in an act of reading it so as actively to produce meaning from the text. This kind of active engagement with the content of the media is one form of media consumption, but the purchase, display and use of media objects such as satellite dishes and television sets can also be described as acts of consumption.

Until relatively recently there has been a trend in the humanities and social sciences to regard consumption as an entity worthy of study only for what it can significantly reveal about production. Consumption was thought to be an inferior by-product of production. Yet studying consumption as an area in itself uncovers a great deal about the importance people place on the social relationship between things and their symbolic meanings. Indeed, the various ways in which people convert or consume objects or goods, by means which are personal to themselves, often act as markers of identity. For example, a domestic space such as the home becomes intensely personalized through practices of consumption. Stevie Jackson and Shaun Moores argue, for example, that consumption works to uphold the ways in which the home is 'symbolically and culturally produced and sustained' (1995, p. 13). But consumption reveals more about people than merely their own preferences for certain consumer goods. Either by buying certain brands of goods or by appropriating or displaying them in highly specific ways, certain groups are able to distinguish, or in some cases even distance themselves from, other communities or social groupings. In doing so they are practising what Lury terms 'positional consumption'; seen in this way, consumption practices are part of the struggle to achieve and maintain social status (1996, p. 80).

This chapter outlines some of the key ideas used in media and cultural studies for thinking about 'positional consumption' and the media. Drawing on Bourdieu's ideas about taste, consumption and social distinction, it outlines the work of writers who have investigated how media tastes are often used as social demarcators. Here, we investigate how positional consumption works across two dimensions. First, social status is often signified through the appropriation of particular media technologies as physical objects. For example, Ondina Fachel Leal (1990), in her ethnographic work on the appropriation of television in working-class and middle-class homes in Brazil, found taste differences in the ways in which television is decorated and positioned. Her research demonstrates key differences in the meaning of television, both as a medium and as a material object, for different social groups in Brazil. And second, through a taste hierarchy of mediums and the media texts associated with them. Watching television, for example, is ranked low down the hierarchy of socially tasteful cultural activities. As Charlotte Brunsdon argues, television texts are rarely regarded as being 'quality' products; indeed, when they are it is because they manage somehow to fit 'high culture' aesthetic criteria (1997).

Theories of consumption and social distinction

In their book *The World of Goods* (1980) Mary Douglas and Baron Isherwood argue that consumption is never related purely to economic factors. Rather, it is a cultural as well as an economic practice. In their account, consumer goods must be analysed within the specific cultural context in which they are acquired, used and exchanged. Their thesis is that people invest symbolic meaning in the most trivial everyday objects. For them, material goods are far more than objects with specific uses: goods also have a cultural role as demarcators of value. The enjoyment, for example, for young people in consuming a pair of trainers goes far beyond using them as a practical form of footwear. Their brand name is a significant bearer of social meaning about their cultural value for the wearer. Moreover, things are saturated with meaning about the people who purchase, utilize and trade them. Goods therefore take on tremendous importance as carriers of social meaning for people, because they are so closely tied to the construction of social identity. In this way, goods act as indicators of how social relations are organized at particular historical moments.

Also central to Douglas and Isherwood's argument is the notion that goods and their relationship to the social status of the consumer are dependent upon consuming them in appropriate and knowledgeable ways. How goods are consumed also confers meaning on the status of those who consume. The purchase of a prestigious wine is a carrier of meaning about social status, but to maintain one's position as part of a particular high-ranking social group one must also have the cultural competence to know about a range of other factors: at what temperature to serve the wine, with what food and so on. This kind of ease with the 'how' of consumption is also a factor which maintains barriers of entry to other social groups which lack the means of recognizing that value is also contained in the correct and appropriate means of consumption.

Pierre Bourdieu's work extends the idea that taste is socially defined, but for him the hierarchies of taste which govern the acquisition and consumption of goods are closely connected to the social class divisions within a society. In his analysis of 1960s French culture, *Distinction: A Social Critique of the Judgement of Taste* (1984), Bourdieu argues that goods possess symbolic significance within the social order and that taste operates as a central organizing principle for how resources are distributed both through and across it. In this way taste has a central role in reproducing and maintaining the dominant order, the effects of which are at least as significant as the political and economic factors which might serve to maintain the unequal distribution of a culture's assets. It is through consumption that people, themselves part of class groups, attempt to gain some kind of social status within what Bourdieu terms the 'cultural field'. The dominant groups in society maintain the eminence of their positions by conferring superiority on their tastes and by dismissing working-class tastes as vulgar and base. In doing so, they affirm their lifestyle choices as distant from those of others who occupy a hierarchically lower position in the cultural field. Class, according to Bourdieu's thesis, is not merely a question of how much economic capital one might possess; it is also defined by one's 'cultural capital'. Cultural capital acts as a form of symbolic wealth in the realm of culture. In this way the middle class cannot only assert greater economic power, they can also confer greater value onto their cultural pursuits. Being conversant with cultural capital is also a requirement for moving easily within middle-class circles, therefore part of one's cultural capital is comprised of the knowledge required to make appropriate discriminations or value judgements about cultural forms. Cultural distinctions lie at the centre of the maintenance of social reproduction, but more particularly for Bourdieu, they play a major role in upholding the unequal class relations in a society.

Central to Bourdieu's theory of taste and social distinction is his notion of habitus. Habitus is the term he uses to describe the system of

competencies and dispositions which govern the social movement of
the individual throughout life. Acquired in childhood, built upon through
the education system and within the context of the family, habitus is
primarily developed by one's class position. It is revealed through the
cultural value of the unconscious, yet seemingly naturalized everyday tastes
of the individual's choices of food, sporting activities, clothing, art, interior
decoration and so on. It is also actually lived out through the body: one's
gestures, facial expression, accent and speech patterns, the amount of
space one feels one has the right to absorb in social encounters – all
these physical manifestations reveal one's habitus. Throughout life in the
cultural field individuals use the 'transposable dispositions' of habitus in
their everyday social encounters to make consumer choices which in the
wider culture are subject to classifications. Habitus allows one to be able
to distinguish between dominant and popular aesthetics. The ability
to make certain choices through consumption, for example purchasing
goods where form takes precedence over function, indicates that one has
the powers to discriminate between legitimate (or elite), middlebrow or
popular tastes. The decision to buy a Dualit toaster, made desirable
because of its chrome formal properties, as opposed to a white two-slice
toaster, indicates the ability to recognize the aesthetic features in even the
most mundane objects, to appropriate one's knowledge of legitimate
culture and to distance oneself from less desirable cultural forms.

Bourdieu argues that the root cause of taste distinctions is directly
related to the material conditions of people's experience of social class in
contemporary society. Legitimate taste is the privilege of the bourgeoisie,
since this is the only group which is economically able to cultivate a
'distance from necessity', or an aesthetic of disinterested contemplation.
The capacity to privilege form over function in virtually every area of life,
to wear clothes that are fashionable as opposed to warm and serviceable,
for example, or to seek leisure and entertainment pursuits with no practical purpose, is to cultivate desires which are distanced from the urgent,
physical needs of working-class people. Yet, as Bourdieu illustrates, the
desire to remain dominant is a continual struggle as different class groups
vie to maintain their cultural capital and to hang on to their position within
the cultural field. Bourdieu's work offers an analysis that insists on the
social dimension of taste. Objects and goods are not intrinsically imbued
with value; rather, taste is historically and socially constructed. And the
classifying systems through which taste is regulated are not fixed; they,
too, are historically contingent and changeable. In this way, his work
provides an historically flexible model for understanding the significance
of taste in the context of societies that are divided by class inequalities.

Bourdieu's work has faced criticism, however, largely because by sin-
gling out class as the most important determinant in consumption patterns
his work is seen to offer a limited and inflexible analytical framework.
Roger Silverstone argues that in *Distinction* Bourdieu gives short shrift to

a range of other social factors such as religion, gender and ethnicity, which undoubtedly also impact on the meaning of consumption tastes – indeed in this chapter we explore the ways in which feminine tastes are often subjected to discriminatory, pejorative judgements. Silverstone also points out that Bourdieu tends to underplay the potential for creativity and resistance in his analysis of consumption: 'he understresses the dynamics: the shifts and turns, the squirming and the resistances which in their significance or lack of significance, do indeed make consumption an active, sometimes creative, process in which individual and social identities are claimed, reclaimed and constantly being negotiated' (1994, p. 117). Indeed, in Bourdieu's work there seems to be little room for the possibility that people might subvert notions of taste in knowing ways which might empower them socially. There is an enormous body of work in cultural studies which charts resistance to the dominant social order through consumption. Silverstone also criticizes Bourdieu for his complete lack of attention to the media as a site where struggles over style and taste are undoubtedly played out. Indeed, the framework of analysis Bourdieu developed in *Distinction* is silent on the role of the media; rather, the onus is on the reader to apply Bourdieu's ideas to examples of how taste operates in relation to the media.

Television: a case study of a 'vulgar' medium

Aspects of the media fit Bourdieu's notion of different taste categories. Radio, for example, is a middle-brow medium. In the context of the multiplex, cinema is a popular medium. The texts these mediums produce are also subject to taste hierarchies. For example, Radio One is a popular station whereas Radio Four is aimed at a more middle-brow audience. In the Art-House cinema independent films are ranked as middle-brow; though art films are often shown in these venues, they aspire to the rank of, and are sometimes legitimated by critics as, elite taste. The media therefore are ranked in terms of taste by particular criteria. Drawing on Bourdieu, in this section we examine the ways in which television has been subject to a specific set of aesthetic criteria. As a result of this, as Charlotte Brunsdon argues, television has become the 'bad cultural object' (1997, p. 114).

Brunsdon (1997) suggests in her chapter 'Aesthetics and Audiences' that there are two traditional ways in which television is considered to be good. First, when it is seen as a democratic medium disseminating 'worthy' programmes presanctioned as legitimate forms of culture according to high- or middle-brow tastes. And second, when it is seen to deliver access to seemingly unmediated events or 'the real'. Examples of this would include documentary footage, news events or sports coverage. In both cases what is significant is that television can only be regarded as 'good' when television itself as a specific form is suppressed or rendered obsolete (1997, pp. 112–13). It is for these reasons, Brunsdon argues, that television is often regarded as a vulgar medium.

In relation to Brunsdon's first point, one can see why certain programmes across the history of British broadcasting are lauded as worthy of the label 'quality', and others not. In the chapter entitled 'Problems with Quality' (Brunsdon, 1997) she charts the specific criteria, manifested in what she terms 'discourses of quality' resonant in the British press, for the high-ranking positions celebrated drama programmes such as *Brideshead Revisited* (1981) and *Jewel in the Crown* (1984) are held. Such programmes are lauded precisely because they correlate with the taste codes of middle- and high-brow audiences. They are made from preordained literary sources, they utilize the skills of the 'best' British actors, they have high production values (importantly, financial resources were spent in line with upper-middle-class taste codes) and, finally, they harbour what Brunsdon calls 'heritage export' – that is, they manufacture a particular notion of upper-class, colonial Englishness.

These criteria demonstrate why programmes aimed at popular audiences like talk shows and breakfast television cannot transcend television as a medium in the same way, and are diametrically opposed to legitimate tastes in terms of both class and gender. Moreover, if we take Brunsdon's second instance of 'good' television one can see a definite gender divide operating between the programmes celebrated for their ability to deliver a sense of the unmediated and most fictional programmes made for television. Therefore news programmes, current affairs, sport and documentaries are associated with masculine taste preferences. Their opposite, fictional programmes which are often demarcated within domestic settings – soap operas, for example – are seen to fall in line with female taste preferences. Programmes divide according to gender because of the socially produced skills of masculinity and femininity. Indeed, ethnographic work conducted in the 1980s which examined the lived cultures in which media texts are consumed found a socially diverse set of 'taste publics' organized along gender lines (Morley, 1986). It is not that female audiences innately prefer soaps; rather, they have the cultural competencies (intuition and a concern with the personal and the domestic for example) to unlock and decode the gendered elements drawn upon by soaps. Moreover, gender is written into television scheduling practices, indicating a split between different taste publics. In this way, while taste is undoubtedly divided along class lines, gender is also a factor in how tastes are constructed. Therefore other kinds of social power apart from class power also impact upon taste formations in society. Following Bourdieu and the research undertaken by Brunsdon, readers' pleasures and competencies can be afforded different value within the cultural economy, and because the hierarchy of preference is generally tilted towards the dominant social groups, female preferences are not as highly valued as the tastes defined as masculine.

Media technologies, taste and social status

Writers such as Brunsdon and Leal also draw on Bourdieu's ideas about taste formations and class in their analyses of media technologies in relation to consumption and taste. Their work focuses on how television and satellite are used within domestic settings as either signifiers of taste, or a lack of it. Their starting point is that while taste might well be linked to personal individual preference, it is actually a profoundly social phenomenon.

In 'Satellite Dishes and the Landscapes of Taste' (1997) Brunsdon makes the point, using the empirical evidence presented by cultural studies writers such as Seiter (1990), Ang (1985) and Radway (1987), that consumers are deeply aware of the cultural and social value of the cultural artefacts they consume and display. In 'Making distinctions in TV audience research: case study of a troubling interview' (1990), for example, Seiter discusses interviewing soap opera viewers who, because of their awareness of Seiter's prestigious social position as an academic, only divulge what they know to be culturally legitimate reasons for their enjoyment of soaps from their repertoire of soap experiences. Similarly, Radway's romance readers find it difficult to admit to the pleasures they derive from romantic novels, preferring instead to suggest that their reasons for reading them is because they are often set in other countries, therefore they are 'educational'. However, an awareness of how cultural products are culturally demarcated is not just the privilege of middle-class consumers; working-class people are also skilled at being able to recognize cultural value. (See, for example, Beverly Skeggs's ethnographic work in *Formations of Class and Gender* (1997). Her findings show that working-class women recognize the negativity of the cultural representations of themselves in circulation and therefore choose to disidentify with what it means to be working class (1997, p. 124).) This kind of awareness of taste and social value is central to an understanding of where people chose to align themselves in the public controversy about satellite dishes in Britain in the late 1980s.

Brunsdon conducted an analytical study of the press and its coverage of the then new satellite dish between 1989–90. Satellite dishes, with their position outside the home, act as conspicuous non-verbal signifiers of taste (see illustration 17.1). Yet, as Brunsdon insists, the conflicts of taste that took place in the press during the late 1980s, the residue of which still informs popular debates about new technologies and taste today, rework previous reactions to technology which are actually really about taste and positional consumption. For example, the satellite controversy evokes and even parallels the public concern about television aerials in the 1950s. For working-class people the aerial signified a sense of purchase on modern, developing consumer durables; for middle-class consumers

Illustration 17.1   Satellite dishes on the urban landscape.
Source: The authors.

it signified a set of unappealing characteristics: Americanization, commercialization and mass-production. Brunsdon uses this context to frame her argument: the meaning of satellite dishes is used to rework these older ongoing historical debates, one's position within which signifies one's position on the taste map. It is taste that figures most highly at the root of such debates, as opposed to genuine technophobia. In fact, questions of taste actually predate the coming of technologies such as satellite dishes.

Brunsdon argues that the public dispute waged in the serious and the tabloid press over the siting of satellite dishes is very revealing about the two sides which partake in the taste war. She identifies two dominant groups which speak in the debate: the 'dish-erectors' and the 'anti-dishers'. Anti-dishers usually have professional occupations and they often speak as representatives of wider committees or institutional bodies which harbour deep concerns about the impact of dishes on the public landscape – bodies such as residents' associations. Significantly, anti-dishers deflect attention away from any possible potential relationship with satellite; instead, they use their social position to present themselves as speaking on behalf of others: 'Anti-dishers, who in Bourdieu's terms are the possessors of, indeed propagandists for, legitimate cultural capital act and speak at a general social level about a matter of public concern' (Brunsdon, 1997, p. 158). They also, as a result of their class habitus, often have some kind of specialized knowledge about town planning or environmental issues which make the dish undesirable. Anti-dishers also never mention the television programmes the dish might provide. According to Bourdieu, it is typical of the bourgeoisie to distance themselves from the immediate, physical pleasures of life; such a response is one that working-class people might make. Rather, their focus is on the potential that satellite dishes have to blight the English architectural landscape. For anti-dishers, satellite dishes are low in the hierarchy of taste; their concern is that they erode the heritage value of the towns and villages they themselves occupy and, in Bourdieu's terms, they are objects they wish to generate distance from.

Dish-erectors, on the other hand, are represented as isolated individuals who speak only on their own behalf about the pleasures of the dish, and the television programmes to which satellite allows them access. For these groups, their value lies in their conspicuousness as home improvements which provide satisfaction in the comparatively shorter term, in relation to the market. But perhaps more importantly, most satellite consumers are presented as working-class people who lack the powers to discriminate between what are the appropriate terms of taste and what are not. This figures most pointedly in those areas of Britain that anti-dishers and a portion of press journalists who are anti-dish believe to be worthy of preservation, areas which by implication working-class people fail to recognize as examples of valuable architecture. For example, anti-dishers object to dishes erected outside houses of historical interest which still have working-class occupancy, such as cottages and Edwardian and Victorian terraced housing.

For Brunsdon, it is through taste in relation to the media that individuals are able to pitch their particular position in relation to either legitimate (architecture) or popular (satellite television) forms of culture. Her analysis of the press debate demonstrates that some people, namely those with enough cultural capital, are able to take up positions from which to speak about taste, technology and value, whereas others cannot. The issue of taste, therefore, is closely tied to questions of power: the power to name and legitimate what cultural forms are valuable and the power to preserve the status quo. Ultimately, as Brunsdon argues, the bid to keep England free of new technologies is a means to preserve an untainted 'vision of England ... as an old country' (1997, p. 161).

In similar vein to Brunsdon's work, but using ethnographic fieldwork in order to access how people consume media technology in the domestic setting, Ondina Fachel Leal discovered interesting expressions of taste and class through the appropriation of television in her study of Brazilian homes (1990). She found that working-class and middle class households have different, yet internally coherent, systems for displaying the television set within the household. Her findings concur with Brunsdon's conclusions about satellite in Britain: that expressions of taste reveal that media technologies have different social meanings for different class groups. Leal found that in working-class homes the television set was a prized possession. Often situated in a position where it could be seen by passers-by from the street, Leal found that the set would be adorned with an entourage of decorative objects:

> The TV is the most important element among the set of objects in the home of the working-class group. The TV sits on its own small table, with the importance of a monument, and it is typically decorated with a crocheted doily. The TV, on or off, represents the owner's search for the social recognition of TV ownership which is why it has to be visible from the street. (1990, p. 24)

Leal's analysis reveals that this entourage of decorative objects is not itself arbitrary, rather it combines to generate an organized set of symbolic meanings for the working-class city-dweller who has immigrated from rural areas. Leal continues: 'All these objects in working-class homes are strategically placed in the most obvious corner of the house's front room. They are arranged around the TV set and they have a common quality: "modernity". They are seen as urban rationality inside the domestic space as an ethos and cultural capital of another class' (p. 24). Leal argues that for working-class people this arrangement of television and entourage represents an attempt to generate meanings of urbanity and modernity, and ultimately to construct a domestic space out of objects, 'which they think are elements of the elite's cosmology' (p. 25).

By contrast, however, the upper-class groups analysed by Leal actively reject the items most prized by the working-class groups as vulgar and tasteless. Whereas in the working-class interior the television acts as the chief source of leisure, the domestic sphere in the upper-class household provides a wide array of leisure pursuits. Watching television is ranked low down the scale of worthy cultural activities; for them, it is not a legitimate leisure pursuit. In order to reflect its low cultural value, the television, almost in direct opposition to its active and proud display within the working-class home, is hidden from view. Usually it is confined to a bedroom, or placed in a separate room so as not to interrupt other activities in the home. If the television is found in the front room it is obscured from view. Moreover the television is never decorated – rather, it is regarded as a functional object, devoid of aesthetic value: 'There is no positive aesthetic value associated with the TV set. In all forms and shapes it is considered a utilitarian object; it is not decorated, nor is it considered a decorative object' (Leal, 1990, p. 26).

While Brunsdon's and Leal's work share similarities about new media technologies, taste and social status, there are significant differences in their findings about the working-class groups they discuss, possibly as a result of the research methods each author draws upon. Brunsdon's press analysis is a discussion of how the press chose to represent different class values in relation to new technologies. Her work therefore shows the mediated responses to satellite dishes in circulation at the time. In the reported reactions and remarks she cites, the ordinary dish-erectors are represented as indifferent, or at least disinterested, in the condescension shown by middle-class groups about their tastes. Her findings might also be read as an attempt by some elements of the press to represent working-class people as naive and unaware; it is often the case that working-class people are represented as childlike (Barker and Petley, 1997). Leal's findings, perhaps as a result of her ethnographic work, suggest on the part of working-class Brazilians an awareness, as well as a desire to mimic the lives of the more socially powerful group: 'the working-class imitates what it takes to be the aesthetic elements of the upper-class, while the upper-class studiously appropriates and labels as "folk" and "art" handicrafts, everyday items, and sacred objects from the others, and reconstructs them as exotic other' (Leal, 1990, p. 27). Crucially, in Leal's analysis the working-class group makes the mistake of believing it can successfully ape the tastes of the middle-class. Yet within their tendency to mimic the taste of middle class groups is doubtless a recognition that items only valued within working-class culture are valueless in the wider societal structure; these strategies are comparable with Skeggs's findings in *Formations of Class and Gender* (1997). The women she interviewed disidentified with the available yet undesirable images of working-class culture.

Both Brunsdon and Leal are concerned with the ways in which new technologies become caught up in lived cultures of consumption – their use enables people to communicate non-verbally a sense of their social identities, particularly in relation to class. Yet ultimately in the taste war, as Leal argues, the power stakes are skewed in favour of the dominant class, since 'Taste, which is often considered to be a very subjective and individual notion, is in fact a social standard that takes for prestigious the established power relations' (Leal, 1990, p. 27). Indeed, reference to satellite dishes and even television aerials as undesirable proclaimers of low culture continues today. In a 'Homes and Gardens' article in a Saturday supplement of the *Guardian*, one headline proclaims: 'The city garden, surrounded by TV aerials and satellite dishes, needs something more majestic than ephemeral perennials to unite heaven and earth' (6/12/97). Here, in the attempt to create a garden, the implied middle-class reader is at odds with the signifiers of base culture that mark the skyline. Such examples only serve to demonstrate the continued importance of theorists like Douglas and Isherwood and Bourdieu for understanding the reproduction and maintenance of class power through taste.

Suggestions for further work

Visit a large newsagent and look at the magazines on offer. How do they potentially provide the opportunity for consumers to display their 'taste' preferences?

What programmes currently showing on television might be considered as 'middle-brow' and why?

Consider recent developments in television hardware (widescreen sets, cinema sound etc.). How do these fit into 'taste' formations?

Further reading

Brunsdon, Charlotte 1997: *Screen Tastes: Soap Opera to Satellite Dishes*. London: Routledge.
Bourdieu, Pierre 1984: *Distinction: A Social Critique of the Judgement of Taste*. London: Routledge.
Lury, Celia 1996: *Consumer Culture*. Cambridge: Polity Press.

18

Public Participation in the 1990s

The increase in audience participation in the 1990s

Media products in the late twentieth century increasingly use audiences as a participating resource in programme design. For radio and television in particular, audience interaction has become a staple part of many of the programmes found in the schedules of the 1990s. And while the use of audiences has perhaps been more commonly associated with light entertainment products, such as quiz and game shows, the public is becoming a major resource in the creation of non-fiction programmes.

Broadly, three different modes of audience participation can be identified in the non-fiction media. First, there has been a wide increase in the use of audience interaction 'segments' on television. For example, breakfast programmes generically have small sections given over to remedying viewers' problems: *GMTV* features Dr Hilary who deals with viewers' 'phone-in medical questions. Current affairs and news-based programmes have 'phone-ins that register opinions on the latest topics or controversy: in mid-1997 *Breakfast News Extra* encouraged viewers to 'phone-in or fax their opinions about the recently discovered condition incalculia (mathematical dyslexia). And there is a whole host of programmes in which viewer participation has become integral: the crime surveillance on *Crimewatch* and the consumer complaints on *Watchdog* are just two examples. Second, programmes that entirely consist of audience participation have proliferated in the late 1990s. In the run-up to the 1997 general election Radio Four and BBC1 simultaneously broadcast *Election Call*, where leading politicians were placed in the hot seat, giving members of the public the opportunity to ask them challenging questions about their policies and beliefs. Radio talk shows, both local and national, consist entirely of audience participation, where the host talks solely to listeners about current issues: examples of these are legion. Third, programmes centred on a live studio audience, mostly drawn from the general public, but which also feature a host, celebrity guests and/or experts gathered together to debate a particular topic. This category includes audience discussion programmes, or 'talk shows' as they are termed in the United States. Programmes of this kind, such as *Kilroy*, *Esther*, *Oprah* and *The Time, The Place* have enjoyed a good deal of popularity in the 1990s.

While audience interaction as a programming device is growing generally, some critics have argued that in the United States the audience discussion programme has now overtaken the soap opera in the daytime schedule popularity stakes (Shattuc, 1997, p. 1). In Britain others argue that audience discussion programmes are already scheduled at times which 'catch' a surprisingly large percentage of the population. Sonia Livingstone and Peter Lunt claim that 40 per cent of the British viewing public are available to watch morning audience discussion programmes. Furthermore, they predict with certainty that programmes like *Kilroy* are sure to expand in the British programming schedules of the future (1994, p. 2).

The growth of audience participation in the media begs important questions. In this chapter we aim to ask what benefits this kind of programming offers to media producers. Is it merely that they wish to offer genuine opportunities to audience members as citizens, to debate a wide range of moral, social and political issues in a public arena? Or are there other more commercially based reasons for the increase in this relatively new mode of product delivery? Second, what are the ideological implications of using audiences as a central resource in programme layout? Are the media, during a time of rapid technological change in which communities are becoming increasingly dispersed, becoming the new 'public sphere', where the members of the public are given an equal stake in debating how society should be governed? Or do these new forms of participation merely offer an illusion of participation and decision-making, without proffering any 'real' political effects?

The benefits for media producers

While it might be tempting to regard the increase in the use of 'real' members of the public in today's current affairs programmes as a philanthropic move towards creating a public forum for people to take established forms of power to task, it is undoubtedly the case that media institutions have commercial reasons closer to heart in their use of audience participation. The institutional production context of the talk show in the United States offers a valuable insight into the financial factors which have made programmes like *Oprah* and *Donahue* invaluable products for a number of interconnected media industries. While British television cannot be compared to television in the United States in terms either of its institutional structure or its programme scheduling, terrestrial, satellite and cable channels in Britain offer a clutch of talk shows, either imported from the United States or discussion programmes produced in Britain, on a daily basis. One satellite channel, Granada Talk, is devoted to discussion format programmes. Further, the decision to reformat Manchester's local BBC radio station GMR as GMR 'Talk' demonstrates the perceived popularity of discussion-format programming for audiences. Parallels can therefore be drawn between the commercial gains talk shows have secured for the media industries in the United States and the groundswell of similar media products which are growing in popularity in Britain.

In her study of the cultural significance of talk shows in the United States, *The Talking Cure: TV Talk Shows and Women* (1997), Jane Shattuc investigates those who stand to benefit from the enormous popularity of the genre. Shattuc suggests that while it might be argued that talk shows represent a potentially radical forum for the voices of marginalized groups to contest established power relations, the industries which produce them are primarily interested in their profitability. Their cultural significance for groups such as women, black people or gay rights activists is only interesting to their producers in so far as they attract larger audiences.

Nicholas Garnham's assertion in *Capitalism and Communication: Global Culture and the Economics of Information* (1990) that distribution is the largest profit-making sector in the media and cultural industries finds backing in Shattuc's analysis of the development of the talk show industry in the 1980s. The most popular talk shows on American television, *Oprah* and *Donahue* for example, are distributed by large corporations which syndicate (sell programmes to exhibitors) the first-run of non-network-produced programmes in exchange for licensing fees and advertising. In the main, these programmes are shown at non-peak periods when women viewers dominate, which is important for garnering advertising revenue. In some cases the shows are produced by syndication companies – Multimedia produces *Donahue* for example. Alternatively, they are made by production companies owned by the host, for example *Oprah* is made by HARPO Productions. Talk shows produced outside syndication companies still need the distribution provided by syndicators, hence HARPO Productions needs the syndication company King World Productions. Significantly, the syndicators own the rights to first-runs, the most desirable and potentially most profitable showing of the programme.

An investigation of the American company King World Productions, the leading distributor of first-run syndicated programming, demonstrates the kind of mega-profits to be gained from talk show programmes. It must be remembered that talk shows generate huge distribution profits not just within the United States, but worldwide. In 1993, for example, *Oprah* was distributed to sixty-four countries outside the United States.

Oprah was responsible for half of King World's profits in 1994 when it grossed $180 million in revenues from the show. King World managed to reap those profits in two ways: first, through fees for licensing the programmes to stations, from which it scooped $144 million; second, for barter agreements where King World traded programmes in exchange for station time which it used for advertising. *Oprah* had captured an 18–49-year-old female audience, the most valuable audience for advertisers. Ultimately, the syndication company took 43 per cent of *Oprah's* profits, or $77 million for the show's distribution.

The most popular talk shows attract huge amounts of advertising revenue. More specifically, as we have noted, advertisers are keenly aware of the predominantly female consumer group of working-class, 18–49-year-olds, who watch talk show television. Shattuc argues that for advertising companies, women constitute the consumer group which many of them actually prefer to reach. First, talk shows deliver this audience to advertisers in a sphere beyond the reach of the display of goods in the shopping complex: the home. Second, they are aware that women within this bracket, even in the 1990s, still purchase the bulk of consumer goods for the home. Third, women within this bracket are, despite changes in the workplace, the largest demographic group available for daytime viewing. This group also makes up the biggest percentage of habitual viewers.

Beyond the advertisement of consumer durables which gratify immediate consumer needs, Shattuc suggests that talk shows also market and commodify a longer-term social practice once considered to be provided by the immediate community: advice. These shows provide an ideal forum for workers in the medical and health industries to promote their products of self-help, counselling and therapy. Publishers also stand to make gains, as guest therapists and experts market self-help publications in the process. These shows therefore exploit the short- and long-term consumer 'needs' of the female viewer.

Shattuc argues that the television industry which manufactures talk shows cares little about the social and political role such programmes might provide for their viewers – that is, until show content or programming style conflicts with the interests of their advertisers. Large companies – Proctor and Gamble and Kelloggs, for example – were afraid of being associated with *Geraldo* because of its liberal values, and MCA cancelled the *Morton Downey Jr. Show* because advertisers refused to be tainted by its populist tabloid approach. It was only when commercial gain came under threat, Shattuc argues, that programme makers stopped to consider the anti-women sentiments of some shows: 'values became an issue only when someone objected' (1997, p. 54).

Yet while these shows yield high profits from distribution and advertising they are relatively cheap to produce. Conscious of their 18–49-year-old working-class market, the producers pack their programmes with all the necessary ingredients to maximize their saleability: their topics are women-centred and they are melodramatic, a mode of production and visual style often constructed to appeal to female audiences. Yet despite their appearance of spontaneity, shows such as *The Jerry Springer Show*, where audiences and guests are known to 'lose control', are made to exact specification. Mass-produced and disposable, they are manufactured under highly rationalized systems of production. The emphasis in production is on speed and efficiency. As Shattuc argues: 'It involves an assembly-line system of codified rules of production, specialized labor, and aesthetic norms and thereby turns out one of the least expensive forms of television to produce – $25,000 to $50,000 each half hour, a fraction of the cost of a unit in network drama' (1997, p. 66). Shattuc's analysis of stringent methods of production, for example talk show production schedules and the division of labour among staff, gives a clear idea as to why talk shows are economical in comparison to drama. But one need only consider the 'cast' of these shows to recognize that 'talk is cheap'; almost all the human resources used in the show content consist of unpaid volunteers. These programme makers have at their disposal a ready-made pool of free labour: ordinary people willing to offer their experiences and views in exchange for a brief moment of fame.

This kind of example demonstrates the full weight of the idea that talk has become an invaluable resource for the media industries. Talk has two benefits for media industries operating in capitalist contexts: it is inexpensive to produce and it makes large profits. However, while the industries make commercial gains on the basis that these programmes construct their audiences as consumers, how far do these programmes offer genuine benefits to audiences as citizens?

The ideological implications of 'talk' for audiences

It might be argued that the proliferation of audience discussion-based programmes, spawned as they are by deregulation, has generated a new climate in broadcasting. Within this view the authoritarianism of public service broadcasting has been replaced by a more democratic, populist style of programming which grants the public a greater proportion of programme space through which they might consider contemporary issues in the light of how they impinge on their everyday lives. In an age of new technologies and dispersed communities, such programmes might be seen to have replaced the public forum or 'town hall discussion': they now constitute the new public sphere. Regarded optimistically, such programmes might seem to offer a range of important public services: they might provide a space where ordinary people take those in authority to task; they could offer a discursive space to those previously marginalized by public domains; and they may provide important educational material on a range of public issues and concerns.

On the other hand, these programmes might be perceived cynically as a downgrading of broadcasting quality, the direct result of the commercialization following deregulation. Viewed pessimistically, they may be seen to celebrate ordinary voices at the expense of expert opinion which could counter their potential value as informational and educational tools. According to this standpoint, far from amounting to part of a genuine public sphere, such programmes are stage-managed products, which, as a result of the pressure to be successful in a market, must be prescribed and media-managed. As a result, the media set the agenda for discussion as opposed to the public. Instead of challenging established forms of power, such programmes divert attention away from the 'real' issues at stake and as a consequence they fall short of providing conclusive and politically active public forums.

Audience discussion programmes: the new public sphere?

If members of the public are to have an active role in democracy, they require access to an institutionally warranted arena where they can air opinions and challenge established power. The notion of what constitutes that kind of democratic forum or public sphere is defined by German philosopher Jürgen Habermas (1989). He characterizes the public sphere as a forum which acts as a mediator between a society and its state; a forum where private individuals can debate public affairs. The public sphere functions to influence state power by producing a critical and agreed public consensus, thereby holding the state accountable to the people.

The notion of a public sphere originated in the democracy of ancient Greece which was comprised partly of a marketplace and partly of a public arena. In Britain in the sixteenth and seventeenth centuries a public sphere was formed out of the onset of capitalism and the concomitant rise in liberal democratic thought. Led by a new rising class, the bourgeoisie, the public sphere was a space where, independent of institutions such as the church, ideas about how civil society should operate were formed and deployed. Public debate was played out in arenas such as universities, salons, coffeehouses and the press. The power of the public sphere rested on its central commitment to debating ideas concerned not with private affairs, but with the public's interest.

During the twentieth century the ideal forum for this kind of participatory democracy might have been the town hall discussion, where members of a community could meet to debate their views to form a critical public consensus. But as we enter a new century, when communications are global and driven by information technology, the local meeting has become increasingly untenable. Instead, the media have become the mediating institution between the state and its citizenry. But how adequately can the media perform their function as an arena for participatory democracy? Moreover, how far can a market-driven entity such as the media act as a public space free from the potentially tainting influences of markets or the government? And, can media products which purport to offer spaces for the exchange of views fulfil the functions of a public sphere?

Habermas argues that the development of monopoly capitalism has destroyed the possibility of offering genuine democratic opportunities for debating citizens. With regard to broadcasting and the market, other critics have voiced mounting fears about the consequences of the demise of the public service ethos in favour of deregulation. Curran (1991) argues that a market-driven media simply cannot deliver what a democratic society should be able to demand of its media. He points out that the market system carries several barriers to this: high entry costs mean that broader social interests are excluded from mainstream media – it is therefore unrepresentative; it also encourages concentrated ownership – a small group of owners is responsible for the ideas that are disseminated in the media. Taken together, these trends amount to 'a narrowing in the ideological and cultural diversity of the media' (1991, p. 47). From this standpoint the media cannot provide an adequately extensive range of economic and political options in a public forum, the very basis of what a democratic media should offer.

However, Habermas takes his deeply pessimistic critique of the modern media further. He argues that as a market-driven entity with vested interests in fragmenting audience markets for profit, the media cultivate a society comprised of private individuals within a dispersed culture. As a result the media cannot provide a real public forum for generating consensus, and therefore cannot challenge existing power relations. Products such as audience discussion programmes encourage passive spectatorship rather than active critical engagement. Instead of addressing audiences as a rational-critical debating public, the media have created a manipulated consuming mass. Instead of providing the space for public matters, the media are saturated with advertising and public relations. Constructing their audiences as consumers as opposed to citizens, the media industries act to divert their attention away from political agency and activism. While programmes which use audience participation offer the impression of 'serving the people', actually they are media-managed products which gatekeep in order to, if anything, protect established power. For Habermas, late twentieth-century media do not constitute a new public sphere. Rather, they amount to what he terms a pseudo-public sphere.

However, there are flaws in Habermas's thesis of a pseudo-public sphere. First, his account falls into the trap of theorizing audiences as uncritical dupes. Central to the notion of the public sphere is the idea that an intellectual bourgeois elite should formulate and lead public opinion. Implicit within that idea is the belief that ordinary people lack the skills to form opinions themselves. It theorizes them as a mass which cannot comprehend the potential dangers and power of the media. Second,

Habermas's theory of the public sphere has attracted sustained criticism from feminists. As Nancy Fraser argues, Habermas's conception of the citizen within the public sphere is a male construct which relies on access to public arenas of debate, forums from which, as a result of their social position, women have been excluded (Fraser, 1989, p. 26). The concept of the public sphere cordons off 'private' issues and, as a consequence, those who have been relegated to the private or domestic domain: namely, women. By bestowing value on public matters, those considered to be 'private' become secondary and the issues which directly impinge on the lives of women, for example political questions about how the family is organized, become 'private' matters of debate and negotiation. Consequently, women have historically been marginalized from the public forum and from setting the agenda of what counts as worthy and important enough for public scrutiny and attention. Nostalgia for a return to the establishment of a public sphere within the media is therefore problematic for feminists, since the concept of the public sphere inherently excludes women.

As a result, feminists have contested the usefulness of using the notion of the public sphere as a critical framework for evaluating media output – such as audience discussion programmes – because they are aimed specifically at female audiences and are consumed within domestic contexts. Fraser argues that the split between private and public domains has served to devalue women, their labour and their activities within the domestic setting. The public/private dichotomy has traditionally served to construct men as producers and women as consumers. Therefore programmes such as talk shows which are designed to reach women within their traditional social settings are devalued first because of their content, often derided as trivial, and second in terms of their audiences, often regarded as mindless consumers as opposed to rational, thinking citizens. As Shattuc argues: 'daytime talk shows, whose audience is predominantly women within the home, are easy to denigrate … as a non-culture. The shows are feminine in that they are experienced as sites of emotion and consumerist values by domestic labour within the home' (1997, p. 90). Instead, feminists have examined the possibility that audience discussion programmes might actually constitute an alternative or counter public sphere.

Audience discussion programmes: an oppositional public sphere?

In the wake of the feminist critique of Habermas's notion of the public sphere, feminists have turned their critical attention to assessing how far audience discussion programmes might actually be regarded as radical sites from which directly to challenge social power. Since audience discussion programmes deal head-on with the 'private' issues feminists have fought to bring into the public arena, can they not be regarded as catalysts for augmenting political action? Further, if the definition of what counts as worthy of public debate is to be challenged, why should Habermas's notion of the citizen, so clearly a 'male' construct, not be brought to account? why must the female viewer of the audience discussion programme be continually defined as a consumer instead of as a citizen? For some feminists, therefore, programmes like *Oprah* might well be defined as a counter public sphere.

For Shattuc, the role of what she terms 'identity politics' has played a key part in bringing issues previously relegated to the private into the public realm (1997, p. 91). Feminism, the civil rights movement and lesbian and gay activists have all campaigned since the late 1960s to advocate the notion both in the United States and in Britain that the 'personal is political'. Bound up with regarding the personal as political is the idea that the requirement for political change begins with one's identity, for example as a woman or as a black person. It means widening the focus out from placing public matters and institutions under scrutiny to include, for example, one's lifestyle, or the power balance of sexual relationships – in short, the cultural politics of everyday life.

For those who regard programmes like *Oprah* as an oppositional public sphere, the impact of identity politics on public life is directly evidenced by the fact that they act as a stage where the personal as political is played out. Such programmes actually operate as an arena for those who have been historically excluded from the bourgeois public sphere to discuss their personal experience in the context of a potentially political framework. The privileged position of knowledgeable experts is overturned by ordinary people concerned with the cultural politics of their everyday lives. Yet, as Fraser argues, while it might be possible to read aspects of the genre radically, particular aspects of the talk show require careful monitoring through close analysis. For example, Fraser encourages the reader to ask: how diverse are the voices that are allowed to speak? and how far are dominant forms of power really brought into question?

While Shattuc argues that aspects of the audience discussion programme do offer radical possibilities to female viewers, she tempers her discussion of the talk show by suggesting that a show like *Oprah* is actually neither progressive nor regressive. Instead, *Oprah* displays radical possibilities which suggest important political progress. However, the show also fosters more conservative elements which tend to harness its aspects of radical potential. Unfortunately they often ultimately serve to delimit the progressiveness of the show.

Shattuc suggests that *Oprah* displays several progressive possibilities which enable it to be part of a potential counter public sphere. Audiences are presented positively as rational, thinking and adjudicating subjects. Moreover, the show validates lower-class forms of participation and argument by allowing space for emotional outpourings, bodily gestures and personal testimonials, forms of communication which have been traditionally frowned upon by public bourgeois institutions. *Oprah* also tends to construct audience scenarios where those who share a particular problem become 'normalized as the majority'. For example, 60 per cent of the audience at an *Oprah* programme on HIV was made up of HIV-positive people. As a result, since both audience and guests were already united by their acceptance of gay people, questions about the morality of gay relationships were avoided, and the debate could extend outwards in more politically useful ways. Hence the show directly references the gains of the identity politics movement, since it offers those who are marginal in most mainstream areas of society the opportunity to take part in a majority discussion.

Moreover, Shattuc argues that the shows are sometimes potentially structurally radical because they refuse to sum up with solutions offered by the guest experts. In some cases *Oprah* concludes in an open-ended way, since a conclusion to the issue or problem simply cannot be achieved: there is no easy solution or way forward. As a result the show works against the idea of closure or an essential single true answer to social problems (Shattuc, 1997, p. 97). Rather, the onus is left with the show's guests and audience, as well as with the home audience, to continue to attempt to resolve the social problem that remains.

However, as Shattuc argues, 'It is naive to assume that daytime talk shows are a public sphere untainted by capitalism, the state, or even the bourgeois intellectual' (1997, p. 109). In some cases, while the show often acknowledges that the problems the public experience are socially determined, the programme frequently closes with a reference to the responsibility of the individual rather than to collective agency as a means to resolve social ills. Even when the show's content covers radical terrain, Oprah Winfrey, acting as the host who controls the main narrative thread of the programme, tends to smooth over the possibility of questioning wider social structures which maintain social inequalities. In many cases her role seems actually to involve circumventing the possibility that the audience might become aware of the wider social and political reasons why social problems exist. For example, in a show about racism entitled 'How Did Black Men Become So Feared?' the black intellectual guests attempted to offer historical and political reasons why people fear black masculinity. Yet Oprah insisted on deflecting the discussion back towards individualism or self-help, as Shattuc describes: 'Dyson describes slavery as a "deeply ingrained tradition in the mores and folkways of American culture." Allen asserts that several myths are operating in the discussion: "equal opportunities," "individualism," and "how one makes it in society." But Oprah maintains her show's emphasis on individualism: "Isn't the bottom line, You have to turn to yourself?"' (1997, p. 107). To return to Fraser's measure of the extent to which talk shows can be considered a counter public sphere, *Oprah* does often contain diverse, and even sometimes radical intellectual, voices, but the host tends to try to 'empty' their radicalism in summing up. *Oprah* generally falls short of allowing the discussion to develop into a genuine forum for contesting the root causes of social problems.

In several respects 'talk' can be viewed optimistically; many programmes which utilize the public as a resource do meet some of the requirements of a genuine public sphere. In some cases members of the public are given opportunities to question power and audiences show themselves to be critical, rational and intellectual. For example, as we have already noted, in the lead up to the 1997 general election in Britain, a special programme *Election Call* gave the public actual opportunities to question leading politicians from the Labour, Liberal Democrat and Conservative parties just days before votes were to be cast. In this programme, while the questions were vetted by the BBC, the politicians were unaware of what they were to be asked, and in several cases the questions were challenging and deeply uncomfortable for the politicians involved. And as feminist critics assert, the influence of identity politics has meant that there is a demand for the media to provide spaces for the voices of the previously marginalized, and that demand is realized by the audience discussion programme. Further, 'talk' does undoubtedly serve an educational purpose, exposing the public to a wide range of important current affairs topics.

Yet while feminists have effectively challenged the basic premises of Habermas's thesis about the pseudo-public sphere, the notion that audience discussion programmes provide a counter public sphere is ultimately questionable. The fact that programmes like *Esther*, *Oprah* and *Kilroy* tend to leave unquestioned the wider social structures which generate social problems means that their contribution to providing oppositional opportunities for members of the public is only partial. The shows themselves are the products of media management and gatekeeping and as a result such programmes, themselves the products of the political economy of the media industries, cannot afford to critique too heavily the capitalist context on which they depend.

Suggestions for further work

List all the media examples you can think of where the public have a prominent role. Attempt to group them in ways that explore 'how' they are used within the programmes (for example, as contestants, as experts, as sources of information). Can you draw any conclusions about the media's attitude to the public from this exercise?

Watch an edition of a TV talkshow. What is the focus of the programme? Does it provide a comprehensive discussion of the issue, or does it leave out certain perspectives?

Further reading

Livingstone, Sonia and Lunt, Peter 1994: *Talk on Television: Audience Participation and Public Debate*. London: Routledge.
Shattuc, Jane M. 1997: *The Talking Cure: TV Talk Shows and Women*. London: Routledge.

Epilogue: Research Methods in Media Studies

What do we mean by research?

Students at university will encounter a range of different forms of assessment. Common to most, if not all of them, is an emphasis on researching around the tasks which they are required to undertake. For example, a student might be asked to complete a discursive essay using a particular theoretical perspective. In this instance, the task would be to select and research the appropriate theoretical 'tool' for the assignment; alternatively, he or she might be required to analyse textually an aspect of the media, for which a research method will need to be selected that will lend the analysis a framework; or illustrative textual examples may have to be collected for a small group presentation. All of these demand that the student finds out information for him or herself. Yet acquiring research skills means more than merely getting a few books from the library. It involves developing a set of adaptable skills which can be utilized in a number of learning contexts. Here, we introduce suggestions and strategies which can be adapted to the needs of a particular learning programme, as well as to students' own personal modes of learning.

Our advice is not wholly prescriptive. As a result, our suggestions are general, yet they frequently acknowledge the specificity of working within media studies as a subject area. We favour a student-centred approach to research which most universities advocate. Therefore our suggestions are designed to encourage students to become proficient at generating their own research skills, so that ultimately they will formulate their own questions about researching the media.

Researching for assignments

During the course of this book we have referred to a number of research methodologies. For example, in chapter 2 we discussed the theoretical underpinnings of semiotics and suggested ways in which semiotics might be applied as a systematic qualitative method for analysing the meaning of textual aspects of the media. Similarly in chapter 4 we discussed content analysis as a quantitative method of gathering data on the frequency of media images. We also examined theoretical approaches, for example political economy, as a means of understanding the actions of media industries. In this section of the chapter we aim, first, to suggest ways of deploying these methods and approaches to the media in the context of writing assignments, and, second, to provide more general approaches to research by, for example, emphasizing the importance of defining the purposes of assignments; or by showing how to select relevant material for assignments.

How to claim ownership of assignments

Most assessed work in higher education is written. However, on occasion a student may be required to give an oral presentation. Therefore, in the main this chapter aims to give advice on written work, since even oral presentations will require the preparation of either cue cards or some kind of script. But it is worth emphasizing that even when an assignment appears to be tightly prescriptive, it can always be defined and researched in such a way that it is recognizably that of a particular student. For example, consider the following typical media studies question: 'Discuss the representation of one social group in the contemporary news media'. There are many ways in which this question might be answered, depending on the perspective that is taken. In order to own this question, it is up to the student to define his or her topic in relation to the question. The next section will suggest ways in which this may be done.

Establishing objectives

Assignments are set as a means by which lecturers can check their students' learning skills; their general aims are tied to the concerns dealt with on the courses or modules for which a student enrols. Specific assessment criteria may also be given which lecturers use both to define the specific purposes of an assignment and to refer to when they go through marking procedures.

These assessment criteria should be followed closely. For example, it may be specified that an assignment be answered within particular parameters, that a particular theoretical perspective should be followed, or that examples from a particular medium are used. Or it may prescribe a word limit. The assessment criteria should be referred to constantly as a checklist during the planning stages; the marker will check that they have been adhered to.

Nevertheless, students are also encouraged to bring their own ideas and interests to an assignment. Lecturers are not interested in having their lectures repeated back to them, nor do they want the activities that have been worked through in seminars simply rehashed. Rather, they embrace well-argued assignments which show a diligent, independent approach to research. This is where students come in. Consider again the typical media studies question above, and notice that it lends itself to being moulded by an individual perspective. One student might be interested in exploring how a particular social group is represented – for example, disabled men or black, working-class women. Another may wish to use certain media texts through which to discuss their chosen social group, with the intention of comparing how that group is represented on satellite and terrestrial television news for instance.

Selecting a topic

Some assignments are general, some have more specific demands. Deciding which angle to focus on means exploring some of the possible options. Students should be prepared to abandon a topic if its possibilities seem confined, and should bear the following points in mind when deciding upon an area of study for an assignment:

- Enthusiasm and interest in a topic. This is important: interest in an area makes it easier to sustain the necessary level of work.
- Students should be prepared to be influenced by available resources. If the chosen area is original and has not yet been written about in academic circles, the student may need to make his or her own academic connections.
- Time constraints should be borne in mind when choosing a topic. Selecting something familiar might save time, though this needs to be balanced against the necessary enthusiasm for a topic. Also, selecting a familiar area can lead to complacency. It certainly does not necessarily mean less work.

Setting the parameters of a topic

Before beginning to track down research materials it is important to identify the entire requirements of the particular assignment. This is a crucial initial planning exercise. In order to set up the scope of the assignment, the following questions should be considered:

What is my specific focus within the topic?
One should always ask oneself, 'what particularly interests me about this topic?' If the aim is to analyse how women are represented in the news media, the focus can be sociologically honed down to be about white working-class women. Another point that needs to be tackled early on is the question of what position or standpoint one intends to adopt in relation to the specific focus. One should ask: 'what do I want to say about the subject at hand?' It is sometimes said that assignments are about constructing arguments, so it is clear that a decision should be made early on as to what those arguments are going to be.

How much breadth or depth can can be covered?
Given the terms of the assessment criteria the following question should be asked: 'How much material can I afford to explore?' Would it be better to explore a number of examples in order to make quantitative claims, or would it be better to explore one or two examples qualitatively?

What approach will I take to the topic?
The words of the assignment heading should be carefully analysed – for example, what verbs have been used to structure the task? Such instructions as 'discuss', 'evaluate' and 'review' will necessarily direct the approach to be taken. It should be found out whether any particular conventions are required for the discursive essay or for the review, and research should be planned with clear objectives in mind.

What research method will I draw upon in order to 'investigate', 'evaluate' or 'review' the topic?
The question, 'which methods best suit the terms of the study?' should be considered. Not all media studies assignments require the use of a specific method, but some do lend themselves to the use of a method-ological framework. For example, two possible research methods that might be used for examining how social groups are represented are semiotics and content analysis. Semiotics can be used for evaluating the meaning of the representations under analysis. On the other hand, content analysis might be used to ascertain the frequency of the occurrence of images. It might be that both research methods could be used, depending on the focus of the study. This question needs be asked in the light of what the student decides in relation to the specific focus of his or her topic, what kind of breadth or depth can be covered, what approach the assignment directs the student towards, as well as the type of argument that is to be constructed.

What overarching theoretical material will I use to investigate the topic?
In this book we explore a number of theoretical perspectives which media studies draws upon, for example Marxism and feminism. It is important that students think about how theory can be applied to their own examples from the media, thereby demonstrating their understanding of theory. In the first instance, students should make note of the basic principles of the theory and ask themselves, 'how can this perspective enlighten my investigation?' More specifically it is important to consider which particular positions within those larger theoretical perspectives it would be most useful to explore. For example, in taking up a Marxist perspective, how useful might it be to explore Althusserian Marxism; or, with regard to feminism, might socialist or radical feminist positions be a help in exploring examples?

What key concepts will I be required to draw upon and define?
As a subject, media studies has its own terminology where key concepts and subject-specific ideas reside. Becoming familiar with concepts, words and ideas, and being able to use them with precision, is fundamental to undergraduate work. One way of beginning to formulate a good working understanding of key concepts is to explore how they overlap and interrelate. In many cases concepts are clearly related: how 'production' is defined as a concept depends on one's conception of 'consumption'. There are a number of useful specialist subject dictionaries available for consultation which will help to clarify individual concepts. However, students also need to begin situating concepts into the wider field of ideas within media studies. They should ask themselves which key concepts might be required to define and demonstrate their understanding of a topic, and work out the ways in which key concepts overlap and feed each other.

What primary resource materials do I need in order to illustrate my piece with examples?
Students should, wherever possible, be able to make an assignment their own by selecting their own examples to illustrate arguments and to demonstrate their understanding of theories and ideas. The question, 'what kind of examples can I glean for my assignment?' should be asked. Interviews might be conducted with experts or with ordinary people with a view to gathering oral evidence. An assignment might require the student to discuss textual examples of their own choosing.

Selecting relevant material

Once the purpose and topic of an assignment have been defined, the question of where to find material for it must be faced. At the most basic level there will have been lectures, seminars and workshops, and reading lists will have been provided, as well as advice from tutors. Students will also, however, be expected to gather their own material, to demonstrate independent learning.

The purpose and definition of the chosen topic should never be forgotten, and should be referred to frequently while choosing material. To stay on the right track there are some points that should be remembered:

- Frequently consult course materials such as the aims and objectives of the course and the assessment criteria of the assignment.
- Refer to the decisions made when selecting a specific topic – these should be a guide during subsequent research.
- Browse with purpose – trawling material can be very pleasurable, but it can also be a time-wasting exercise if clear objectives are not kept in mind.
- Be prepared to search for material that is not recommended but is clearly usefully related to the topic.

Often, the end result is that there will be a great deal of material at one's disposal, perhaps overwhelmingly so! It is therefore important to decide which material is of most use.

Judging the selection

Even if all the material appears to be relevant, does it directly serve the purposes of the particular assignment? Students should be ready to discard what aspects don't fulfil their objectives. Some materials might be pertinent, but they might lack complexity. Sources should be at an appropriate level of study for the assignment.

Some sources might be written for another kind of audience, for example, journalistic books, biographical information or the Internet. This material is not necessarily irrelevant, but students need to demonstrate an awareness of its context. When using materials of this kind, students should ensure that they fashion the information into a form that serves their academic purposes.

Hints for compiling research materials

When gathering research it is useful to:

- file information into a system which makes the material accessible when it comes to writing up the assignment;
- file information into sections which allow further ideas and notes to be added as the project progresses;
- keep bibliographical and source information. All material from printed journals or books will need to be recorded in the bibliography.

Using libraries

The library remains the dominant mode of gathering research in institutions of higher education. Libraries often house a vast range of information resources. This section is about making the best use of the resources they offer. It also aims to help students to select material they might require for researching around a chosen topic.

While the main university library is often the starting point, it is always possible to find relevant material in other libraries. For example:

- the departmental library;
- libraries in other departments – consider, for example, the material that might be found within the following subject areas: cultural studies, sociology, women's studies, gender studies, history;
- local college libraries;
- the local public library;
- government department libraries;
- specialist libraries belonging to societies or voluntary organizations.

Clearly, some of these libraries will be more useful than others. The main university library might well have a range of key relevant sources. However it might not entirely cater for the entire scope of a topic. It is also possible that these resources may be under heavy demand from other media studies students, in which case it may well be useful to visit other college or university libraries or local libraries. If the main university library does not stock a particular book or article, it might be able to obtain it via the inter-library loan system.

Making maximum use of library resources

Libraries contain a wealth of resources which broadly divide into two categories: printed and non-printed resources.

Printed resources
These might include:

- books;
- periodicals or journals (current ones on display and back issues either shelved or on microfilm);
- newspapers and magazines;
- a reference collection which might include: specialist encyclopedias or dictionaries, for example, *International Dictionary of Films and Filmmakers*; resource directories such as *A Journalist's Guide to Sources*; year books and annual reports which contain current statistical information, for example, IBA annual reports and ITC annual reports;

- indexes, bibliographies and abstracts – often housed in the reference collection, these are invaluable for finding references on a particular topic. In order to make full use of indexes and abstracts, a list of terms that are central to the topic should be planned before visiting the library.

An index is a list of terms on a particular subject, and usually refers to periodicals. For example, *British Humanities Index* and *Design and Applied Arts Index.* A bibliography is a selected list of both books and journal articles on a particular topic. Abstracts are a short summary of books and articles on a particular subject. Abstracts are also indexed. For example, *Communications Abstracts.*

Indexes and abstracts are now also widely available on CD-ROM. For example, *Art Index and Film Index International.*

Non-printed resources
These might include:

- CD-ROM. Besides the abstracts and indexes, full text of the daily broadsheet newspapers is also available on CD-ROM, for example the *Guardian* and the *Independent;*
- microform, which can either take the form of a reel of film called microfilm, or a flat sheet of film, about the size of an index card, called microfiche. Microform is used in preference to storing bulky items such as newspapers where the image is photographically reduced onto the film or fiche and then enlarged onto a screen using a special reader;
- audio-visual material such as videos, audiocassettes and slides;
- computers and a range of computer software, for example the Internet which can be accessed from any networked computer. Increasingly, colleges and universities are now linked to the Internet by JANET. There are gateways and subject resources available which might offer help with research topics. However, the Internet must be treated with caution. It is possible to 'surf the net' for long time-periods with little gain, since much of the material available will lack sufficient academic grounding. In addition, information on the Internet is not regulated, is not checked for accuracy or reliability – nor is the material necessarily up to date.

Getting to know the library and locating the relevant items

Contemporary library users are increasingly encouraged to be self-reliant. Below are the first steps towards becoming an independent library user:

- Students should familiarize themselves with the library's layout, thus enabling them to become fully aware of what the library has to offer, and helping them to access the materials they require quickly and efficiently. Most libraries have user-friendly maps which are designed to guide users around the library space.

- Become acquainted with the library's systems. For example, how to order an inter-library loan, or the terms under which audio-visual materials may be borrowed.
- Find out what system the library uses for classifying, indexing and shelving its collection. Most libraries will use an on-line catalogue. If there are difficulties in locating an item, check the entry for spelling!
- Time-manage use of libraries. Gaining access to specific materials can be very competitive. It is important therefore to begin a materials search well in advance of assignment deadlines. It might be useful to reserve some items, and some items might only be available on loan for short time-periods. Ensure that the assignment planning allows for these constraints on resources.
- Ask the librarians if specific materials cannot be located. They are the experts on what the library contains, but ask them only as a last resort. Finding the means to locate the materials that are needed independently is the only way to developing sound research skills.

Writing up

Once a topic has been defined and rigorously researched it should be ready to be written up in assignment form.

Prepare to plan

Most academic writers would agree that planning written work is an imperative. But it is sometimes at this stage that one feels absolutely saturated with ideas, examples and arguments and it is possible literally to become lost in all the notes. A useful preliminary to writing a plan is to brainstorm points onto a large sheet of paper. During this stage these points will be random and incoherent, but the idea is to get them down on paper. Afterwards they can begin to be ordered into assignment form. After the brainstorm phase and before actually constructing a plan, it might be necessary to remember a few basic but crucial points:

- Think again about the aims and objectives behind the assignment. Ask, 'What is the point of writing this assignment?' and 'Why did I choose to focus on this particular topic or area?'
- Before starting, encapsulate the argument or the case that is to be built and try to develop a sense of what perspective is intended in relation to the topic.

- Remember that every assignment is an act of communication with an implied audience. Bear in mind therefore that it must communicate precisely what is meant in a coherent and concise form in the manner the audience expects.

Constructing a plan

There are two key objectives in writing assignments: work must be structured and thoughts must be clearly expressed. The plan should include everything that is to be included in skeletal form. In this way, at the final stage, the student will remain constantly aware of the direction the assignment will take and will therefore be able to concentrate on ensuring that the arguments are as lucid as possible. Aim to plan in sections, using the following points as a structuring principle:

The introduction
This is a brief section introducing the reader to the arguments that will follow. It should include:

- the main argument or case;
- the perspective, standpoint or position;
- a brief encapsulating statement which explains what the assignment is about;
- a signposting brief which takes the reader through the assignment's structure.

The main body
This section includes the main material used to argue the case. Remember to order main points strategically; it might be the case, for example, that some ideas would be more effectively used towards the end of the assignment. Remember too that if there are any key concepts which require definition, it is best to provide the reader with that information early on in the assignment. Aim to make this part of the plan as detailed as possible – plan the main body with a paragraph-by-paragraph breakdown. Clearly, if the assignment requires the use of a particular theoretical framework or research method, these need to be developed in the main body, as they are key ingredients and will shape the entire content of the final work. Each paragraph should include:

- a key point;
- an idea of the relationship it has to other key points;
- reference to the theoretical/conceptual framework;
- evidence of the deployment of research methods;
- supporting evidence or primary source examples;
- reference to secondary sources and how you intend to use them.

As each paragraph is planned, the question should be asked: 'How does this material provide an answer to the question set by the assignment?' If it is clear that it does further the argument in some way, ensure that each paragraph contains some kind of signposting statement which reminds the reader why the information provides answers to the question. This will also ensure that the objectives of the assignment remain at the forefront of the mind of both student and assessor.

The conclusion

This encapsulates what has been argued. It should draw together and reflect back upon the main points of the assignment and in this way should refer back to the introduction. The conclusion should also aim to end smoothly to round off your assignment.

Writing up the plan

The process of writing itself is time-consuming and requires considerable work; an assignment cannot be expected to be finished in one brief sitting. It is always necessary to write up the plan in the form of at least one, and sometimes even several, drafts. It is possible to experiment with different ways of writing up the plan. For example, it may be sensible to write the main body first, and the introduction afterwards. It is always useful to write a draft and come back to it several days later – in that way weak phrases and cloudy expression become apparent. When the final draft is finished, it should be checked very thoroughly. The following checklist might be useful:

- Is the content entirely relevant? Does it sufficiently develop an understanding of the key points?
- Is the assignment analytical as opposed to descriptive? If theoretical/ conceptual material is used, is it applied in ways which demonstrate a clear understanding?
- Is the argument clear and coherent throughout? Is the argument sufficiently evidenced with clear supporting examples?
- Is the bibliography entirely consistent, accurate and complete? Are sources appropriately cited using bibliographical referencing? Most courses will issue a handbook that will outline the system that should be adopted.
- Does the assignment effectively express the intended argument? Are spelling and grammatical and syntactical construction of sentences accurate?
- Is the assignment neatly and clearly presented?

Even though it might well be the case that this checklist has been satisfied, it is still essential that the final draft is very carefully proofread.

Conclusion

The structuring of this book around the three broad areas of textual analysis, media institutions and media audiences is clearly a conscious one. It has enabled us to cover a range of important and central ideas and approaches within contemporary media studies, and to include, particularly within the audience section, some areas of academic work that are sometimes overlooked in overviews of media analysis. As we state within the audience section, many of these approaches are drawn from, or utilize methods associated with, what might broadly be called cultural studies. One of the things that marks out cultural studies approaches to the media and other aspects of contemporary life is its willingness to draw from a range of methods and disciplines in order to arrive at the fullest possible understanding of the object of study.

It is to this willingness to cross academic divides that we now want briefly to turn. Academic approaches to the media often offer a variety of contrasting and contradictory 'positions'. These might be presented in contexts, conferences papers, books and journals, which create a sense of opposition between differing positions and offer critiques of seemingly 'incorrect' approaches. For example, in *Cultural Studies in Question* (Ferguson and Golding eds, 1997) a series of contributors debated whether political economy approaches or cultural studies approaches are the most valuable and appropriate for the analysis of contemporary culture. Within this collection of essays Douglas Kellner argues for what he terms a 'multiperspectival' approach. He sees this method, which draws on a number of traditions, as a way of overcoming what he calls 'the great divide' between political economy and cultural studies approaches (p. 103). He states that the division and differences between culturalist approaches to culture and communications research has meant that 'These conflicting approaches point to a division of the field of media communications into specialized sub-areas with competing models and methods, and, ironically, to a lack of communication in the field itself' (p. 103).

Kellner also outlines his multiperspectival approach in his contribution to another publication, *Cultural Methodologies* (McGuigan ed., 1997). He sees this approach as one that can lead to a fuller understanding of contemporary, global media cultures and developments. This approach is able to do this through the utilization of a variety of critical perspectives. These involve, broadly speaking, political economy, textual analysis and audience studies. In a sense, then, Kellner's multiperspectival approach to the media breaks down the distinctions that structure this book, arguing that elements from all three sections should be drawn on and embraced in order to comprehend fully the contemporary media and their place within modern societies.

An important facet of Kellner's approach is that it stresses the importance of a politicized approach to the media. He argues that whatever perspective one takes to understand contemporary media industries, they must be acknowledged as operating in the context of corporate, international capital. Therefore, the media is a site where the interests of owners, capital and profit are of great importance. He also argues, therefore, that even if one approaches the media as an example of, say, postmodernity, the centrality of global capital to postmodern society cannot be ignored. Kellner also states that even when considering audiences it is important to consider the influence of economic interests, in the shape of production and distribution patterns, upon them. For example, audiences only have the option to see films at the cinema which distribution companies see fit to purchase and place in circulation. This means that whatever the audience response to such films, their availability is directly influenced by the distribution companies, and exhibitors desire to make as much profit as possible. Similarly, when approaching close textual analysis, the influence of production and distribution upon textual material needs to be acknowledged. For example, Hollywood films are put through a strict process of previews, the responses to which often inform the final cut of major blockbusters. To understand fully how audiences can respond to and use these films one has to acknowledge the influence of these profit-seeking forces. Kellner also argues that the links between textual construction and capital can be explored through the organizing codes and conventions that operate within the media industries such as genre:

> The encoding of media artefacts is deeply influenced by systems of production so that study of the texts of television, film or popular music, for instance, is enhanced by studying the ways that media artefacts are actually produced within the structure and organization of the culture industries ... This economic factor explains why Hollywood film is dominated by major genres and sub-genres, explains sequelmania in the film

industry, crossovers of popular films into television series, and a certain homogeneity in products constituted within systems of production with rigid generic codes, formulaic conventions and well-defined ideological boundaries. (Kellner, 1997, p. 32)

It is important for us as we conclude this book to reiterate how false the divisions within it are. Media studies should draw from a range of perspectives and it is the job of students confidently to select and utilize the approaches they feel the most suitable. The divisions within this book are maintained in order to make the material as accessible to its target readers as possible, thereby, we hope, reflecting some of the divisions students will encounter in the structure of their undergraduate modules. As we have already stressed, however, having reached this point in this book, the student should be ready to begin overcoming these somewhat false divides. We therefore end by arguing for an approach to the study and analysis of the media which draws on a number of the approaches outlined in this book, as well as others that students may come across from other sources as they progress in their studies. It is worth finally quoting Kellner, who argues with regard to cultural studies something that we feel should be equally applicable to the analysis of the media:

The major traditions of cultural studies combine – at their best – social theory, cultural critique, history, philosophical analysis and specific political interventions, thus overcoming the standard academic division by sur-mounting arbitrary disciplinary specialization. Cultural studies thus oper-ates with a transdisciplinary conception that draws on social theory, economics, politics, history, communication studies, literary and cultural theory, philosophy and other theoretical discourses. (Kellner, 1997, p. 25)

Bibliography

Allaun, Frank 1988: *Spreading the News: A Guide to Media Reform*. Nottingham: Spokesman.

Alloway, Lawrence 1971: *Violent America: The Movies 1946–1964*. New York: Museum of Modern Art.

Althusser, Louis 1971: *Lenin and Philosophy and Other Essays*. London: New Left Books.

Altman, Rick 1987: *The American Film Musical*. London: British Film Institute.

Alverado, Manuel, Gutch, Robin and Wollen, Tana 1987: *Learning the Media: An Introduction to Media Teaching*. London: Macmillan.

Ang, Ien 1985: *Watching Dallas: Soap Opera and the Melodramatic Imagination*. London: Methuen.

Armes, Roy 1988: *On Video*. London: Routledge.

Barker, Martin 1989: *Comics: Ideology, Power and the Critics*. Manchester: Manchester University Press.

Barker, Martin and Petley, Julian (eds) 1997: *Ill Effects: The Media/Violence Debate*. London: Routledge.

Barthes, Roland 1972: *Mythologies*. London: Cape.

Barthes, Roland 1977: *Image-Music-Text*. London: Fontana.

Berelson, B. et al. 1954: *Voting: A Study of Opinion Formation in a Presidential Campaign*. Chicago: Chicago University Press.

Betterton, R. (ed.) 1987: *Looking On: Images of Femininity in the Visual Arts and Media*. London: Pandora.

Blumler, J. G. 1969: Producers' attitudes towards television coverage of an election campaign: a case study. In P. Halmos (ed.), *The Sociology of Mass Media Communicators*, Keele: The Sociological Review, 85–115.

Bobo, Jacqueline 1988: *The Color Purple*: Black women as cultural readers. In Deidre Pribram (ed.), *Female Spectators: Looking at Film and Television*, London: Verso, 90–109.

Bobo, Jacqueline 1992: The politics of interpretation: Black critics, filmmakers, audiences. In Gina Dent (ed.), *Black Popular Culture*, Seattle: Bay Press, 65–74.

Boddy, William 1990: Building the world's largest advertising medium: CBS and television, 1940–60. In Tino Balio (ed.), *Hollywood in the Age of Television*, London: Unwin Hyman, 63–90.

Bordwell, David and Thompson, Kristin 1986: *Film Art: An Introduction*, 2nd edn. New York: Alfred A. Knopf.

Branigan, Edward 1985: Color and cinema: problems in the writing of history. In Bill Nichols (ed.), *Movies and Methods Vol. 2*, Berkeley: University of California Press.

Briggs, Asa 1960: *The History of Broadcasting in the United Kingdom*. London: Oxford University Press.

Brunsdon, Charlotte 1997: *Screen Tastes: Soap Opera to Satellite Dishes*. London: Routledge.

Brunsdon, Charlotte and Morley, David 1978: *Everyday Television: Nationwide*. London: British Film Institute.

Bourdieu, Pierre 1984: *Distinction: A Social Critique of the Judgement of Taste*. London: Routledge.

Burnett, Robert 1996: *The Global Jukebox: The International Music Industry*. London: Routledge.

Burns, Tom 1972: Commitment and career in the BBC. In Denis McQuail (ed.), *Sociology of Mass Communications*, London: Penguin, 281–310.

Burns, Tom 1977: *The BBC: Public Institution, Private World*. Basingstoke: Macmillan.

Buscombe, Edward 1970: The idea of genre in American cinema. Screen, 11, 2.

Buscombe, Edward 1985: Sound and color. In Bill Nichols (ed.), *Movies and Methods Vol. 2*, Berkeley: University of California Press, 83–91.

Cameron, Ian and Pye, Douglas (eds) 1996: *The Movie Book of the Western*. London: Studio Vista.

Caughie, John (ed.) 1981: *Theories of Authorship*. London: British Film Institute.

Collins, Jim 1993: Genericity in the nineties: eclectic irony and the new sincerity. In Jim Collins et al. (eds), *Film Theory Goes to the Movies*, London: Routledge, 242–64.

Connell, Ian 1983: Commercial broadcasting and the British left. Screen, 24, 6, 70–80.

Cook, Jim and Lewington, Mike (eds) 1979: *Images of Alcoholism*. London: British Film Institute.

Cook, Pam (ed.) 1987: *The Cinema Book*. London: British Film Institute.

Cormack, Mike 1992: *Ideology*. London: Batsford.

Cottle, Simon 1993: *TV News: Urban Conflict and the Inner City*. Leicester: Leicester University Press.

Courtney, A. and Whipple, T. 1983: *Sex Stereotyping in Advertising*. Lexington: Lexington Books.

Crisell, Andrew 1986: *Understanding Radio*. London: Methuen.

Cubbit, Sean 1991: *Timeshift: On Video Culture*. London: Routledge.

Culler, Jonathan 1990: *Saussure*. London: Fontana.

Curran, James 1991: Rethinking the media as a public sphere. In Philip Dahlgren and Colin Sparks (eds), *Communication and Citizenship: Journalism and the Public Sphere in the New Media Age*, London: Routledge, 27–57.

Curran, James and Seaton, Jean 1991: *Power Without Responsibility: The Press and Broadcasting in Britain*, 4th edn. London: Routledge.

Curtis, Liz 1984: *Ireland: The Propaganda War. The British Media and the Battle for Hearts and Minds*. London: Pluto Press.

Dent, Gina (ed.) 1992: *Black Popular Culture*. Seattle: Bay Press.

Douglas, Mary and Isherwood, Baron 1980: *The World of Goods*. Harmondsworth: Penguin.

Driver, Stephen and Gillespie, Andrew 1993: Structural change in the cultural industries: British magazine publishing in the 1980s. *Media, Culture, Society*, 15, 2, 183–201.

Dworkin, Andrea 1981: *Pornography: Men Possessing Women*. London: The Women's Press.

Dyer, Richard 1986: *Heavenly Bodies*. London: British Film Institute / Macmillan.

Dyer, Richard 1990: *Now You See It: Studies on Lesbian and Gay Film*. London: Routledge.

Dyer, Richard (ed.) 1977: *Gays and Film*. London: British Film Institute.

Eagleton, Terry 1991: *Ideology: An Introduction*. London: Verso.

Eco, Umberto 1984: A guide to neo-television of the 1980s. *Framework*, 25, 18–27.

Elliot, Philip 1972: *The Making of a TV Series*. London: Constable.

Elliot, Philip 1973: Uses and gratifications: a critique and a sociological alternative. Mimeo: Centre for Mass Communications Research, University of Leicester.

Elliot, Philip 1977: Media organizations and occupations. In James Curran et al. (eds), *Mass Communication and Society*, London: Edward Arnold, 142–73.

Ellis, John 1992: *Visible Fictions: Cinema: Television: Video*, 2nd edn. London: Routledge.

Erens, Patricia 1977: *Sunset Boulevard*: a morphological analysis. *Film Reader*, 2.

Giddens, Anthony 1990: *The Consequences of Modernity*. Cambridge: Polity Press.

Fell, John L. 1977: Vladimir Propp in Hollywood. *Film Quarterly*, 30, 3.

Ferguson, Marjorie and Golding, Peter (eds) 1997: *Cultural Studies in Question*. London: Sage.

Fiske, John 1987: *Television Culture*. London: Methuen.

Fiske, John 1992: The cultural economy of fandom. In Lisa A. Lewis (ed.), *The Adoring Audience: Fan Culture and Popular Media*, London: Routledge, 30–49.

Flichy, Patrice 1995: *Dynamics of Modern Communication: The Shaping and Impact of New Communication Technologies*. London: Sage.

Fraser, Nancy 1989: *Unruly Practices: Power, Discourse and Gender in Contemporary Social Theory*. Minneapolis: University of Minnesota Press.

Gallafent, Edward 1994: *Clint Eastwood: Actor and Director*. London: Studio Vista.

Gallagher, Margaret 1982: Negotiation of control in media organizations and occupations. In Michael Gurevitch et al. (eds), *Culture, Society and the Media*, London: Methuen. 151–73.

Garnham, Nicholas 1990: *Capitalism and Communication: Global Culture and the Economics of Information*. London: Sage.

Gillespie, M. 1995: *Television, Ethnicity and Cultural Change*. London: Routledge.

Glasgow University Media Group 1976: *Bad News*. London: Routledge and Kegan Paul.

Glasgow University Media Group 1982: *Really Bad News*. London: Writers and Readers Publishing Co-Operative.

Grant, Charles 1995: *Whirlwind*. London: Harper Collins.

Gray, Anne 1992: *Video Playtime: The Gendering of a Leisure Technology*. London: Routledge.

Greimas, A. J. 1966: *Sémantique Structurale*. Paris: Larousse.

Gross, Larry 1989: Out of the mainstream: sexual minorities and the mass media. In Ellen Seiter et al. (eds), *Remote Control*, London: Routledge, 130–49.

Habermas, Jurgen 1989: *The Structural Transformation of the Public Sphere: An Inquiry into a Category of Bourgeois Society*. Cambridge: MIT Press.

Hartley, John 1982: *Understanding News*. London: Methuen.

Hall, Stuart 1973: Encoding and decoding in the television discourse. *CCCS Stencilled Paper*, 7, University of Birmingham.

Hall, Stuart 1980: Encoding/decoding. In S. Hall, D. Hobson, A. Lowe and P. Willis (eds), *Culture, Media, Language: Working Papers in Cultural Studies 1972–79*, London: Unwin Hyman, 128–38.

Hall, Stuart 1981: Cultural studies: two paradigms. In Tony Bennett, Graham Martin, Colin Mercer and Janet Woollacott (eds), *Culture, Ideology and Social Process: a reader*, London: Batsford, 19–37.

Hall, Stuart 1981b: Notes on deconstructing 'the popular'. In R. Samuel (ed.), *People's History and Socialist Theory*, London: Routledge, pp. 227–40.

Hall, Stuart 1982: The rediscovery of 'ideology': the return of the 'repressed' in media studies. In Michael Gurevitch, Tony Bennett, James Curran and Janet Woollacott (eds), *Culture, Society and the Media*, London: Methuen, 56–90.

Hall, Stuart (ed.) 1997: *Representation: Cultural Representations and Signifying Practices*. London: Open University/Sage.

Hall, S., Critcher, C., Jefferson, T., Clarke, J. and Roberts, B. 1978: *Policing the Crisis*. London: Macmillan.

Hall, Stuart, Held, David and McGrew, Tony (eds) 1992: *Modernity and its Futures*. Cambridge: Polity Press/Open University.

Halloran, James 1970: *The Effects of Television*. London: Panther.

Haskell, Molly 1987: *From Reverence to Rape: The Treatment of Women in the Movies*, 2nd edn. Chicago: University of Chicago Press.

Hawkes, Terence 1977: *Structuralism and Semiotics*. London: Methuen.

Hebdige, Dick 1988: *Hiding in the Light: On Images and Things*. London: Routledge.

Hobson, Dorothy 1980: Housewives and the mass media. In S. Hall et al. (eds), *Culture, Media, Language: Working Papers in Cultural Studies 1972–79*, London: Unwin Hyman. 105–14.

Hollows, Joanne 1995: Mass culture theory and political economy. In Joanne Hollows and Mark Jancovich (eds), *Approaches to Popular Film*, Manchester: Manchester University Press, 15–36.

Hollows, Joanne and Jancovich, Mark (eds) 1995: *Approaches to Popular Film*. Manchester: Manchester University Press.

Hood, Stuart 1980: *On Television*. London: Pluto Press.

Horkheimer, Max and Adorno, Theodor 1979: *The Dialectic of Enlightenment*. London: Verso.

Jackson, Stevie and Moores, Shaun (eds) 1995: *The Politics of Domestic Consumption: Critical Readings*. London: Prentice Hall.

Jameson, Fredric 1985: Postmodernism and consumer society. In Hal Foster (ed.), *Postmodern Culture*, London: Pluto Press, 111–25.

Jancovich, Mark 1992: David Morley: the *Nationwide* studies. In Martin Barker and Anne Beezer (eds), *Reading into Cultural Studies*, London: Routledge, 134–47.

Jancovich, Mark 1995: Screen theory. In Joanne Hollows and Mark Jancovich (eds), *Approaches to Popular Film*, Manchester: Manchester University Press, 123–50.

Jenkins, Henry 1991: It's not a fairy tale anymore: gender, genre and *Beauty and the Beast*. The Journal of Film and Video, 43, 1 and 2, 91–2.

Jenkins, Henry 1992: *Textual Poachers*. London: Routledge.

Johnston, Sheila 1987: Film narrative and the structuralist controversy. In Pam Cook (ed.), *The Cinema Book*, London: British Film Institute, 222–51.

Jordan, Glenn and Weedon, Chris 1995: *Cultural Politics: Class, Gender, Race and the Postmodern World*. Oxford: Blackwell.

Katz, E. 1959: Mass communication research and popular culture. *Studies in Public Communication*, 2.

Katz, E. and Lazarsfeld, P. 1955: *Personal Influence*. New York: Free Press.

Kellner, Douglas 1997a: Critical theory and cultural studies: the missed articulation. In Jim McGuigan, *Cultural Methodologies*, London: Sage.

Kent, Raymond (ed.) 1994: *Measuring Media Audiences*. London: Routledge.

Klapper, J. 1960: The Effects of Mass Communication. New York: Free Press.

Kosicki, G. M. et al. 1987: Processing the news: some individual strategies for selecting, sense-making and integrating. Paper presented at the International Communication Association, Montreal, Canada.

Kozloff, Sarah 1992: Narrative theory and television. In Robert C. Allen (ed.), *Channels of Discourse, Reassembled*, London: Routledge, 67–100.

Lazarsfeld, P. et al. 1944: *The People's Choice*. New York: Columbia University Press.

Leal, Ondina Fachel 1990: Popular taste and erudite repertoire: the place and space of television in Brazil. *Cultural Studies*, 4, 1, 19–29.

Livingstone, Sonia and Lunt, Peter 1994: *Talk on Television: Audience Participation and Public Debate*. London: Routledge.

Lull, James 1980: The social uses of television. *Human Communications Research*, 6, 3, 197–209.

Lull, James 1990: *Inside Family Viewing: Ethnographic Research on Television's Audiences*. London: Routledge.

Lull, James 1995: *Media, Communication, Culture: A Global Approach*. Cambridge: Polity Press.

Lury, Celia 1996: *Consumer Culture*. Cambridge: Polity Press.

Lusted, David 1996: Social class and the western as male melodrama. In Ian Cameron and Douglas Pye (eds), *The Movie Book of the Western*, London: Studio Vista, 63–74.

McCabe, Colin 1974: Realism and the cinema: notes on some Brechtian theses. *Screen*, 15, 2, 7–27.

McDonnell, James (ed.) 1991: *Public Service Broadcasting: A Reader*. London: Routledge.

McGuigan, Jim 1992: *Cultural Populism*. London: Routledge.

McGuigan, Jim 1997: *Cultural Methodologies*. London: Sage.

McLeod, Jack M., Kosicki, Gerald M. and Zhongdang, Pan 1991: On understanding and misunderstanding media effects. In James Curran and Michael Gurevitch (eds), *Mass Media and Society*, London: Edward Arnold, 235–66.

McQuail, Denis (ed.), 1972: *Sociology of Mass Communications*. Harmondsworth: Penguin.

McQuail, Denis 1994: *Mass Communication Theory: An Introduction*, 3rd edn. London: Sage.

McRobbie, Angela 1991: *Feminism and Youth Culture: From Jackie to Just Seventeen*. London: Macmillan.

McRobbie, Angela 1994: *Postmodernism and Popular Culture*. London: Routledge.

Maltby, Richard with Craven, Ian 1995: *Hollywood Cinema: An Introduction*. Oxford: Blackwell.

Marx, Karl and Engels, Friedrich 1974: *The German Ideology: Part One*. London: Lawrence and Wishart.

Medhurst, Andy 1989: Introduction. In Therese Daniels and Jane Gerson (eds), *The Colour Black: Black Images in British Television*, London: British Film Institute, 15–21.

Moores, Shaun 1994: *Interpreting Audiences: The Ethnography of Media Consumption*. London: Sage.

Morley David 1980a: *The 'Nationwide' Audience: Structure and Decoding*. London: British Film Institute.

Morley, David 1980b: Texts, readers, subjects. In Stuart Hall, Dorothy Hobson, Andrew Lowe and Paul Willis (eds), *Culture, Media, Language: Working Papers in Cultural Studies 1972–79*, London: Hutchinson, 163–73.

Morley, David 1986: *Family Television: Cultural Power and Domestic Leisure*. London: Comedia.

Morley, David 1992: *Television, Audiences and Cultural Studies*. London: Routledge.

Murdock, Graham 1982: Large corporations and the control of the communications industries. In Michael Gurevitch, Tony Bennett, James Curran and Janet Woollacott (eds), *Culture, Society and the Media*. London: Methuen, 118–50.

Murdock, Graham 1997: Base notes: the conditions of cultural practice. In Peter Golding and Marjorie Ferguson (eds), *Cultural Studies in Question*, London: Sage, 86–101.

Nava, Mica 1992: *Changing Cultures: Feminism, Youth and Consumerism*. London: Sage.

Nava, Mica and Nava, Orson 1992: Discriminating or duped? Young people as consumers of advertising / art. In Mica Nava, *Changing Cultures*, London: Sage, 171–84.

Neale, Stephen 1980: *Genre*. London: British Film Institute.

Negrine, Ralph 1990: *Politics and the Mass Media in Britain*. London: Routledge.

Negus, Keith 1992: *Producing Pop: Culture and Conflict in the Popular Music Industry*. London: Edward Arnold.

Nichols, Bill (ed.) 1985: *Movies and Methods*, vol. 2, Berkeley: University of California Press.

O'Sullivan, Tim, Hartley, John, Saunders, Danny, Montgomery, Martin and Fiske, John 1983: *Key Concepts in Communication*. London: Methuen.

O'Sullivan, Tim, Hartley, John, Saunders, Danny, Montgomery, Martin and Fiske, John 1994: *Key Concepts in Communication and Cultural Studies*, 2nd edn. London: Routledge.

Oakes, Ted 1995: Campaigning camcorders. In *Viewfinder*, 25, 95.

Paterson, Richard 1990: A suitable schedule for the family. In Andrew Goodwin and Garry Whannel (eds), *Understanding Television*. London: Routledge, 30–41.

Perkins, Tessa 1979: Re-thinking stereotypes. In Michèle Barrett, Philip Corrigan, Annette Kuhn and Janet Wolff (eds), *Ideology and Cultural Production*, London: Croom Helm, 135–59.

Perkins, V. F. 1976: The cinema of Nicholas Ray. In Bill Nichols (ed.), *Movies and Methods: An Anthology*, Berkeley: University of California Press, 251–61.

Petley, Julian 1992: Independent distribution in the UK: problems and proposals. In Duncan Petrie (ed.), *New Questions of British Cinema*, London: British Film Institute.

Poster, Mark 1995: Postmodern virtualities. In Mike Featherstone and Roger Burrows (eds), *Cyberspace/Cyberbodies/Cyberpunk*, London: Sage, 79–95.

Prince, Gerald 1987: *A Dictionary of Narratology*. Lincoln: University of Nebraska Press.

Propp, Vladimir 1968: *Morphology of the Folktale*. Austin: University of Texas Press.

Radway, Janice 1987: *Reading the Romance: Women, Patriarchy and Popular Literature*. London: Verso.

Rimmon-Kenan, S. 1983: *Narrative Fiction: Contemporary Poetics*. London: Methuen.

Robins, Kevin 1995: Cyberspace and the world we live in. In Mike Featherstone and Roger Burrows (eds), *Cyberspace/Cyberbodies/Cyberpunk*, London: Sage, 135–55.

Robins, Kevin and Webster, Frank 1990: Broadcasting politics: communications and consumption. In Manuel Alverado and John O. Thompson (eds), *The Media Reader*. London: British Film Institute, 135–50.

Rosen, Marjorie 1973: *Popcorn Venus: Women, Movies and the American Dream*. New York: Avon.

Rosenau, J. 1990: *Turbulence in World Politics*. Brighton: Harvester Wheatsheaf.

Saussure, Ferdinand de 1974: *Course in General Linguistics*. London: Fontana.

Scannell, Paddy 1990: Public service broadcasting: the history of a concept. In Andrew Goodwin and Garry Whannel (eds), *Understanding Television*, London: Routledge, 11–29.

Schlesinger, Philip 1987: *Putting Reality Together*. London: Methuen.

Schlesinger, Philip, Murdock, Graham and Elliot, Philip 1983: *Televising Terrorism: Political Violence in Popular Culture*. London: Comedia.

Seiter, Ellen 1990: Making distinctions in TV audience research: case study of a troubling interview. *Cultural Studies*, 4, 1, 61–84.

Seiter, Ellen 1992: Semiotics, structuralism and television. In Robert C. Allen (ed.), *Channels of Discourse, Reassembled*, London: Routledge, 31–66.

Seiter, Ellen, Borches, Hans, Kreutzner, Gabriele and Worth, Eva-Maria (eds) 1989: *Remote Control: Television, Audiences and Cultural Power*. London: Routledge.

Seymour-Ure, Colin 1996: *The British Press and Broadcasting Since 1945*, 2nd edn. Oxford: Blackwell.

Sharma, Ashwari 1990: Do they think we're aloo? In Janet Willis and Tana Wollen (eds), *The Neglected Audience*, London: British Film Institute, 61–5.

Shattuc, Jane M. 1997: *The Talking Cure: TV Talk Shows and Women*. London: Routledge.

Silverstone, Roger 1985: *Framing Science*. London: British Film Institute.

Silverstone, Roger 1994: *Television and Everyday Life*. London: Routledge.

Skeggs, Beverly 1997: *Formations of Class and Gender: Becoming Respectable*. London: Sage.

Snead, James 1994: 'Black independent film': Britain and America. In Colin McCabe and Cornel West (eds), *White Screens/Black Images: Hollywood from the Darkside*, London: Routledge, 121–30.

Stam, Robert, Burgoyne, Robert and Flitterman-Lewis, Sandy 1992: *New Vocabularies in Film Semiotics: Structuralism, Post-structuralism and Beyond*. London: Routledge.

Stevenson, Nick 1995: *Understanding Media Cultures: Social Theory and Mass Communications*. London: Sage.

Stoddart, Helen 1995: Auteurism and film authorship. In Joanne Hollows and Mark Jancovich (eds), *Approaches to Popular Film*, Manchester: Manchester University Press, 37–58.

Strinati, Dominic 1995: *An Introduction to Theories of Popular Culture*. London: Routledge.

Thompson, John B. 1990: *Ideology and Modern Culture*. Cambridge: Polity.

Todorov, Tzvetan 1977: *The Poetics of Prose*. Oxford: Blackwell.

Tolson, Andrew 1996: *Mediations: Text and Discourse in Media Studies*. London: Edward Arnold.

Tunstall, Jeremy and Palmer, Michael 1991: *Media Moguls*. London: Routledge.

Turner, Graeme 1988: *Film as Social Practice*. London: Routledge.

Turner, Graeme 1990: *British Cultural Studies: An Introduction*. London: Unwin Hyman.

Twyman, Tony 1994: Measuring audiences to radio. In Raymond Kent (ed.), *Measuring Media Audiences*, London: Routledge, 88–104.

van Zoonen, Liesbet 1991: A tyranny of initimacy? Women, femininity and television news. In Peter Dahlgren and Colin Sparks (eds), *Communication and Citizenship: Journalism and the Public Sphere*, London: Routledge, 217–35.

van Zoonen, Liesbet 1994: *Feminist Media Studies*. London: Sage.

Wallerstein, I. 1991: *Geopolitics and Geoculture*, Cambridge: Cambridge University Press.

Weedon, Chris 1987: *Feminist Practice and Poststructuralist Theory*. Oxford: Blackwell.

Williams, Raymond 1974: *Television: Technology and Cultural Form*. London: Fontana.

Williams, Raymond 1976: *Keywords*. London: Fontana.

Willis, Paul 1990; *Common Culture*. Milton Keynes: Open University Press.

Winship, Janice 1987: *Inside Women's Magazines*. London: Pandora.

Wollen, Peter 1976: *North By North-West*: a morphological analysis. *Film Form*, 1.

Wood, Robin 1980: The Incoherent Text: narrative in the '70s. *Movie*, 27 / 28, 24–42.

Wright, Will 1975: *Sixguns and Society*. Berkeley: University of California Press.

Index